Skills and Knowledge for Life Story Work with Children and Adolescents

also by this author

Life Story Work with Children Who Are Fostered or Adopted
Creative Ideas and Activities
Katie Wrench and Lesley Naylor
ISBN 978 1 84905 343 3
eISBN 978 0 85700 674 5

Helping Vulnerable Children and Adolescents to Stay Safe
Creative Ideas and Activities for Building Protective Behaviours
Katie Wrench
Foreword by Ginger Kadlec
ISBN 978 1 84905 676 2
eISBN 978 1 78450 183 9

Creative Ideas for Assessing Vulnerable Children and Families
Katie Wrench
ISBN 978 1 84905 703 5
eISBN 978 1 78450 225 6

of related interest

Innovative Therapeutic Life Story Work
Developing Trauma-Informed Practice for Working with Children, Adolescents and Young Adults
Edited by Richard Rose
Foreword by Deborah D. Gray
ISBN 978 1 78592 185 8
eISBN 978 1 78450 468 7

Life Work with Children Who Are Fostered or Adopted
Using Diverse Techniques in a Coordinated Approach
Joy Rees
ISBN 978 1 78592 229 9
eISBN 978 1 78450 504 2

Skills and Knowledge for LIFE STORY WORK with Children and Adolescents

KATIE WRENCH

Jessica Kingsley Publishers
London and Philadelphia

First published in Great Britain in 2024 by Jessica Kingsley Publishers
An imprint of John Murray Press

1

Content Warning: This book mentions abuse, alcoholism, addiction, child neglect, drugs, homelessness, incest, rape, self-harm, sexual violence, suicide, and violence.

A CIP catalogue record for this title is available from the British Library and the Library of Congress

ISBN 978 1 83997 616 2
eISBN 978 1 83997 617 9

Printed and bound in Great Britain by CPI Group

Jessica Kingsley Publishers' policy is to use papers that are natural, renewable and recyclable products and made from wood grown in sustainable forests. The logging and manufacturing processes are expected to conform to the environmental regulations of the country of origin.

Jessica Kingsley Publishers
Carmelite House
50 Victoria Embankment
London EC4Y 0DZ

www.jkp.com

John Murray Press
Part of Hodder & Stoughton Ltd
An Hachette Company

Acknowledgements

Writing this book while working full time has been a slog. But I felt all along that this little book would address all the life story challenges I hear about on a weekly basis, so I hope you will agree it was worth it.

Just a few people to thank.

Lesley Naylor, Mary Carter and Jo Robinson are all excellent social workers who have given of their time freely to read chapters and offer suggestions, vignettes and support. For that I am incredibly grateful.

Alison Ferguson, as my non-social work reviewer, has checked for excessive use of the word 'might', clarity and plain English, and ensured as a result that the book reads much better.

Vicky Holland gave an invaluable parent's perspective.

My son Louis did a sterling job of cross-referencing all citations with the References – obviously for a fee, but I am thankful, nonetheless.

Stephen has held the fort at home when I have been squirrelled away in the garden room writing.

Many others have offered reassurance and encouragement, sometimes gently, and sometimes rather more forcefully, but all were extremely important in getting me across the finish line.

And finally, an apology to Honor...the summer of 2023 has been a bit rubbish because your mum has spent every weekend and day off writing. I promise I will never do this again!

Contents

INTRODUCTION

In the years since the publication of our little pink book, *Life Story Work with Children Who Are Fostered or Adopted* (Wrench and Naylor 2013), there have been developments in my learning and in fostering and adoption practice. I now spend at least a day every week training diverse teams around the United Kingdom in life story work, and regularly hear about the common challenges of undertaking this crucial work and of writing life story books for children placed for adoption or in special guardianship arrangements.

The advent of the Adoption Support Fund (ASF)[1] in 2015, and the decision within their framework to fund therapeutic life story work has also meant that therapists with clinical training in art and play therapy, for example, have begun to offer life story work too. They bring invaluable therapeutic skills that undoubtedly enhance therapeutic life story work, but without good supervision, training and a model for practice, they may not always feel confident and competent enough to be able to offer the support children and their families need in relation to understanding their stories.

Many more guides and resources have been published to support the delivery of life story work for children and young people since our first book was published, but they haven't addressed many of the most common barriers to providing high-quality life story work that I hear about in training every week (Golding 2014; Rees 2017, 2018; Rose 2017; Ryan and Walker 2016; Shotton 2020). Although there are undoubtedly brilliant pockets of practice, this is still not consistent across teams, agencies or counties. I still hear of children being told a parent in prison is 'working

1 In December 2023, the ASF was renamed as the Adoption and Special Guardianship Support Fund (ASGSF). www.gov.uk/guidance/adoption-support-fund-asf

away'. I know of children in special guardianship arrangements who have not been given any information about their first family – and who are led to believe that they are living with their birth parents. Although they know this is not true on a bodily level, no one has given them the words yet to understand their stories or their origins. And if they are not supported to understand who they are, where they fit into the world or why they were separated from their birth parents, the implications for these children are potentially catastrophic.

The feedback we have received about the model for practice we introduced in *Life Story Work with Children Who Are Fostered or Adopted* (2013) has been positive. We aimed to create a containing model for practice for practitioners and families, and this remains valid today. We expanded the notion of life story work beyond focusing solely on information sharing, and encouraged practitioners to think more creatively about meeting the needs of individual children and young people. The accessibility and simplicity of the book mean that it is still a great 'entry-level' resource, but inevitably, in keeping it brief, there were aspects to the work we were not able to cover and, of course, in the intervening years my thinking has developed, and research has offered us new insights and understandings, particularly from adoptees and people with care experience. Therefore, I use our original practice model as the foundation for this new book, but also address the most common issues that arise when doing this work. In order that this book can stand alone, however, I will briefly outline the rationale for the practice model in Chapter 1, which is being used in teams across the UK. I will then explore the complexities of planning an intervention, undertaking the work and creating a product at the end, typically a life story book.

In Chapters 2 and 3 I offer advice on getting started, galvanising the team around the child and family, collating the information bank and collaborating with parents or carers. Then stage one of the direct work, described in Chapter 4, focuses on helping it feel safe enough for children to go back and explore their story. This includes psychoeducation around the impact of trauma, strategies for co-regulation and the development of emotional literacy. Stage two of the work, described in Chapter 5, explores how to nurture a sense of connectedness, belonging and identity for the child, all of which will enhance their self-esteem and resilience. Then finally, in Chapters 6 to 8, stage three focuses on information sharing and integration, including thinking about how to talk or write about distressing and traumatic events. (Please note that Chapter 7 contains material that some readers may find difficult or distressing, including references to sexual abuse, death by suicide and self-harm.) From here we also think about ending the work and looking to the future with hope and optimism. Finally, Chapter 9 considers the creation of the life story materials, including a life story book.

It is important to be clear at this point that it is inevitable that there will be generalisations in this text. This does not mean, however, that I am making assumptions about people's lived experience of care or adoption. Having care experience as a child or adult may mean that they share commonalities with others, but I understand that care experience varies as widely as the experience of adoptees – and understanding of that experience may also shift and change throughout the lifespan.

I have been thoughtful about my use of language throughout the text. While I generally refer to 'child' or 'children', this also includes 'young person/people'. I keep my descriptions of children gender-neutral. I refer throughout to 'parents or carers' – to encompass adoption, foster and kinship care, residential care and special guardianship arrangements. To make a clear distinction I refer to 'birth families' and 'birth parents' in talking about the families children were born into. I am mindful, of course, that many birth parents would prefer to be known simply as their child's parents, and that others favour the use of 'natural' or 'first parents'. In undertaking work of this sensitive nature, it is always important to use the language that fits for the individual child and their caregiving system.

I have included brief, illustrative vignettes throughout, rather than longer case studies, to share practice examples that will enhance the reader's understanding of this way of working. They are written in such a way that the child or young person cannot be identified, and details have been changed or omitted to maintain anonymity. Where there are direct quotes from parents or carers, adoptees or adults with care experience, these are clearly referenced. I have also found insights from blogs, autobiographies and memoires written by adult adoptees and adults with care experience a useful tool in illuminating key points.

One final point relates to what this work is called, and there are clearly variations. In Wales[2] and in some English local authorities, 'life journey work' is favoured to describe the process. Nicholls (2005) refers to 'life work', while Rees (2018), Ryan and Walker (2016) and Shotton (2020)

2 www.adoptcymru.com/life-journey

prefer 'life story work'. Rose (2012, 2017) has developed a model known as 'therapeutic life story work' (TLSW). We are all describing the same thing, and for consistency in relation to this model for practice, I will use the terms *life story work* in relation to the process, and *life story books* in relation to the product.

If you are ever in doubt about the necessity of this work, please consider the impact of not doing it.

If an adult or professional had asked me how I felt about doing some life story work when I was in care over 13 years ago, I would have guessed they were talking about me being born, how many siblings I had or random parts of my life that may have been of interest to a professional at the time. Sadly, I had no real understanding of what this work really was and what it meant until I trained to become a social worker. It was only when I became a social worker that I realised there was so much of my life that I had very little sense of and so many muddled memories. If someone had taken the time and effort to complete life story work with me, I may have felt less uncertain and wobbly myself when I transitioned into adulthood, especially prior to accessing my file as an adult.

My past is complex; so much of it still doesn't make sense to me, and there are so many questions that flood my brain in times of distress. Having no family members there to help in this matter, it's really tough. Those that I know are still around I remain estranged from, and they would probably have a narrative that fits their own needs.

I, like many other care-experienced young people, have experienced much separation and loss in life. The impact is still very apparent today within my intimate relationships and in the way I view people around me. If I had the opportunity to have life story work, would the separation and loss have been understood better? Would it have paid to handle some of the deep-seated emotional difficulties and barriers that have felt at times unmanageable? I am not suggesting it would have made my head feel less full, and nor do I think it was the answer to all my problems at the time. We know that for life story work to be meaningful and effective for children an internal sense of safety is needed, and the importance of timing and feeling ready to complete the work is pivotal. I was likely to not have been at this stage, but would it have helped adjust the way I see the world? I am assuming yes.

Life story work really matters. I needed to hear my story, have those gaps filled. I wanted to be heard and I needed someone to remind me of the good things that I had forgotten, rather than all the things that went wrong. How was I able to explore the meaning of these events? When I moved on to my new families throughout my teenage years, I could have moved with a clearer sense of my world – in a place in which important decisions were made with care and with a more coherent narrative of my own life.

Mary Carter, care-experienced senior social worker

1

THE ORIGINAL MODEL FOR LIFE STORY PRACTICE

In 2013, frustrated by inconsistencies in social work practice in the local authority where we worked, my colleague Lesley Naylor and I began to think about how we could support more life story work to happen in a meaningful way for children in care and adoption. We were working as therapeutic social workers, and both had additional training in play therapy (Lesley) and art psychotherapy (Katie). We became interested in how we could integrate therapeutic approaches into what had traditionally been a social work task. We saw many things getting in the way of life story work in the area social work teams: time to prepare and then do the direct work was a key factor, but so, too, was not knowing where to start, worrying about 'making things worse' and feeling anxious about how to find the right words to help children begin to explore their stories. There was a sense that this work was the preserve of specialists or therapists, and not of social care staff.

Yet it is social workers and social care staff who are tasked with writing life story books and later life letters when a child is placed for adoption. It is social workers who should support children in care in the UK to understand their journeys; it is still unusual to have access to specialist teams supporting life story work. With the advent of the Adoption Support Fund (ASF),[1] psychological therapists are also now being funded to work with adoptees, children subject to special guardianship orders (who were previously looked after) and their families. But my sense is that life story work is a core social work task. Any child who has experienced

1 www.gov.uk/guidance/adoption-support-fund-asf. See previous footnote on the fund's renaming.

disruption, separation or loss has the right to understand their story, and to have support from someone they trust to explore their feelings about it.

Our six-part model for practice is simple (Wrench and Naylor 2013), and was designed to scaffold practitioners and help them first think about where to start and then how to tailor life story work to meet the needs of individual children and young people. For each stage we offered suggestions of six simple, low-resource, creative activities as a starting point. We stressed that there was no standard formula to follow, and avoided offering a manualised approach or session-by-session guide because we felt the work should always reflect the uniqueness of the child and their caregiving system. I stand by this position now, and feel the model stands the test of time. However, with new learning, it is also important to think about how it could be improved, and this is the aim of this book.

For readers who are not yet familiar with the model, I will recap the six parts to the model here.

PART 1: BUILDING A SENSE OF SAFETY FOR THE CHILD

Our focus initially is on supporting children to feel safe enough in their brains, bodies and relationships to be able to explore their stories. Even where children know on a thinking level that they are safe, their brain and central nervous system may continue to respond as if the trauma is ongoing. 'We have learned that trauma is not just an event that took place somewhere in the past; it is also the imprint left by that experience on mind, body and brain' (van der Kolk 2015, p.21). If we don't first offer support to children to manage their hypervigilance so that their body and brain can recognise that the danger truly has passed, it is neither realistic nor ethical to think about going back to explore those early traumatic experiences.

Critical for many children to this stage of the work is the involvement of attuned parents or carers. I explore the ways in which it might be possible to work dyadically in Chapter 2.

PART 2: EMOTIONAL LITERACY

A primary aim of life story work is for a child or young person to express their feelings about what has happened to them and their family, and to have those feelings validated. In the original model, the focus was on assessment of the child's emotional literacy skills, with activities to look at whether they could name feelings and connect those feelings with things that had happened to themselves and others. We were also interested in whether children could tune into their body's communication about emotions – were they aware of how and where feelings were held in their body? Were certain feelings easier to locate or name? Did certain feeling states dominate or threaten to overwhelm at times?

In this book I will combine these parts 1 and 2 of the model as they are inextricably linked. I explore this in Chapter 4 under the umbrella of *helping it feel safe enough to go back*. This is stage one of the work. Even where it might not be possible to think with a child about their experiences, we should still be able to work on resource building and consider this a critical element of life story work. In so doing, we will be supporting the development of a sense of felt safety, providing opportunities for co-regulation, and helping children to experience a sense of connectedness and belonging that is essential for wellbeing.

PART 3: RESILIENCE AND SELF-ESTEEM

We wanted building resilience and self-esteem to be a theme throughout the work: to support the child to thrive despite early adversity, and to focus on the strengths within them and their family systems, including their birth family. This is important because we know that where children have had interpersonal experiences that have been negative and undermining, this will impact their self-esteem. We are also gaining more understanding of the link between self-esteem and belonging.

This part of the work is also about reinforcing the belief that a child is more than the sum of their difficult stories. It is a commitment to celebrate the child's strengths, achievements and positive threads of connection with friends, family and community. Their story and this work should never be purely saturated in trauma. Like Shotton (2020), I have been influenced by narrative psychology, understanding that if we only ask about the child's difficult life experiences, 'a thin description of what happened emerges' (2020, p.xii). Instead, we should seek to understand how the child responded to these challenges, recognising their strengths and resilience, which have often been overlooked, as well as successes in other aspects of their life.

PART 4: IDENTITY

Traditionally the family is the source of all information about a child, but where these links have been broken or lost, their personal history becomes fragmented, and they risk losing consistent access to crucial information about themselves, their lives and their families. We focused on the importance of positive threads of connection to a child's birth family. We also explored those things that make a child unique, who the child most identifies with, stories that are special to that child, together with their experience and understanding of 'family'.

In this book, I will seek to combine these two aspects of the work, and explore them in Chapter 5 under the umbrella of *nurturing connectedness, belonging and identity*. This is stage two of life story work.

PART 5: INFORMATION SHARING AND INTEGRATION

It is important to emphasise that what historically is thought of as life story work in its entirety – information sharing or filling in the gaps in children's understanding of themselves and their lives – is only one-fifth of our six-part model. To safely support children in this phase of the work, it is imperative that we first lay the groundwork securely, and for that, we need a stable base.

Trauma interrupts a child's narrative so there will be stops, starts, inconsistencies and missing pieces rather than a coherent flow that supports understanding. I always emphasise that it is not enough to simply present a child with a story that has been written for them and think this will suffice. This approach will not support them to integrate their story, to express how they feel about what has happened to them, to gain clarity where there may be misunderstandings or to manage what they do not know or is too painful to acknowledge. Nor will it be their story – it will not have their perceptions, their feelings or their process represented in it. Children should not have a story that has been constructed for them without being an active participant, unless they are too young to contribute, or other factors prevent them from doing so.

It will also not be enough to present the *facts*. This is the space to explore multiple perspectives or truths. (We explore information gathering in its broadest sense in Chapter 3.) It is the opportunity for words to be put to experience, sometimes for the first time in a child's life. As a result, it is commonly the phase of the work that adults find the most challenging. Therefore, in Chapter 6 I consider the basic principles for information sharing and support for the integration of this material. I then explore how to have difficult conversations about traumatic events in Chapter 7, considering the most common issues children have faced, including parental mental health, addiction and domestic abuse.

PART 6: LOOKING TO THE FUTURE

The final part of the model is concerned with looking ahead to what comes next, with hope and optimism. The child and their parents or carers should now have a clearer sense of the child's history and what this means for now and the future. We hope the child will also have had experiences that enhance their sense of self, and their experience of connectedness, belonging and permanence where possible. We think about the ways in which we might mark the ending of the work, acknowledging any feelings that might emerge about saying goodbye. We also look to the future, exploring hopes, dreams and aspirations, with the explicit invitation to continue to build the life story – life does not end when the life story work ends.

In Chapter 8 we will think in more detail about the ending process and how to encourage the idea of continuing to add to the story and look to the future. We also think about how we might pull together the experience of the life story work into a product or life story materials, in Chapter 9, which we didn't cover the first time around.

2

GETTING STARTED

The investment we make in thorough preparation for life story work, before beginning direct work with the child, is a good indicator of more positive outcomes for children. It is all about the groundwork and scaffolding, both for practitioners and for the system around the child. This will look different in fostering and adoption contexts, and should look different depending on the individual needs of the child.

WHAT DOES THE GUIDANCE TELL US?

Children in care or looked after children

Under the 1989 Children Act, the term 'looked after child' refers to all children and young people being looked after by a local authority, namely:

- Those subject to care orders or interim care orders (under Sections 31 and 38 of the 1989 Act).
- Those children who have been placed, or are authorised to be placed, with prospective adopters by a local authority (Section 18(3) of the 2002 Children Act).
- Those who are voluntarily accommodated under Section 20 of the 1989 Act, including unaccompanied asylum-seeking children. Where children are accommodated under this provision, parental responsibility remains with the parents.
- Those who are subject to court orders with residence requirements (for example, secure remand or remand to local authority accommodation), in accordance with Section 21 of the 1989 Act (DCSF 2010).

If you are supporting children in care, life story work is highlighted in the NICE quality standards (2013) pertaining to looked after children. Quality statement 4 requires looked after children and young people to have ongoing opportunities to explore and make sense of their identity and relationships. Life story work is also included in the NICE guidance (2021) in respect of working with children in care. Unfortunately, no routinely collected national data for this measure has been identified, so it is impossible to know how much of this work is happening, or what the quality of that work might be.

There is also no mention of the importance of carers being aware of and supporting life story work in *Fostering Services: National Minimum Standards* (DfE 2011), and only a brief mention in the *Guide to the Children's Homes Regulations* (DfE 2015, p.16) in relation to providing a safe and supportive environment for children: 'The importance of understanding who we are and where we come from is recognised in good social work practice, for example through undertaking life story work or other direct work. Staff in children's homes should play a full role in work of this kind.'

The decision-making forum in relation to starting life story work for children in care is the child looked after review, chaired by the independent reviewing officer for children in care or with a plan for adoption or special guardianship. Care planning and reviewing is about bringing together children who are looked after and their families, carers and relevant professionals from health, education and social care to plan for the care of the child and to review that plan on a regular basis. Parental responsibility is shared between the local authority and the child's parents, who therefore should be consulted before the life story work begins.

Adoption

There is much more clarity regarding life story work where there is a plan for adoption. The adoption statutory guidance in England (AAR 13 2.22) states that: 'as far as is reasonably practicable – which will of course be influenced by the age and understanding of the child – the agency must ensure that the child is provided with counselling and information about adoption (including written information) in accordance with AAR 13' (DfE 2013, p.37). Furthermore, any support:

> should help a child – subject to age, background, and development – to

> understand over time what adoption would mean for them now and in the longer term. The child should be helped to understand why the agency considers they should not stay with their own family or current carer and why adoption is the preferred option for their permanence. They also need to know about the implications adoption may have for contact with their parents, brothers and sisters, wider family members and others (AAR 13 2.23). (DfE 2013, p.37)

Regulation 35 makes specific reference to the life story book as a tool to support children to understand 'their early history and life before their adoption'. It stresses the need for collaboration with the prospective adopter so 'that the language and terms used are agreed...before the book is handed over'. It is also made very clear that the child's birth parents, family, foster carers and other people who know the child well should be encouraged to become involved in putting together the contents and providing significant information and 'objects' for a memory box, such as the child's hospital birth wristband, teddies, letters and celebration cards; first drawings and paintings; and photographs of birth parents, siblings, family members and other people who are important to the child.

The guidance is clear that these resources should be coordinated by one person, preferably the child's social worker, and that they do *not* have to be given to the child and prospective adopter all at once. The directive in relation to a competed life story book is that it should be shared within 10 working days of the adoption ceremony, that is, the ceremony to mark the making of the adoption order. This allows sufficient time for the child and their prospective adopter to begin to become a family, and for adoptive family stories to also be integrated into the life story book or materials. However, in practice I see two extremes: stories written and shared when the children are first placed, with no input from the adoptive parents, or no story at all, even years post the adoption order. As long as adopters understand the child's story from the point of placement, and they are supported and encouraged to create an environment in their families where children feel safe to talk and think about the fact they have another family, this is enough of a starting point. More details about their new lives together can be added over time to the life story book.

The regulations (AAR 35) also give direction about the use of later life letters. The life story book does not need to include information about everything that has happened in the child's life. It may be that some information is more appropriate to share when they are older, which is where a later life letter comes into its own. It should be written by a social worker who knows the child, preferably the child's social worker (AAR 35 5.51), and should explain the child's history from birth and be sufficiently detailed so that in adolescence or young adulthood they will have access to a higher level of factual details about their birth family and their life before adoption. The timescales for completing this are the same as for the life story book, within 10 working days of the adoption ceremony. It is also important to consider asking the child's birth family either to write their own letters to the child or to make contributions to the agency's letter (DfE 2013).

THE TEAM AROUND THE CHILD

Is it the right time for life story work?

Irrespective of the context, anyone undertaking life story work with a child or young person must engage and collaborate with the caregiving system and professional network to plan the work together initially, and to ensure that the young person is supported appropriately throughout the process. While getting everyone involved around the table to think about these things can be a challenge, it is imperative that decisions are made that everyone in the network agrees with.

The child's network must include their adoptive parents or carers, and, where appropriate, will also include their social worker (for children in care or in receipt of post adoption support), teacher, any health professionals involved such as CAMHS (Child and Adolescent Mental Health Services), therapists and any other professional involved in supporting the child or young person. In a planning meeting, the systemic network should work together to decide whether it is the right time to begin the life story, and to agree roles and responsibilities within this process. Although it is important that one person (usually the social worker) coordinates the work, it is critical that all stakeholders see themselves as fundamental to the process and understand their role within it, with the child at the centre of the thinking, *before beginning the work*. Similarly, if tasked with writing a story for a younger child prior to the making of a special guardianship or adoption order, a planning meeting is critical for thinking about who will contribute, together with timescales for completion.

In this meeting, consider the motivation for instigating the life story work: who is driving it, and for what purpose? Is it a child's questions or curiosity about their story? Is it professionals' or parents' or carers' concerns about behaviour? Is it a box-ticking exercise as part of the review process for a child in care because it is long overdue? In deciding whether it is the right time to begin direct work, it is important to consider factors relating to the child, their caregiving system and the professional network. You will also need to garner crucial information to help you decide where to start from the systemic network. Even if there is resistance to sharing difficult information because a carer is worried about the impact this might have on the child's mental health, for example, this does not mean nothing should be done. It simply means working with the child and their parent or carer to identify helpful ways in which they can manage those feelings (see Chapter 4).

This planning stage is also the time to consider who is the right person to be speaking to the child about whether they would like to engage in life story work, and also, who is responsible for subsequently gathering the information, doing the direct work and curating the life story materials.

1. Explore the child's circumstances

If there is no overt indication that the child is either interested in exploring their story or asking questions, but adults in the system think it is a good idea, you will need to explore whether the child would be open to life story work. Think about who is the right person to have this sensitive conversation – either yourself or someone the child trusts. We explored these issues briefly in relation to building strong, secure foundations for practice in our first book (Wrench and Naylor 2013, pp.17–23), but it is important enough to say again, and to expand on with some questions you should consider:

- Is the child asking questions about their experiences or family history?
- What is their placement status? It is a myth that life story work should never begin until children are in a permanent, secure and settled placement. It is never too soon to begin (even informally) supporting children to understand decision making while changes

are happening or very soon afterwards (Burnell and Vaughan, 2008, p.227).

- Are they about to undergo a major change in circumstances in relation to family time, where they are living, or where they go to nursery/school/college?
- Do they have other priorities just now, like exams? Or have they recently experienced a significant loss?
- Do they have a good enough relationship with a parent/carer/keyworker who could support the life story process?
- Do they have any additional needs or access issues that may need to be considered in planning the work? Will an interpreter be needed? Do they have additional communication needs? If so, what needs to be done to best able support or engage them?
- How stable is home life? School life?
- What is their availability? What is going on for them outside of school hours?
- How do they experience family time/contact with extended family, including letter exchange?
- In the case of sibling groups, what are the potential implications for children who will not be involved in life story work, and how could this affect the work with the child? What if one child wants to know more about their history but the other child doesn't? Or if there is a big age difference, which means that the level of information that is appropriate to share is vastly different, how will this be managed?
- If the child or young person has other challenges, such as significant self-harming behaviour, violence against others, is regularly running away or using drugs or alcohol, this needs to be addressed and the child supported to stabilise and feel safer before beginning any life story work. Ideas from stage one around helping it feel safe enough for the child to think about their story could be a good starting place.

2. Explore factors related to the caregiving system – parents (birth, adoptive) or carers (foster/kinship, special guardian, children's home)

- Is the caregiving system robust enough to support a child through the process of life story work? There is plentiful evidence that the task of parenting a child who has experienced development trauma can have a significant impact on wellbeing and on parenting capacity (Hughes, Baylin and Siegel 2012; Morwen 2020; Ottaway and Selwyn 2016; Skandrani, Harf and El Husseini 2019). As a result, some may show signs of burnout or compassion fatigue. If it looks as though the parent or carer is meeting their child's basic care needs but is also exhausted, both physically and emotionally, then before expecting them to support life story work, first make sure there is support for the parent or carer. This is essential if they are to find compassion and empathy for themselves and their children and to be available for co-regulation. Priorities therefore would first be to find an empathic listening ear and ally with whom the parent or carer can share their feelings without fear of judgement or blame; to build in essential self-care as part of their daily routine; and to have a break from parenting – for 10 minutes or for a weekend.
- Does everyone agree it is the right time to start?
- Can you agree what information to share, and how?
- Does the parent or carer see themself as critical to the process? Can they make themself available to join sessions? (See p.33 for assessing caregiver capacity.)
- Is the caregiving system under stress – health, bereavement, challenges in caring for another child, moving house, instability in the staff team?
- Would the parent or carer be willing and able to do life story-related 'tasks' between sessions?
- What is the parent or carer's view of the child's birth family?
- Does the parent or carer have a good understanding of the child's journey themself? How do they feel about it?

3. Explore the roles different workers might play and the necessary skills required

- Who is the right person to facilitate the direct work with the child?
- Is this person confident in working with a parent or carer and the child together?
- Do they have the time to commit to the work, so that it is of sufficiently high quality to meet the child's needs? Often-cancelled or irregular appointments are not an option.
- If the child is engaged in another therapeutic intervention, does this need to end before the life story work begins? Or in certain circumstances, could the therapist play a role in the work?
- Who is going to supervise the direct work? It can evoke strong feelings in the adults as well as in the children, so it is important to have an outlet for this and support when it comes to making decisions about how to share information. As a network we need to be convinced that if we decide to withhold information it is in the best interests of the child, and not because it is unbearable to us. This sometimes means taking the time to process the impact of what has happened in the child's life, especially if it resonates with personal life experiences.
- If something feels too challenging, consider whether it is right that you should do it. When professionals lack confidence in the work, this has a potential impact on how well they can support the child and their family. If it is not an essential part of the work, do not do it – can someone else in the network fulfil the role? If it is essential, it is important not to go beyond your level of competence.

INFORMED CONSENT AND A TRIAL RUN

Given that some social work professionals and therapists might not be clear themselves about what life story work entails, we should not expect that children and young people will understand either without some help to do so. Given that no two pieces of life story will look the same, this further complicates the issue of 'informed consent' to a more formal piece of work. Children should be involved in a decision to start life story work while recognising that some may subsequently choose not to access information about their early life. They should never be forced to do so – be mindful of the strategies children rely on to get through the day, and avoiding thinking about upsetting things that have happened might be one of those defences. Remember the core principles of restorative practice – working *with* not doing *to* or *for* (Wachtel 2016).

If a child or young person does want to begin life story work, it is important to agree clear expectations about the scope of the work from the outset with a working agreement, so that whatever follows is a consensual activity (Baynes 2008; Hammond and Cooper 2013; Wrench and Naylor 2013) (for ideas about how to do this, see Chapter 4, p.63). These expectations can be revisited during the work, if necessary, but I often find that inviting children to first be part of a 'trial run' can be helpful – about four to six sessions in which I can begin to assess where the child is – and they can also test me out to see if they think we can work together. For many children this feels like a much less onerous undertaking, and they have an early 'get-out clause' if they need it.

I have worked with several children who, at the end of the trial run, have then opted out. As frustrating as this might be for the network around the child, it is imperative that the child is listened to and their position respected. They may have other priorities at that time, or may not be ready to explore their stories. One child in kinship care told me, 'I know what happened and I see no point at all in going back over it. I just want to get on with my life.' Another adopted child with a life story book written at the point of placement, which was insufficient to explain why two adopters had become one soon after they came home, did not want to proceed because they already had a life story book – so why bother? I suspect that both children, in different ways, were invested in not thinking about the pain of their stories at that time, and these defences were both powerful and protective. The reality is that 'the content of the history of most children who have been removed from their birth families is very distressing and that the very process of doing the work invokes unresolved traumatic memories' (Burnell and Vaughan 2008, p.224). I hope that when *they* are ready, rather than when the system deems them to be ready, they will be able to ask for help understanding their journeys, having had their views respected.

I often get asked what we should do if it's clear children would benefit from life story work, but they say no, or they are not able to work with us. Maybe they are asking their parents or carers lots of questions, but the adults feel ill-equipped to answer them. This has happened to me when working with adoptees a couple of times. On one of these occasions, English was not the adoptive parent's first language, and the original life story book didn't contain good enough explanations of the 'why' for the parent to feel they could confidently answer their child's questions. When it became clear during the 'trial run' that this little one was struggling to engage because they were so anxious, the answer was clear. I needed to support their parent to feel more confident in engaging with life story conversations with their child as and when the child instigated them, and not when I turned up once a week.

The parent and I subsequently worked together to re-write the child's life story book, integrating information from their life in the adoptive family, giving more detail to explain why they couldn't live with their birth parents and integrating the work we had done together. This gave the parent both a useful tool and the language they needed to support their child to make sense of their journey.

VENUE

Think carefully about the venue, although I appreciate you might not have much of a choice. You will need a consistent, predictable space where you will not be interrupted, and where the child can learn to feel safe enough to engage. Ideally, I like to have some natural light, room to move around if needed, and not too many distractions in terms of games and toys. I also like us to be able to make a bit of a creative mess without worrying about getting glitter on the carpet. I have worked in my own therapy room, in family homes, in local authority buildings and in schools. Just please be mindful about what will become associated with the space for the child when you introduce traumatic material, especially to what are otherwise 'safe' spaces.

Also consider the *timing* of the session. For example, if you are working together in school, try to meet so you finish the session at break or lunchtime, or even better, at the end of the school day, so the child is not having to go immediately back into class, potentially full up with big feelings. Be mindful of what lesson the child will be missing, and avoid their favourites if you can. Some schools will also understandably ask you to avoid key lessons like phonics in the morning for little ones, or core GCSE subjects in high school.

ASSESSING PARENT OR CARER CAPACITY TO BE INVOLVED IN THE WORK

The more of this work I do, the more convinced I become that the involvement of a child's parent or carer is critical, and this view is shared by others who think and write about life story work (see, for example, Burnell and Vaughan 2008; Kagan 2009; Rose 2017; Shotton 2020). However, as with all aspects of life story practice, there is no *one-size-fits-all* approach. As a practitioner, you may have limited experience of parent–child work, which can inevitably impact confidence; this was certainly the case for me. However, you sometimes need to be prepared to take a risk to allow your practice to evolve. Your skills can quickly develop by reading around the subject and getting appropriate support, training or supervision. The potential benefits to the child and to the relationship between the child and their parent or carer are immeasurable.

Parent–carer engagement and involvement is something to be discussed at the initial planning meeting, and then followed up when you meet them on an individual basis. After gaining a sense of the appropriateness of working with the dyad from the system's perspective, it is also important to hear the child and parent or carer's view. When there is a specific focus to the work, such as creating narrative coherence, enhancing regulation or processing a particular event, it can be incredibly helpful to collaborate with parents or carers and build their skills so that they can take an active role in the life story work. They can then provide a bridge between sessions and a sense of safety for the child in the work, but it is critical to plan and prepare.

Arrange to meet with the child's parent or carer at the earliest opportunity to explain the life story process and to gather information about the child's life. It is important that from this earliest engagement you are working in a collaborative way, respectful of the fact that they are more expert in their child than you are, and building confidence in this way of working. I rely heavily on this insider knowledge parents and carers bring to plan the intervention together. You will need to see yourselves as a team, with both parties bringing critical knowledge and skill to the work. Of course, in working with the parent or carer, not only will you be gathering information, you will also be sharing information and preparing them, which includes identifying any potential triggers for parents or carers. They may need time to process their reactions to the child's history before they are able to be available to support their child.

In this early meeting, begin to think about parental or carer capacity, as there are diverse ways in which they might contribute to the life story work. In setting up the work, it is critical that you agree what this will look like. During your time together, think about the relationship between the parent or carer and the child. Is the relationship or family system under stress? Would the life story process benefit from the parent or carer first having a space where they can think about the child's emotional world and their experiences before joining their family? This is even more pertinent when children are living with kinship carers – the child's story is often also their own story too.

> I supported Ron and Elise[1] who cared for their niece and nephew, who they hadn't known growing up after becoming estranged from their father, Ron's brother. However, when they were first introduced before the children moved in, nobody told these children, then aged four and five, that Ron and Elise were relatives. Elise recalls:
>
> > We were very nervous about discussing family ties. And we both had feelings of anger when we found out what had happened to the kids. We thought, 'How could he?' It was very difficult for us to face those emotions, but also to deal with the children's emotions, because ultimately, it's the children's emotions that are most important. The biggest worry was about their capacity to really understand those family relationships because they had never met any other family before us. Would they think Ron was like their dad? He even looks like him! Would they think that's how all dads behave? We had to deal with our feelings first and then put them to one side so we could support the children.

Where parents or carers have some capacity for thinking about and supporting their child, life story work can play an important role in

1 Please note that pseudonyms have been used here rather than real names.

strengthening the relationship between children in care, adoptees and their parents or carers: 'The empathy and understanding that can emerge when you travel a life story journey with a child cannot be underestimated and can sometimes be enough to stabilise placements' (Wrench and Naylor 2013, p.12). Therefore, it is important to involve parents or carers in this work where possible, so that the opportunity for this positive impact is not lost. Indeed, there are multiple goals that can be met in relation to the engagement of the parent or carer, not least ensuring they have access to full details and understanding of the child's history. From here you can link the past to the present to help both the child and the parent or carer to understand how early life experiences continue to impact the child in the here and now.

Indicators for working with the parent or carer and child in the room together

When planning the work, there are many considerations in respect of working with the dyad. You will get a feel for these factors as you get to know each other in your early meetings, and as you talk about the parent or carer's relationship with their child and their understanding of the child's history. It may be that one parent or carer demonstrates these qualities in abundance, but the other less so. The priority for the life story work is that the parent or carer who is going to join the sessions:

- has the capacity and curiosity to think about the child
- is empathic and understanding of the child's early history, and can make connections with their presentation in the here and now
- sees themselves as a key agent of change for the child
- retains some capacity for playfulness, and can enjoy time with their child
- is aware of and can manage their own emotions or, when necessary, can be supported to recognise, contain and eventually understand them. This can be of particular relevance to kinship care where there often is a direct personal connection to the narrative
- possesses a high enough level of reflective function
- is available to the child for co-regulation

- can be sensitive to the child's needs. Do they empathise with the child's position? You need a parent or carer who is aware of the 'signals' from the child related to need, who can make an accurate interpretation of them, and give an appropriate and prompt response to them. They need to be able to tune into the child's needs, and not become overwhelmed by them
- has capacity for collaboration and is open to working with others and hearing their view.

Possible barriers to working with the parent or carer and child in the room together

- Starting or continuing with dyadic work if the parent or carer cannot think about the child and their needs and/or is too preoccupied with their own difficulties at that time. Can the parent or carer contain the story? Will it overwhelm their coping mechanisms and render them unavailable for the child?
- Where a parent or carer is in a state of blocked care, they tend to be judgemental towards the child and themself, and can find it hard to be empathic. They may need support to top up their own tank first, before being able to sit alongside the child's pain (Baylin and Hughes 2016).
- Where the parent or carer cannot be in the space without first giving an account of everything that has gone wrong since you last met, they will need some containment, and may benefit from some therapeutic parenting support or a call before the dyadic session to hand over information they feel is critical.
- Time – can they regularly commit to meeting with you and prioritise the work? Are they in full-time employment, or do they have other caregiving responsibilities?
- Is the child or young person adamant they do not want their parent or carer to be present in the room? It is important if so to understand why not, and to think creatively about how to ensure that there is a feedback loop that everyone agrees to.
- Do you find yourself taking sides, or overly identifying with one

half of the dyad? It is important in this case to have space to reflect on this in supervision.

- Family dynamics – including within the placement and with the birth family. Is the parent or carer too busy with other caring responsibilities or the needs of other children in the family to fully commit to the work? How do they talk about the child's birth family?

MODELS FOR DYADIC WORKING

When planning dyadic work there are multiple considerations. This checklist will help you to formulate a plan:

- Consider the structure of sessions, which will always be determined on a case-by-case basis – will they be directive or non-directive?
- Ensure that the parent or carer understands their role in the session – to follow the child's lead, not take over the activity and maintain an attitude of playfulness and curiosity.
- Rules of thumb are useful, for example, about who is responsible for maintaining the boundaries or whether to bring issues from home into the session.
- Agree what will happen if one week the parent or carer is not able to join the session. Will you cancel, or see the child individually that week? How will relevant information then be handed over?
- Is the parent or carer's role to witness the process at first hand, gain insight and provide a sense of safety for the child, or is it to directly contribute to reflection and understanding? Is it a more active co-worker role? Do you think it might be possible to have reflective, curious conversations together that might benefit the child?

> I worked with an eight-year-old child, 'B', and their foster carer. They struggled to verbalise how they were feeling in the here and now, but also found it hard to talk about their terrifying experience living with a birth parent. Sometimes 'B' would be playing in the sand tray or with soldiers and a fort, while the carer and I had some curious

conversations. We wondered how baby 'B' might have felt when they heard shouting or had a hungry tummy. We imagined into what that experience was like. Sometimes 'B' said nothing. Sometimes 'B' interjected briefly to correct or concur with us, often non-verbally with a little nod or shake of the head. Sometimes 'B' was able to show us through art-making what they were thinking and feeling. This process of mentalising or mentalisation, where we learn to see ourselves from the outside and others from the inside, is critical to human development. 'B' had the opportunity, which they had sadly lacked as an infant, of us trying to understand their state of mind and connecting those states to feelings and behaviour.

If, for some reason, it is not possible for the parent or carer to be present for logistical reasons, because the child doesn't want it, or because you assess it not to be in the child's best interests at that time, think about how you are going to communicate with them throughout the work. Consider the following, and agree this clearly with the family at the beginning of the work:

- Could they join for 10 to 15 minutes at the end of the session? You and the child then agree what needs to be 'handed over'. This ensures that the child will get a 'soft landing' when they get home if needed, and that a parent or carer is available for support to discuss any issues that have arisen during the session that week. Remember that the process of integrating the material does not stop when the session ends.

- If they are not involved in transporting the child to/from the session, could you agree with the child what needs to be handed over and call the parent or carer when each session ends or later the same day? Could they be available once a month for a joint session? If anything urgently needs to be shared in the interim period, you can agree that you will do so through a phone call or secure email.

I worked in the family home with a care-experienced young adult who was still living with their foster carer. They didn't want their carer to be directly in the room during the sessions, but they would always be home, busy in the kitchen making dinner or watching TV. Before we finished the session, we would agree what was important to hand over

> to the carer. The young person would then leave, allowing me to share what was important to share, without them having to be physically present. There was an acknowledgement that it was important for the foster carer to be aware of what we had been thinking about that week, but also that it felt too difficult for the young person to directly witness the sharing of information.

It is important in any case to build in regular reviews with parents or carers where relevant. You then need to continue to give them the support they need throughout the work to be able to support their children, and to jointly plan and prepare for the work. Consider, also, whether a supervising social worker might be available for foster carers, or a post adoption support worker for adoptive parents.

3

GATHERING INFORMATION

Good life story work depends on having access to what I think of as the 'information spine', the stories of the child's life and experiences. This is also sometimes known as the 'information bank'. Lauerman (2015) references the fact that 'growth in the availability of information from written, electronic and social media sources, only increases the complexity and challenges that will be only too well known to anyone who has tried to extract information and create a coherent narrative even from a range of written material'. Effective and impactful work in relation to children's life stories cannot be undertaken unless information contained in records is sufficient as a basic starting point.

Information is not only written or oral. Recognising that adolescents communicate differently from younger children, Hammond and Cooper (2013) suggest incorporating a range of accessible digital technologies to provide interactive and practical activities to support workers to empower young people to take the lead in the creation of, and reflection on, their own story. You might also think about video or audio recordings of interviews with other key individuals as part of this process.

Gathering information should come right at the beginning of your work, following your planning sessions, and before you start the formal work with the child. You will need a comprehensive understanding of the child's story yourself first, as well as knowing where the gaps might be, if you are to instil confidence in parents or carers and in the child. You are not expected to know everything, of course, but you do need to hold a coherent narrative in your mind as you shape the work. This is not something to rush into without thorough preparation.

> Working with a nine-year-old adopted child, we worked towards an exchange of video messages with a birth parent, with me as the

'go-between'. By this stage we had worked on the reasons why the child hadn't been able to live with their birth parents. The questions that remained were not necessarily going to be found in a chronology. For example: 'Why did you pick my name and choose that spelling of it?' 'Was I a planned baby?' 'How old was my birth mum when she started puberty?'

INFORMATION FROM THE LOCAL AUTHORITY

In training social care staff, I am forever talking about how the time to begin to think about record keeping that will support the development of a coherent narrative for a child is the day we first become involved in a family's life. Waiting until a decision is made about whether a child will come into care or not return home is far too late. Everyone working with children and young people in the care system should recognise that their recordings may later contribute to life story work. From those records we need to be able to understand the basis of decision making, see explanations of and justification for any actions and direct interventions in family life, as well as the context within which any decisions were made or not.

Everyone involved in the child's life must also be mindful that what they record might be read by the child when they reach adulthood. The MIRRA Project (MEMORY – IDENTITY – RIGHTS IN RECORDS – ACCESS)[1] was based in the Department of Information Studies at University College London (UCL) and undertaken in partnership with the Care Leavers' Association (CLA), a care leaver-led charity. It focused on access to care records and noted that trends had emerged suggesting that revisiting childhood experiences often coincided with significant moments of reflection, for example, when leaving care, moving into a new career, being in prison, following the birth of a child or on retirement: 'The coincidence of these key events with the turn to memory is consistent with understandings of how the self is reconstructed at moments of personal change' (Hoyle *et al.* 2020, p.938). It is disappointing that one of the project's findings was 'a lack of consideration for the identity and memory needs of care-experienced children, young people and adults in England' (p.942), due to inadequate record keeping and inconsistencies in access and release protocols. The project also found that developments in social

1 https://blogs.ucl.ac.uk/mirra/about

work record keeping since the 1980s, such as the introduction of life story work and participatory report writing, had not translated sufficiently to practice in such a way as to make a difference to care-experienced people. Only five of the 21 care-experienced adults interviewed remembered life story work, and sadly, only three had access to it as adults. The impact of this can be long lasting and is a theme of many reflections from care experienced adults.

> I needed this work; in all honesty I still need this work. I'm 27 and still to this day feel very alone with my story, very confused and things remain very unclear; 1000 pages of my files have not given me the closure I expected. Although it has helped me understand some of the decisions, I was also left feeling even more muddled. (Mary Carter, care-experienced adult)

So, when thinking about record keeping, think about its short- and longer-term function, including being proactive in seeking out reflections and memories. In relation to life story work, for example, if a birth parent is attending family time, ask the contact supervisors (with the parent or carer's permission) to take plenty of photographs, which can then be uploaded to your shared recording platform, together with some short videos of their interactions. Make sure the parent or carer gets a copy too. Give supervisors ideas of the kinds of questions to ask during family time, so that they can gather some softer information that way, or encourage foster carers to ask one or two questions in the contact book that can be used to exchange information between the foster carer and birth parent. This can be as simple as 'What is your favourite TV programme/colour/song?' 'What stories did you enjoy when you were little?' Think about developing a format for family time supervisors, child protection chairs or the independent reviewing officer to capture their memories of the child and family. They will often know both the parents and the child well, and in many cases could contribute the most beautiful letters that may later prove to be invaluable to the child's understanding of themself and their birth family.

Accessibility to social care files will depend on your role and whether you work for the same local authority responsible for the child or not. If not, request access at the earliest opportunity, through the child's social worker or post adoption support social worker who has commissioned the work, if you are in private practice. Viewing files is a lengthy business, so be sure to give it sufficient time at the beginning of the process. Sometimes you need to review everything; sometimes you might approach the task with key questions in mind to support you to fill in the gaps.

> In working with an adoptive family and their child, I benefited from the fact that the adopters had face-to-face meetings with their child's birth parents. The child permanence report and other reports were detailed and of good quality. They had maintained a positive relationship with their child's foster carer.
>
> The reports consistently referenced how family time for this infant was incredibly distressing. The foster carer advocated strongly for a reduction in family time being in the child's best interests. The gap in information for the life story work was a better understanding of what might have been happening during family time that was causing such distress. When accessing the files, I was directed to the contact supervisor's records as a starting point.

There are also key documents that might be helpful to be signposted towards. The chronology prepared for the court as part of care proceedings will document the child's journey to care. There may also be police reports or transcripts of interviews, psychological assessments or psychiatric reports. Adopters may also have other documents such as the child permanence report (CPR), which is also a useful source of information about the child and their birth family. If you are supporting older adopted children, they may already have a life story book and later life letter, which can also be useful in the planning stage.

INFORMATION FROM INTERVIEWS

One of your next jobs is to identify who to interview or to contact to gather information, because case files will only ever give you part of the story. I contact any professional who has been involved with the child over time, specifically previous social workers, supervisors of family time, the independent reviewing officer, child protection chairs, family support workers and social work team managers. These people should have memories about the child and their family, and will hopefully be able to share different stories to those you will find in a formal case record. And this is at the heart of good life story work: gathering all the facts, fantasies, hopes, dreams and anecdotes that are specific to the child.

I know people are busy, so I tend to ask them to share a memory that is special to them about the child or their family – something that makes them smile, something they admire about the child or have learned from them. These are like golden nuggets for children whose lives have been so fractured, whose memories have sadly not always been held precious. These reflections should all be integrated into your work with the child and/or into the product (the life story book) together with some golden nuggets of your own.

> I used to collect a child to bring them to the life story session. We got into a little habit during this brief journey after I had downloaded a new album. We would listen to their favourite track, then my favourite track, and then choose a random third song, and by this time we had usually arrived at our destination. We wouldn't just listen; we'd joyfully sing our hearts out, and this would help with the transition. This is the kind of detail I'm looking for. Stories of connection that are specific to the child.

Then consider how and where you are going to conduct the interviews. You might want to ask the interviewee if you can record the session so you can be fully present and not preoccupied with note taking. You could offer the chance to meet over a video call and ask permission to make a recording. Remember that information gathering does not have to be the responsibility of just one person. At the planning stage agree who is the most appropriate person in each case to approach different people.

INFORMATION FROM BIRTH FAMILY MEMBERS

Contributions from wider birth family members, not just parents, are priceless when you are writing life story books or undertaking direct work with children to understand their stories. Consider who within the family system might be able to be part of the work, and think in the initial planning stages about who the best person would be to facilitate these conversations. This is important for so many reasons, but what seems to me to be imperative is, that *if it is safe to do so*, the child can hear about more than just what 'went wrong' in their birth family directly from their family. Post adoption order, the child's adoptive parents would need to agree to contact being made with birth family members. There then needs to be an explicit agreement made about what, if any, information can be shared about the adoptee with birth family members before an approach is made.

There is much more emphasis now on more open contact arrangements in adoption, acknowledging the lifelong impact of adoption on a child's identity development. At the very least this should include the option of birth and adoptive parents meeting or exchanging letters. While ongoing direct contact between children and their birth family members remains the exception rather than the rule, there is growing acceptance 'that well managed contact can help everyone involved' (Green 2019, p.133). This includes birth parents who are given the opportunity to provide information, offer reassurance their child is remembered and loved, but also receive updates on the child's progress.

> I met with a birth parent who agreed to write an explanation of how they felt their mental health impacted their parenting capacity when their child was still living at home. After we met, they agreed to write an explanation of how they felt at that time and how their mental health impacted their parenting capacity. I would argue this account was far more accurate a representation of events than I could ever have provided. It gave the parent an opportunity to contribute towards a greater understanding for their child of their story, which felt incredibly important to them given the lack of direct contact. The parent also had their own experiences and feelings validated, which they acknowledged felt unusual based on previous experiences of working with professionals.

If the child is subject to a special guardianship order or is in care, their birth parents will retain parental responsibility, and should always be consulted about life story work and invited to contribute, even if they choose not to be involved. In both scenarios, for birth family members to be able to meet the identity and life story needs of their child, they first need to experience having their own needs understood and supported.

My approach is simple. I should already have access to a chronology that details why a child couldn't safely remain with birth parents. If parents would like to give their perspective on these events, then I am more than happy to listen. In so doing, however, I am mindful of taking parents back to a time in their life that is likely to have been difficult. We have a responsibility towards everyone who played a part in the story, and to ensure they are supported after we leave. It is not our role to be judge and jury, but simply to gather what might be a different perspective to that in the social work files, and accept it for what it is. It can be more powerful for children to hear their birth parents' views in their own words than it can to hear our interpretation of them.

> A child suffered a significant non-accidental injury as a baby inflicted by a birth parent but didn't know the detail of what or how it had happened. As they were still having supervised family time, it was important to talk to the parent *before* talking to the child about the nature of the injury. Initially they were upset, angry and concerned that if their child knew how the injury had been inflicted, they would stop all contact.
>
> I offered the parent support to write the child a letter to explain what was going on in their life at the time of the incident – there were multiple stressors that contributed to losing control and lashing out, and this parent wanted their child to understand the context.
>
> However, the parent also took responsibility for the actions that led to the injury. They explained their deep regret for what had happened, acknowledged they deserved the punishment they received and expressed hope for forgiveness.

Sometimes in cases like this it might be possible and appropriate for parents or family members to make a direct contribution to life story work or to the book. Where birth parents are willing and able to take responsibility for their role in the child being in care or adopted, this can be so much more powerful than when we say the child was not to blame for their losses. For example, where a birth parent is able to explain, in their own words, what life was like when they were experiencing domestic abuse or struggling to break free of an addiction, this is likely to hold more meaning for the child. Keep an open mind about how this might happen.

Most commonly, what I ask of parents and other birth family members is to share the *other stories*, the stories I won't find in the case files. These are precious threads of connection between them and their child that might otherwise be lost. Don't forget the simple things that many of us take for granted, such as who we look like or take after:

> While I was growing up I hated looking in mirrors, as I didn't resemble anyone. Looking in a mirror just accentuated the fact that I was adopted, and I looked like a stranger. I found looking in mirrors hard and it was something I avoided.
>
> When I began my reunion journey, I thought I really don't mind who I look like, I just want to be able to look at my biological family and say, 'Yes I can see you in me.' (Danielle 2021)

I seek the anecdotes and the tales that are special to them because we know that they tend to have positive meaning for children and birth parents alike, and most children love to hear stories about themselves. Walker (2020) suggests offering birth parents ideas about how they might record things themselves, for example, completing

> a baby book for their child who will go on to be adopted, complete with photos of themselves as children, photos of relatives, and pregnancy scan pictures. If parents are not comfortable writing things, ask if they could record themselves on their phones and then help them to send this to foster carers or family support workers if they are not happy to send it directly to the social worker. Help them think of things to record and whether they have any objects or baby clothes they want to share.

Social scientist Debbie Watson was involved in a project with Coram where they talked to adoptees about the things that mattered most to them, remarking on the emotional value of objects and mementoes from the birth family:

> These biographical objects unsurprisingly hold deep significance for the child. The act of being able to touch, hold and explore baby clothes, ribbons indicating length at birth, drawings, toys, souvenirs from family outings and gifts from birth family members seem to be of real importance in helping them feel more emotionally connected to their pasts. (Watson 2015)

This project led to a small study of adopted children, trialling a digitally enhanced memory box (Watson, Meineck and Lancaster 2018) exploring the significance of these objects that are often too big to include in a memory box or life story book:

> There is some empirical evidence to suggest that physical objects are important as memory prompts in enabling adopted and looked after children to narrate the self and develop a sense of identity...children who misplace, lose or have possessions kept from them through their care journey report feelings of ongoing loss and instability beyond loss of family, foster carers and other people in their lives.

It is therefore critical that you give yourself plenty of time and be prepared to meet birth family members if necessary for a second or third time. It can be helpful to have a general outline of the kinds of questions or topics you would like to cover. This might be based on questions the child has, or to fill in the knowledge and understanding you have where there are significant gaps. I love the fact that during these conversations we often have the freedom to go off on tangents and hear the detail of the stories, but equally I do not want to come away disappointed that I missed an opportunity to ask about key information.

Here are some ideas, with some borrowed from Nicholls (2005, pp.106–121). You'd be surprised by how often children in care and adoption don't have *basic information about family members*. Evidently be mindful of including information in stories for children where there may be a risk ascribed to a child making contact with their birth family (for example through social media) without support, so think carefully about including full names, dates of birth and addresses – this information can still be given to adoptive parents or foster carers where appropriate, but doesn't need to be in the life story book. Do think about asking for details about other things, such as:

- Height?
- Weight?
- Build?
- Shoe size?
- Hair colour?
- Eye colour?
- Complexion?
- Do they wear glasses?

- Health issues and medical history?
- Left- or right-handedness?
- Talents, hobbies or interests?
- Favourite things: to eat, to do in free time, to watch on TV/at the cinema, places to visit, holidays, animals, colour, pets, music to listen to, clothes to wear, etc.?
- Religious or political beliefs?
- Personality?

It is important to be able to say who this child takes after, looks like and shares characteristics or personality traits with. We are back to the threads of positive connection again. Where is the common ground? These are all issues that were identified as important in research with adolescent adoptees (Wrobel and Dillon 2009).

You might want to ask about *their childhood or experiences growing up*:

- What did they like/dislike about school and what/who was their college/favourite subject or teacher?
- Happiest memories or stories passed down through the generations?
- Friendships and games they liked to play?
- Holidays, birthdays and special occasions, such as Christmas and Easter, and how they were celebrated – were there any traditions, and if so, where or who did they come from?
- Important family members – who did they spend time with as a child?
- Family rules or values and where they came from?
- Favourite toys/books/music/interests?
- Family pets?
- Nicknames?

Then don't forget the *here and now*. Even for children who have ongoing connections with their birth parents, either through direct or indirect contact, it is still important to include these questions. Children tell us it is not always easy to ask during family time. It is often a delicate balance to get right. If children are aware of the reasons their parents couldn't care safely for them when they first came into care, it makes sense that they might still worry about or become preoccupied with understanding whether their parent is still using drugs, still in an abusive relationship or homeless, for example. We don't want to add to children's worries but nor should we sanitise the situation and lead children to feel all parental difficulties are resolved when they are not. So you could ask about:

- Who they live with?
- What they do, day to day?
- What they enjoy – TV/film/socialising/reading/music/fashion?
- Current friends/important relationships?
- How they get along with other family members – who do they see and when?
- Any positive life changes or who is helping them with their challenges?
- Hopes for the future?
- Health and wellbeing?

Ask about the birth parents' relationship:

- When and how they met...what they remember about that day – the weather, what they had been doing, how they came to be in the place they met, who introduced them?
- What were their thoughts about each other when they first met? What did they like about each other?
- What did they enjoy doing together? Did they have a favourite place?
- How did they treat each other? What was life like for them day to day?
- How and when did they decide to live together/get married? When did this happen?

- If their relationship ended, how, and when?
- What would they have changed?

Ask the birth family for stories about the child:

- How did they feel when they found out about the pregnancy? How was it? Were there any complications?
- Was the child born at term? Birth weight? Place of birth? Who was there? How long was the labour? How long did they both stay in hospital? First thoughts when they held the baby in their arms?
- How did they choose the child's name? Any significance to it?
- Developmental milestones – feeding, motor development (sitting, crawling, walking), sleep, play, weaning?
- Favourite stories, rhymes, toys, teddies, people?
- What would they have changed? Hopes and dreams for the child? Any funny stories or anecdotes?

This is not an exhaustive list, but should get you started. Remember that not only are you hunting for unique and special stories, you are also potentially anticipating the kinds of questions children might have about their birth family in the future.

> A 10-year-old believed that their father had played no part in their life. The story from the birth mother was that he was 'no good', and other than a name, she had previously refused to share any further information about him. This fed into the child's narrative about not being 'good enough', about being abandoned, not worthy of care.
>
> Review of the care files revealed more – that the father had jointly parented this child for the first six months of life and was considered by social workers to be a protective parent. There were no contact details for him, but when I approached the mother, I explained how hard it was for her child to feel like there was a part of them that was missing, that a belief that all that was 'bad' was in their father had left the child feeling they, too, must be 'bad'.

> She didn't share much more with me...the father's place of birth, his footballing allegiances, and his job as a gardener. This was enough at that time. It allowed us to establish a thread of connection between father and child through a shared love of growing vegetables. Maybe this talent came from their father?

These family stories can be the most enlightening and remarkable aspects of family history, and no matter how unusual or far-fetched they may seem, they all help to form our sense of self. They are the threads that connect family members – the things that many of us with enduring familial relationships and opportunities to share and revisit stories with our brothers, sisters and parents take for granted, yet can be denied to adoptees and children in care. I always come back to the idea that if all you know about your birth family are the difficult stories, what does that say about you? The positive threads of connection may be hard to find and may sometimes be tenuous, but children deserve for them to be unearthed. It is important that this process happens *alongside* hearing about the more difficult and challenging parts of a child's story. It shouldn't be a case of one or the other – children need both, wherever possible.

I accept that this is not always a realistic option. It may prove impossible to contact family members, or indeed not be safe to do so. If you do make contact, they may choose to withhold information, or sadly may not remember. They may find the idea of revisiting the past too painful. They may not be able to accept that they are responsible for harms caused to their children or accept the risk factors. They may still be incredibly angry with the social worker or legal system, and feel that the child should still be in their care. This may well get in the way of agreeing to further discussions, but these views should be integrated into the work, nonetheless (see Chapter 6). If the person does not want to speak to you, for whatever reason, you could send them a questionnaire or a list of questions to look at when they feel ready, or ask for copies of photographs. Also consider whether there are organisations locally that offer support to parents whose children are in care or adopted (sadly this provision is far from universal). These organisations can, in some cases, support parents to participate in the life story work, or support them with how they are feeling after contributing.

But remember that, even if family members cannot contribute, there may be others in the network who could share valuable anecdotal information about the child. Supervisors of family time and independent reviewing officers can often offer good insights (and may well have been the most consistent people in the professional network), as can family support workers who may have played an important role in trying to support children to safely remain within their birth family.

> Working with an adolescent in care, I wanted to offer their parent an opportunity to contribute to the life story work. The family support worker was the only person in the network to have maintained a working relationship with this parent over many years, albeit through many ups and downs. Although ultimately we were never able to speak – we made appointments for calls that were never answered – even getting this far was only possible by using the family support worker as a go-between. It would have been easy for me to listen to the common narrative about this parent, that they blamed social workers for the loss of their children, would never cooperate with me and could never see anyone else's perspective. However, I felt it was important to be able to demonstrate to the child that I had done all I could to support this parent to contribute, even if things didn't work out as I'd hoped.

Tempting as it might be to access an open social media profile to gather information about a birth parent, be mindful that social workers have a duty to consider and respect confidentiality and people's right to privacy. This means only accessing a social media account with a parent or carer's consent. If you work for a local authority, please familiarise yourself with their social media policy and any policy that relates specifically to social work practice, although this seems most commonly to relate to surveillance practices in gathering evidence in safeguarding.

INFORMATION FROM ADOPTIVE PARENTS OR CARERS

Consider previous foster carers or residential care workers, and ask for their contributions. Again, in training I stress the importance of safeguarding children's stories – not just taking photographs and putting them in an album, but deep-diving into the experience – what could they see, smell, hear, taste and touch on that day, in that place? Always think about how we can bring the memory back to life using our sensory experiences or immersing the child in a memory.

> I worked with a child many years ago who was now living back with a family member, but who had been in care as an infant.
>
> I discovered that the foster carers were still fostering for the local authority and wrote to them, curious to know if they remembered this child. They were on the phone to me within minutes of receiving the letter, and offered to meet up with me and the child, if the child was interested in so doing. They remembered their time together fondly, and had many stories to tell.
>
> We did indeed visit. The whole extended family, including their now adult children, was there to greet us and to share memories. Even the cot they had slept in was still there! There was also a photograph in the dining room on their 'picture wall' of this child, beaming down at us. What a way to see, as well as hear, that they mattered, they were remembered, and they were still important to the foster carers.

There may occasionally be times where it would be inappropriate to go back to previous carers to gather these memories, if, for example, they have caused the child harm or there has been an allegation made against them by the child. However, even where things have not worked out, or where placements have disrupted, this is not always a reason to avoid including them in the information-gathering phase. Where there have been ruptures in relationships, sometimes there is a beautiful opportunity for repair as part of life story work.

> An adolescent had more foster placement moves than anyone would wish for. One such home was with a newly approved carer. It was never going to be a good match on paper, but choices are not always available to us as social workers, are they? They shared a home for a few months. They enjoyed some positive experiences together, but there were challenges, too, which led to the carer ultimately feeling they weren't the right person to provide care in the longer term.
>
> As part of life story work, contact was made with this foster carer who was able to share their highlights of having got to know this child. They also acknowledged, 18 months on, that they hadn't had the skills or experience to know how best to support the young person at the

> time. They were open to meeting up and it was a positive reunion in which mistakes were acknowledged on both sides. Over time there was repair to the relationship, which would not necessarily have happened without the life story process.

Talk to adoptive parents or carers, and encourage these kinds of contributions within and outside of the direct work, even where children are newly placed: 'Day-to-day carers – especially foster carers, residential support workers and adoptive parents can offer the best informal life story work – at least that which covers their shared care experience. They have the information about the day-to-day events in the child's life, their milestones, and achievements' (Lauerman 2015).

OBJECTS AS MEMORIES

Stories do not only have to be verbal. Objects, if the story goes along with them, can also be invaluable resources: 'In family settings stories, photographs, and memory objects support narratives of identity and belonging. Such resources are often missing for people who were in care as children. As a result, they may be unable to fill gaps in their memories or answer simple questions about their early lives' (Hoyle *et al.* 2020, p.935). In his work around object-based social work, Doel (2017, 2019) explores how the stories and associations that attach to an object can make it significant in developing an understanding of ourselves in the world. An object can provide a focus around which precious stories can wrap.

> One parent met with me to share stories of their child's early life. The only stories I had about this person from the social work files were grim. But they took me up into a spare bedroom, and there I encountered a treasure trove of memories. There was the baby nest all the children had snuggled inside as infants. There were paintings brought home from nursery, first shoes, hospital bracelets, and so much more. In exploring the objects together, I was privileged enough to also hear these stories and pass them onto the child, who was surprised to learn that through many, many house moves, their parent had safeguarded these possessions and memories. These objects served as tangible evidence that the child was precious to their parent.

Where foster carers, residential staff and adoptive parents collate objects in memory boxes, be sure to ask for the story that goes with the photograph or the ticket stub, because that is where the magic lies. We need to know, for example, who is in the photograph, where was it taken, when and by whom. The photograph or the object should not just be a snapshot in time, but also recognised for its potential story-telling power. They are important because 'care leavers may have very few photographs, keepsakes or memory objects from childhood, and they lack a chronology of their childhood, often compounding the trauma that they faced before they came into care' (Shepherd 2022).

'LIFE APPRECIATION DAY' OR 'UNDERSTANDING THE CHILD DAY'

It is common practice in adoption to bring the network around the child together to celebrate their life and share information with prospective adopters. These sessions are designed to offer the child's new family an opportunity to meet people who have been an important part of the child's life to date, and to share their memories and experiences. They are a perfect opportunity for gathering information for a life story book, because one person's memories will often trigger another's. Invitees might range from the social worker who brought the child into care, to the nursery keyworker, to the old nextdoor neighbour or babysitter. If you are planning how to gather information in this way for children in care, there is no reason why you couldn't organise a similar event.

MAKING SENSE OF THE INFORMATION

There are several ways in which to do this depending on what feels most useful. Irrespective of how you record and make sense of the information, the most important thing is that you do so before you begin the work with the child and their family. Make time to go through it with the parent or carer before the work begins:

- Create an *integrated chronology* that pulls together all the source material. I colour-code the entries dependent on the source – for example, social work files in black ink, health records or reports in green ink, information from birth parents in purple ink.

- Draw out a *timeline* on a roll of lining paper – again, you can colour-code the information depending on the source.
- Create a *trauma-nurture timeline* table. This draws on a full and thorough information search including case files, foster carer records and any medical information available. You will then be able to quickly see detailed information about a child's experience at each stage of life, and really appreciate the full depth of that experience. Begin the timeline pre-birth, to include the child's in utero experiences, date the experience, but also begin to relate what is known and what is suspected of the potential impact on the child. For example, if a mother is using drugs or alcohol during pregnancy, or experiences high stress because she knows the plan is for the baby to be removed at birth, what is the impact of that on the child at a particular developmental stage?
- Rose (2012, pp.79–81) suggests using *movement boxes* in a similar way to break down the story into chunks and to identify the relationships between different events. Record the event – for example, an assault on the mother by the father when she was 32 weeks pregnant. Then consider what the practitioner needs to know – was the assault reported to the police? Who else was present? Was the father prosecuted? What injuries were sustained? Did this assault contribute to the child's premature birth? Next, ask yourself if, or in what way, this is relevant to the child now. What might the child need to know? Was anyone else hurt? Why did their dad hurt their mum? What happened after they were born? Then finally, is there any detail about this event that is not appropriate to share at this stage? As you assemble the questions for each 'box', you will see the value of interviewing key stakeholders. This will support you to ensure that the stories you share with the child are as accurate as possible and attributed to the correct source.

4

STAGE ONE OF LIFE STORY WORK

HELPING IT FEEL SAFE ENOUGH TO GO BACK

One of the most important considerations at the beginning of your work with any child or young person and their family is to begin to build a relationship and to assess what they will need from you during the life story work. Although I think of this part of the work as an assessment, I don't use that terminology with children. I ask them to think about spending some time together as a bit of a *trial run*. It's a way of me beginning to get to know the child and their parent or carer, but is also essential if I am to establish where the focus of the work should be. It should also, of course, be an opportunity for the child to get to know me, so they can decide whether they'd be happy for us to work together in the longer term. Sometimes the 'fit' might not be right, and children and their parents or carers need to feel empowered to say if they feel this is the case.

Before beginning this first phase of the work, I will have already met with the child's parent or carer at least once, and usually more than that. We will have explored the child's history together, to ensure they know what I know, and vice versa. I will have taken advice about what will work best for their child, including where to meet, what time, where to sit, whether to have a creative focus or more talking. We will have decided collaboratively how we think we might work together (see Chapter 2).

MEETING WITH THE CHILD

Before beginning the life story sessions, I meet with the child just to say 'hello'. During this meeting, some children like to introduce you to their home and show you their toys or pets. Others might like to play some games to begin to get to know each other, read a favourite story or draw together. Sometimes I introduce a game to support safe sharing of information about each other. This could be using Sentence Completion Cards that help me learn more about the child before starting the work proper (Treisman 2017b) or even Rory's Story® Cubes from the Creativity Hub.[1] Other children connect better with a shared game on a console or watching funny videos together on YouTube.

ICEBREAKER GAMES

M&M'S

One of my favourite icebreaker games, if food isn't a trigger or a contentious issue, is played with M&M's or other multicoloured sweets, and it's good to include parents or carers too. There are lots of ways to play the game to get to know each other better. Option one is to first prepare a list of six questions (see 'Ideas for questions' below) and to sit in a circle or around a table together. Pass around the bowl of M&M's and tell each person to take a small handful, but not to eat any yet. If this feels too high an expectation, an adult can take charge of the sharing, or prepare some little pots or bags with sweeties in before beginning. Then, for each sweet that everyone has in their hand, they have to share something about themselves. Each colour M&M will have a different subject to share about, and each time you share something, you get to eat the M&M it's related to – continue this until everyone has shared enough for all their M&M's to be eaten.

Ideas for questions

There are usually six colours in a packet of M&M's – red, green, blue, yellow, orange and brown – so you need to devise a list of six questions. You could agree safe and engaging subjects with the parent or carer before you arrive. These can be about anything you like, but here is a list of some different ideas to get you started:

- favourite snack
- role model or someone you look up to
- hobbies

1 www.storycubes.com/en

- dream job
- something you like about another person playing the game
- favourite story, book or TV programme
- best thing to have for dinner
- best ever holiday
- most exciting video game to play
- ideal pet.

When you've decided on the six subjects, write them down so that you can refer to the list during the game, and allocate a colour to each one.

Option two is a simpler variation. Empty a small bag of M&M's into a little jar or tub. Pass the jar around the group, asking each person to choose one and to hold onto it. Then take turns answering questions that correspond to the colour, but in this instance, have the colour sheet already prepared. For example, a red M&M means you share your favourite memory from the last school holidays, or an orange M&M means you talk about your top three desserts.

BEACH BALL/BEAN BAG GET TO KNOW YOU

Sometimes movement is good if you have enough space, and for this game you'll need an inflatable beach ball or a bean bag (nothing that will cause too much damage) that is big enough to catch fairly easily. Stand in a circle and have one person start by holding the beach ball. The person with the beach ball begins by saying someone's name and throwing the beach ball to that person (for example, 'Katie'). Whoever catches the beach ball must repeat their own name and share one thing about themself. For example, 'I'm Katie and I like watching football.' Next, they say the name of somebody else in the session and toss the beach ball to that person, with the game continuing until everyone has caught the beach ball. You can then go for a few more rounds, but this time the thrower says, 'This is for Katie who likes watching football' as they throw the beach ball to Katie.

TEDDY BEAR/PUPPET INTRODUCTION GAME

For younger children, you can use a teddy bear or puppet to help. Explain that you will be playing a game where each person pretends to be a teddy bear. Everybody will then use the teddy bear to introduce themselves and share one of their favourite things. To start, hold up the teddy bear and pretend it is talking for you: 'Hello, my name is Katie, and my favourite colour is green.' Feel free to be as playful as feels comfortable as you pass the teddy bear around the circle and give everyone a chance to create their persona for the teddy bear. There is then scope for the child to use this teddy bear to speak for them during the work, if that feels helpful.

HOW MANY FACTS IN 90 SECONDS?

Pair up and ask each other to share interesting facts about each other with a timer of 90 seconds. You might need to have a list of questions on little cards as prompts for some children.

BEING CLEAR ABOUT WHY WE ARE HERE

Although it is important to have some fun, during this initial meeting I will also ensure that the child understands who I am, why we are meeting, and talk about what the work *might* look like. I stress the word 'might'. Within this model, every child will need the focus to be on different areas and will move through those stages of work at different rates. This is why I always struggle to definitively say how long a piece of life story work will take, and why I don't favour manualised approaches to the work. As the lead worker you will not be responsible for completing all this work, but you do need to establish the starting point and coordinate the different strands of life story work.

I often start with fortnightly meetings because this allows space in between the sessions for other work to happen. This might be developing skills and competence around regulation or working towards a sense of felt safety at the beginning, or processing material later in the work. Some young people prefer to meet weekly, which is also fine if you can regularly commit to this frequency of contact, but I would avoid leaving too big a gap between sessions as you can lose momentum quickly. You also risk children being left with big feelings that need some containment, or with unanswered questions for extended periods, which is unhelpful and potentially destabilising. Follow the child's lead around what they can manage, which means never prioritising the task over the child's capacity on the day. You must be prepared and confident enough to be flexible and change the plan from what you had intended, including potentially working at a much slower pace than you had originally planned.

I cannot stress enough the need for this work to be given the priority it deserves, which I know is often a challenge if you are working in a local authority. Placement disruption, court hearings and strategy meetings are always deemed more important, and the impact of cancelling life story sessions is not always fully understood. It is always better to under-promise in terms of the frequency of sessions than over-promise. Perhaps be explicit about the fact that sometimes emergencies happen, and explain how you will let each other know in these circumstances.

These are all things to consider when you are setting up the work in your initial parent or carer sessions, but also in your early meetings with the child:

> Remember that children who have experienced relational trauma will have a belief that the world and others are unsafe, so building routines and rituals into your interactions can help decrease feelings of insecurity and vulnerability. You may need to pay attention to the child's need for control around your interactions. If, for example, you bring a structured activity of your choosing, it can be helpful to also factor in time for some free play or an activity of the child's choice. (Wrench 2018, p.36)

This is not wasting time; it is ensuring that the pace is right for the child, and that they feel regulated enough to be alongside you.

A WORKING AGREEMENT

A working agreement for the life story work is a good starting point in helping it feel safe enough for a child or young person to begin this work, because we know that consistency and predictability are critical. There is safety in sameness. The most important factor is coming to an agreement about how you will work together moving forward, with transparency of aims and goals from the outset for the child and their parent or carer. Having established strong, clear boundaries as part of the much-needed structure to the life story work, these boundaries must then be held firmly. Remember that if you give children an instruction rather than making a request, there is much needed clarity rather than confusion. A request can be easily misinterpreted as a choice or an option, and if it is not really a choice, this can be difficult for children to manage and does not set them up for success.

You will only need basic resources to make a working agreement, such as paper and pens. Other collage and craft materials are nice to have, but not essential. The working agreement becomes a document that sets the ground rules for your sessions with the child and their parent or carer. I encourage the child to take ownership by drawing or writing on the agreement themselves, and try to incorporate some of their interests too. For example, you could use a gaming theme, sport or a favourite TV programme, which aids engagement by valuing the child's interest. Coming prepared with images you know the child is more likely to connect with also gives a strong message of having been held in mind by you.

> I worked with a young person who loved *EastEnders* and enjoyed drama classes. On their working agreement the 'rules' were contained in speech bubbles spoken by the current cast. I simply downloaded some images before the session and used them as a resource when making the image. This simple act made the activity more accessible, and gave this autistic child an opportunity to share one of their interests.

The child might like to contribute their ideas about the work, such as playing a quick game at the beginning of the session, and agreeing a way of letting you know when they need to stop. It can be reassuring to explicitly be asked 'How will you let me know if you need a break?' Or 'How will you tell me if you feel unsafe or can't talk about something just now?' This is harder than it sounds for many children – they may show you through behaviour (getting up and leaving the room, or beginning to fidget), but it is important they know it is okay to say they don't want to do an activity or have had enough for today. Sometimes you might need the help of a parent or carer in this, who is likely to tune into non-verbal cues much quicker than you. This can prevent a child becoming overwhelmed or dysregulated. As you get to know the child and they, too, begin to understand their early warning signs better, this may shift over time, but in any case, permission to take a break is vital, as is permission not to return to the session after that break. They may need more time and to start afresh the next time you meet.

The working agreement should include key information about what to expect from the life story process and from each other. If children have engaged in therapeutic work before, I always ask what they found helpful and what they found unhelpful. You could also ask if they have any suggestions for the agreement, or any questions about what is going to happen.

> I was the third person from my team to attempt to work with a 10-year-old child in a children's home. Both previous attempts had only lasted for a few sessions before they refused to come any more or became incredibly dysregulated at home. I asked if they could share what they had liked and not liked so I could make sure I didn't make the same mistakes. I took responsibility for the fact we hadn't got it right for them yet. They were immediately clear that one of the 'rules' should be that I did not mention the name of their birth dad, whom they had chosen not to see. I explained that life story work is tricky if we don't ever talk about birth family. But also, that I would leave it up to the child to decide when they were ready to do so. We wrote this explicitly into the working agreement: 'Do not talk about X until [child's name] is ready.' Allowing them to feel in control of their story meant that within weeks they brought him into the work. Over time we were able to think and talk about their life together, and the child's ambivalent feelings about their parent could be explored and validated.

Considerations for content for your working agreement should include:

- Practical arrangements, such as where and when you will meet.
- How many sessions you will have together and for how long. Some children will benefit from a visual timetable marking down the sessions with a tick or a sticker, for example.
- Confidentiality and the limitations of information boundaries. Explain with whom information about the work will be shared, especially if it is not possible to have the parent or carer in every session. Discuss what will happen if a safeguarding concern is raised.
- What kinds of things you might talk about, and anything the child does not want to talk about yet.
- Expectations of each other, for example if someone is ill or running late – how will you let each other know?
- Whether you will have a drink or a snack, and who is responsible for bringing it.
- The importance of physical safety where applicable, for example, rules about respecting the room, resources, each other.

- Permission to make mistakes.
- Agreement about the use of mobile phones – for children and for adults!
- Understanding about what happens to the materials, artwork or objects you make during the activities. I keep them safe between sessions in a large plastic box or art folder, and this is non-negotiable. I will offer to take a photograph and send it to the parent or carer, if the child really feels they need it now, but the physical object stays safe with me until the end of the work. This is for three reasons. First, because we often come back to do more work on something in subsequent weeks, and once things go home with a child, in my experience they rarely come back, meaning opportunities for further exploration are lost. Second, these materials form a record of the life story journey, and I always find it helpful to reflect on this at the end of the work, looking at what has been created from start to finish, and agreeing together what, if anything, will go into the book. Third, these materials are often 'containers' for challenging and traumatic material. It is important that I can physically and emotionally contain this material for the child for the duration of our work together.
- Agreement about the structure of the sessions, which should be maintained with a clear beginning, middle and end, even if the primary activity has to be altered from the original plan to meet the child's needs on the day. If the beginning and ending of the session remain consistent throughout the work, this helps promote a feeling of safety and predictability (adapted from Wrench 2016, pp.18–20).

ACTIVITIES TO EXPLORE WORRIES

At this stage it is often helpful to acknowledge that it is natural that even willing participants, who consent to the work, may also have fears or anxieties about what life story work might be like, or how it will leave them feeling. In my experience, many children anticipate that 'big secrets' might have been withheld from them. On being contacted via social media by a relative she had not seen since childhood, Kerry Hudson (2020, p.15), in her memoir *Lowborn*, acknowledged the fear that swept over her, fear of 'everything I can't remember' about a childhood lived in poverty and at times in foster care, because 'not knowing is scary'.

So it is important to think about the ways in which you can support the child to bring those worries into the open, to normalise them and to problem solve or resource the child to manage them where appropriate at the beginning of the life story work process.

Stories for younger children

There are many picture books that can help begin conversations with younger children about worries and anxiety, which can serve as an introduction to the direct work activities.

Ruby's Worry by Tom Percival (2022) is a sturdy board book from his Big Bright Feelings series, and is perfect for children in discussing childhood worries, big or small.

My Monster and Me by Nadiya Hussain (2020) explores how to make friends with the part of us that sometimes feels worried. It is about a little boy whose worry monster follows him everywhere so he feels he cannot escape his worries.

The Very Hungry Worry Monsters by Rosie Greening (2020) is an interactive touch-and-feel story about children naming worries and sharing them by writing them down.

The Huge Bag of Worries by Virginia Ironside (2011) is a story about a little girl whose worries follow her in a big blue bag wherever she goes and whatever she is doing. When I use this story with children it often leads to us drawing the child's own huge bag of worries, and working out how we are going to deal with them together.

COLLAGE

Have a selection of magazines, newspapers and craft materials so the child can cut or tear out images and words that represent their worries. These can be stuck on a large piece of paper or cardboard to create a Worry Monster collage. This activity allows children to externalise their worries and gain a sense of control over them, nurturing a sense of empowerment. The parent or practitioner can offer help if needed. While you are cutting and gluing, you can be exploring the nature of their worries.

SENSORY BOTTLE

Fill a clear plastic bottle with water and add a few drops of food colouring and some glitter. Encourage the child to add small objects, such as plastic stars, beads, shells or small pebbles or gems that represent their worries. Seal the bottle tightly and give it a gentle shake, explaining as you do that the swirling glitter and objects inside symbolise or represent their worries. As you watch the glitter begin to settle, you can use this opportunity to remind the child that worries do eventually settle too.

WORRY JAR

For this activity you just need an empty glass jar and a pen and paper. Encourage the child to write their worries onto small pieces of paper, fold them, and add them to the jar. As they are written down, you can explore whose worry it is and what actions can be taken to ease that worry. When putting the worry into the jar, ask the child to imagine the worry leaving with the paper and becoming trapped inside the jar – both you and the jar will then provide some containment for the child's fears or worries. Another option is to pop the worries into a Worry Monster toy, or to make and decorate a Worry Box with a little letterbox opening to post the worries through.

WORRY DOLLS

You can either use pre-bought traditional Worry Dolls, which are small handmade dolls made originally by people in Guatemala, where it is tradition that if a child feels worried they would be given a Worry Doll to tell their worries to – or even better, let the child make their own. *Silly Billy* by Anthony Browne (2007) is a great story about a boy who eases his worries by telling them to his Worry Dolls, and it might be useful to read it alongside this activity. The idea, then, is that if the child feels worried during or even before the work starts, their Worry Doll can help them to find a trusted adult to tell those worries to. Think together about who that might be, and whether there is somewhere safe to keep the Worry Doll/s, because it is okay to make more than one.

All you need for this activity is a pipe cleaner (or a twig, ice cream or lollypop stick); string, wool, scraps of fabric or paper; pen or pencil; glue or tape. Begin by creating the doll's body using any craft materials that feel appropriate, such as a pipe cleaner, lollypop stick, twig or even a simple rolled-up piece of cardboard. If the child feels confident in making this themselves, then great, but if not, their parent or carer or the practitioner could lend a hand. Then decorate the doll using string, wool or scraps of fabric to wrap around the body. Tie or glue fabric or paper to create clothes for the doll, and then draw or stick on a face. Once the doll is made, think of a name for it. It is better not to give the doll the name of someone the child knows. It is important to reinforce that if they subsequently feel worried, their Worry Doll is there to help tell an adult they trust how they are feeling.

WORRY TREE

This activity can be as simplistic or as creative as you choose. Give the child the option of doing the drawing, cutting and sticking independently, or having some help from one of the adults if they prefer. Here are some options:

1. Draw a tree, draw on the leaves and write the worries on the leaves.
2. Draw a tree, cut out some leaves from green card, write the worries on the leaves and glue them to the tree.
3. Use twigs in a simple vase or tie the twigs together with twine to represent a tree. Then write the worries on card luggage labels (you can also buy multicoloured ones, which look much more interesting).

GOAL-BASED OUTCOMES

In these early sessions, I like to set some goal-based outcomes (GBOs) for the work (Law and Jacob 2015). These can be the child's goals, the parent or carer's goals or shared goals. GBOs help focus the work, bring transparency to what we are trying to achieve in life story work, and provide a way of tracking whether we are making progress towards achieving those goals. They are also a good tool for shared decision making, which is important when working with children who have been so disempowered in their abuse. Over time you can compare how far a child, or their parent or carer, feels they have moved towards reaching a goal they set for themselves at the beginning of the life story work.

The GBO tool can be used with any intervention or therapeutic modality, which is important if you plan to integrate other therapeutic approaches, such as play therapy, art psychotherapy or EMDR (eye movement desensitisation reprocessing) into the life story work. The

GBO can also be used alongside other measures, together with your own clinical judgement, to track progress across the work. You can monitor this in the sessions with the child or young person and their parent or carer, as well as for your own reflection or in supervision. The life story process therefore begins with a shared understanding of the goals of the intervention. Some children and young people have a clear idea of the goals they want to achieve through life story work, while others might take a little longer to decide.

Ensure that the goals set are consistent with what is possible to achieve through life story work, and don't be afraid to make suggestions or support decision making so they are realistic and there is the potential to make progress. Generally, aim to record up to three goals, and once they are agreed, agree how close the child or parent or carer feels they are to reaching the goal on a scale from 1 to 10, where 1 means the goal is not met in any way, 10 means the goal is met completely, and 5 means they are halfway to reaching the goal. Ideally you should aim to agree and score them within the first three sessions. You can rescore at the midway point and at the end of the intervention to record again how close to reaching the goal the person now feels they are (adapted from CORC n.d.).

Examples of goals in life story work for the child or young person are:

- 'To work out why I came into care and couldn't live with my parents.'
- 'To understand why I was adopted and my brother wasn't.'
- 'To share my story with my foster carer or adoptive parent.'
- 'To have help to manage my big feelings.'
- 'To understand why I feel this way.'
- 'To find out more about my birth family.'
- 'To know more about who I take after or look like.'

It can be helpful to record the goals on a sheet that looks something like this:

Session	Date	Today I would rate progress to this goal: (Please circle or highlight the appropriate number below) *Remember that a score of 1 means no progress has been made towards a goal, and a score of 10 means a goal has been reached fully.*									
GOAL ONE											
Initial		1	2	3	4	5	6	7	8	9	10
Midway		1	2	3	4	5	6	7	8	9	10
Final		1	2	3	4	5	6	7	8	9	10
GOAL TWO											
Initial		1	2	3	4	5	6	7	8	9	10
Midway		1	2	3	4	5	6	7	8	9	10
Final		1	2	3	4	5	6	7	8	9	10
GOAL THREE											
Initial		1	2	3	4	5	6	7	8	9	10
Midway		1	2	3	4	5	6	7	8	9	10
Final		1	2	3	4	5	6	7	8	9	10

UNDERSTANDING THE IMPACT OF TRAUMA ON THE DEVELOPING CHILD

In attempting to create a sense of safety from the outset of the work, you will first need to understand how the child sees themself, and how they manage life and relationships in the context of their early trauma. You will already have important information from your discussions with the parent or carer, and you will also come to understand the child better during these initial sessions. Until you understand how the child functions in relation to their experiences of relational and developmental trauma, you will not know where the developmental gaps are, and you cannot ethically or safely plan your intervention.

All the following elements come together in stage one of the work, and it is essential you take time to explore them:

- Consider how aware the child is of the impact trauma had, and is continuing to have, on their development, relationships, state of mind and behaviour. *Psychoeducation* is critical to children and young people of all ages for developing an understanding of themselves that is empowering rather than pathologising.

- Understand the child's shame responses and reactions to stress, and how to help them remain regulated. What do they look like both within their *window of tolerance* and when they are close to the edge or beyond their window of tolerance? (If you are unfamiliar with this term, see p.75.) Observe the child's responses, and closely monitor for changes, for example, in skin tone, breathing and attention, which might signal them moving outside of their window of tolerance.
- Understand the *coping strategies* the child uses to manage stress or big feelings, and identify key support people for the child.
- Understand the child's *attachment style* – this will be key in influencing how you approach the work for that child in terms of building a relationship (if you don't have one already). Does the child have a secure base – someone to support with co-regulation for and with the child, and who can create a safe enough space in which to make sense together of the child's history, behaviours and associated feelings?
- Understand the child's emotional world and assess their *emotional literacy* (see p.94 for more on this). Without emotional literacy skills, the child is not likely to be able to explore their feelings about their story, or to manage the feelings that emerge when thinking about what has happened to them.

Trauma psychoeducation

Trauma psychoeducation helps children (and sometimes their parents or carers too) understand the impact of trauma and how it affects the brain and body. Sally Donovan, in her story for children, *The Strange and Curious Guide to Trauma*, describes knowing about trauma as a superpower because it 'means we can understand and take care of ourselves and other people better. It can help us understand that experiencing trauma is not our fault and doesn't make us bad or weak' (2022, p.94). This, in turn, can help children learn to manage the impact of trauma and make sense of how they feel.

This is relevant to building safety into the process of life story work because it is important to know that our brains have many important jobs, one of which is to keep us safe. As we move through life, our brain converts experiences into memories so that we can embrace things that feel good, and avoid things that feel unpleasant or frightening. Each memory becomes a blueprint to help us learn, recording valuable facts such as where we were, what we could smell, what we saw, who was there or what we were feeling at the time. In his memoir *Plot 29*, Allan Jenkins (2017), a care-experienced author and journalist, recalls sitting at a fancy dinner as an adult and being transported back to the time when he had just moved to live with his foster carers Lilian and Dudley:

> I notice my face is wet. I am quietly crying. Ferran Adria's peas have burst in my mouth... I am maybe six, in shorts and stripy top, on the pink porch of our Devon house. Lilian is there with me, in her yellow patterned summer dress with blue butterfly-wing brooch, sitting, smiling, patiently podding peas into her dented colander. And as I pick up a pod and help her, I know this is what safety will forever taste like: garden peas freshly picked from the lap of your new mum. (Jenkins 2017, p.16)

Trauma psychoeducation can take many different forms depending on the needs of the child and their family, and could include the use of stories, imagery or metaphor, but also diagrams, illustrations or lists. You could focus on recognition of triggers or introduce somatic resources such as grounding or breathwork. It can also be helpful at times to use examples of success the child has already experienced that offer hope and encourage progress towards future goals or reframing of survival strategies as resources that helped keep them safe at one time.

Critically, psychoeducation can support survivors of trauma to understand their natural responses, symptoms and coping skills, while hopefully also reducing the powerful feelings of isolation, guilt and helplessness that often accompany traumatic childhood experiences. I often talk to children about the fact that they are experiencing an entirely predictable, normal response to having experienced incredibly abnormal events.

Understanding how the brain and central nervous system respond to trauma and work out what to do in an emergency

Working out how to respond in a situation that is perceived to be dangerous or an emergency happens in a split second; it is an unconscious process of choosing the best way to keep yourself safe. When someone is feeling under threat, there is no time to think about what approach would be best to secure safety. The nervous system responds instantly to make these choices for you based on previous experiences. You might not always understand the choice, but your body is always working hard to try to keep you safe the best way it can. This is how it works:

> First you identify a threat. Then you ask:
>
> Can I escape?
>
> YES – flee/flight – if you can get far enough away from the threat quickly enough, you might be able to escape and avoid the danger altogether.
>
> NO – can I overpower it?
>
> YES – fight – if you attack the threat before it attacks you, you might be able to weaken it and stop it attacking again in the future.
>
> NO – can I make it lose interest in me?
>
> YES – freeze – if your body closes up, becomes rigid and doesn't move, you might be able to stop the threat from noticing or becoming interested in you.
>
> NO – collapse/flop – if you disconnect your mind/brain from your body, by dissociating or even by fainting, you might be able to avoid feeling so much pain (adapted from nicabm n.d.).

However, if you are dealing with traumatic memories, the brain wants to keep you safe so badly that it works overtime. It trusts these blueprints of memories from the past, creating a sense of danger in the present, long after the immediate threat has passed. For example, if a parent has repeatedly physically hurt a child, the child's flight response is activated, but they cannot flee and are effectively trapped. Their flight response is shut down. The fight response will be also activated, but the urge to fight is neither safe nor effective. The child's abuser is likely to be too big and strong to fight off, so the child's fight response is truncated – it, too, is stopped. The only survival mode this child can access is to shut down inside – to go into a state of collapse. However, the truncated fight-and-flight responses are stuck, unfinished, in the child's nervous system. As they grow older, they may continually have the urge to fight or run away. Their nervous system is constantly trying to repair the early experience by completing their truncated responses (Beacon House 2021).

The 'window of tolerance'

The 'window of tolerance' (Siegel 1999) refers to the zone of arousal where we function optimally and where we can be our best selves. We are in a psychological space that allows us to manage day-to-day tasks without feelings and/or thoughts overwhelming us or interfering with our performance. When we are in this space, our brain is working most effectively. It is efficiently processing what is happening around us, our thoughts and our feelings. In this state, we can play, learn, be in relationships and connect with the world around us. Each of us has our own unique window of tolerance, and it is normal to move in and out of the space where we are functioning best, as we experience stressors throughout the day.

Stressful experiences and trauma can cause the window of tolerance to shrink. Some people use the analogy of floating down a river. When the river narrows, the flow is faster, and it can be unsafe to navigate. When it widens, the flow slows down and it is more possible to feel in a balanced and calm state of mind, relaxed, in control and better able to manage any challenges up ahead. It is important that where our river tapers, we work actively to expand the window of tolerance, or our 'comfort zone'. Children who have experienced complex developmental trauma can experience triggers in the here and now that remind their body and brain of the past, thereby activating the nervous system into believing that it is under attack again. This can lead to them moving quickly out of the window of tolerance into hyper- or hypoaroused states.

The 'window of tolerance'

Hyperarousal Fight or flight – increased responsiveness Anxiety, panic, overwhelm, hyperactivity, rage, struggles to relax, runs away
Window of tolerance 'Just right' state Present, grounded, flexible, able to access reason, curious
Hypoarousal Freeze – decreased responsivenss Exhausted, numb, shut down, depression, shame, disconnected, passive

Until we help children and their parents or carers to function within their window of tolerance, they will not be able to readily receive, process and integrate information and respond to the demands of everyday life without great difficulty. Their ability to contribute meaningfully to the life story process will inevitably be compromised, and indeed, you may inadvertently cause more distress and difficulty. Everyone's window of tolerance is different and can be impacted by their environment, but in general terms, individuals are better able to remain within their window when they feel supported and safe.

Polyvagal theory and neuroception

The other clinician working in this field that it is important to be aware of is Stephen Porges, an American psychologist and neuroscientist who, in 1994, proposed the polyvagal theory in a talk to the Society of Psychophysiological Research, taking its name from the vagus nerve, which is the primary component of the parasympathetic nervous system. Porges published his work the following year (1995) in a simplified representation of an extremely complex system. He described three distinct nervous system states – *ventral vagal*, *sympathetic* and *dorsal vagal* – which are activated in a particular order. You will notice a connection with the idea of the window of tolerance here. It is the ventral vagal state that helps us feel safe, communicate and connect with other people; it is the place where most of us would want to be, much of the time, to *rest and digest*. The sympathetic state is the energy of *flight or fight* (hyperarousal) that helps us take action to survive in dangerous environments or situations. If we cannot fight or flee, the dorsal vagal system leads us to *shut down*, flop or psychologically cut off to protect ourselves from harm.

'Neuroception', a term coined by Porges in 2011, is the process of our nervous system doing a speedy risk assessment by automatically scanning the environment for cues of danger that we might not be consciously aware of, by noticing and tuning into messages from inside the body, the environment and in the interactions and communication between people around us. This brain circuit is 'dedicated to assessing safety and trustworthiness in other people...in the fast and furious range of thirty to 100 milliseconds, faster than the time required for me to consciously "know" I am seeing you' (Baylin and Hughes 2022, p.5). It is neuroception that determines whether we are in a ventral vagal, sympathetic or dorsal vagal state, depending on our environment. These states are not entirely separate, because we move through the continuum throughout each day, and although they are controlled by different parts of the nervous system, ultimately, all three states are directly managed by the vagus nerve, which runs all the way from the base of the brain to the gut, connecting the brain to the body. The vagus nerve therefore plays an integral role in regulating our heart rate, breathing and digestion, as well as our emotional state.[2]

Dana (2018) describes this concept using the metaphor of a hierarchy ladder – you can climb up and down the ladder by activating the stimulating or relaxing branches of the autonomic nervous system, based on neuroception. A neuroception of safety brings you into a ventral vagal state, up at the top of the ladder. In this state you will experience the world as a safe place – it is the zone of social engagement, in which to feel and be connected to the world and people around you. But when something happens internally or externally to warn you of danger, you enter the sympathetic nervous system state of *mobilisation* and take a big step down the ladder, what is known commonly as 'fight or flight'. Where a child is entering this state, you might notice them looking flushed, sweating, with dilated pupils or their heartbeat starting to race. Because the body is physiologically getting ready for fight or flight, internal resources that we're not consciously aware of are redirected. Blood shifts away from the digestive system and to the muscles and limbs, in readiness for action. Cortisol and adrenaline are released, and the body's resources are focused on survival. The nourishing but non-essential functions humans need are temporarily suspended to prioritise staying alive.

Going down another step on the ladder, with a neuroception of extreme danger, neurologically you enter the dorsal vagal state of *immobilisation*. Imagine a turtle drawing its head inside its shell or a hedgehog rolling up into a tight ball to keep itself safe. In this state the child might feel motionless, anaesthetised, alone and without hope, because the world is not a safe place to be in that moment. This is sometimes referred to as the 'faint' response because blood flow to the brain reduces, which can lead to an episode of fainting.

The autonomic nervous system shuts the body down and conserves energy. Heart rate and blood pressure drop. Movement is frozen, which

2 Adapted from www.polyvagalinstitute.org/whatispolyvagaltheory

lowers the metabolism and reduces the need for food. Endorphins are released to numb anticipated pain.

Humans are constantly shifting through the different states working their way up and down the ladder, but these states can only be moved through in sequence. For example, if you are immobilised, you cannot jump straight to safe and social without first passing through mobilisation – however briefly. If you are lucky, you will live predominantly in the ventral vagal zone, but if you have experienced developmental trauma, you are more likely to spend much of your time on the lower rungs of the ladder, and it might be much harder to climb back up into the social engagement zone. The more time you spend in any part of the ladder, the more likely it is that you might get 'stuck'.

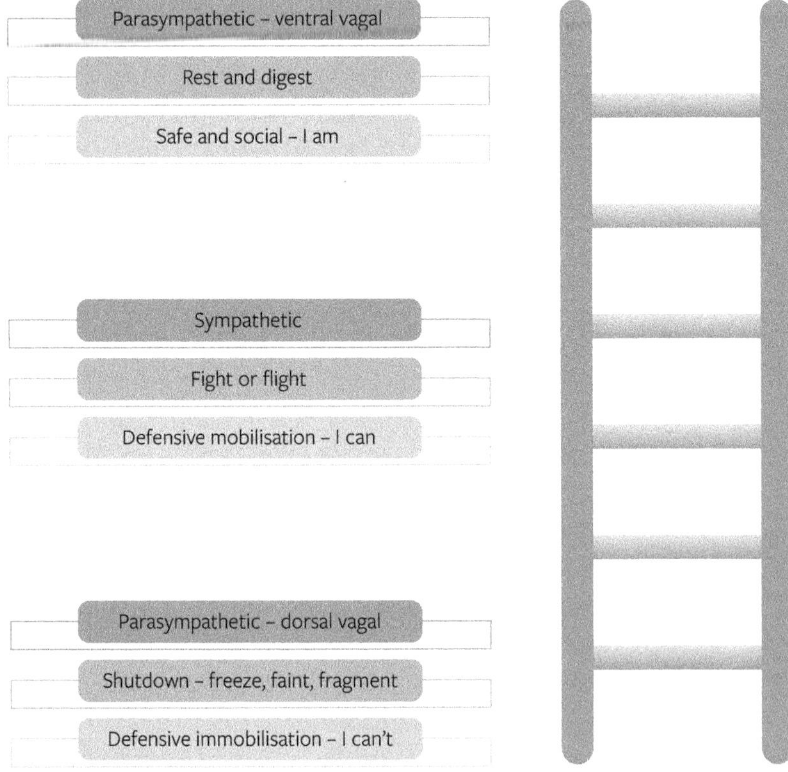

THE POLYVAGAL LADDER

Explanations for children and young people

There are many ways to approach trauma psychoeducation for children of different ages and developmental stages, but if we can help them understand how their brain and central nervous system function, they will be so much better able to face everyday challenges, including those inherent in life story work. Many approaches make use of metaphors that can 'give a young person a way of understanding an experience by helping them to organise what they experienced. The same metaphor may provide useful ways of thinking about a variety of experiences', especially if the parent or carer is involved (Shotton 2020, p.30). This way, the metaphors can become part of an ongoing shared understanding.

Beacon House (2020) offers training using the analogy of the *survival animals* inside all of us to help children and their families to understand how and why we each have survival behaviours, and how each of the survival animals work hard to keep us safe from danger:

- Tiger: our fight survival mode.
- Cheetah: our flight survival mode.
- Rabbit: our freeze survival mode.
- Sloth: our collapse survival mode.

In so doing, they explore some basic premises:

- We all have an internal alarm system that alerts us both to real and perceived danger.
- Children who have experienced trauma and loss can often have a super-sensitive alarm system.
- The brain's alarm system 'wakes up' or activates survival behaviours in everyone, which are designed to protect us from hurt and harm.
- Our survival behaviours were helpful at one point in our lives, but over time, they can cause us many problems.
- We can learn how to tame our survival behaviours so that we can feel more in control of how we behave and react and how we feel.
- Children need the help of safe adults around them to support them to do this tough work.

Family Futures has produced a series of animations called 'The Brain Game'.[3] They are designed around video game imagery with child-friendly language. The animation is divided into five sections, with each one designed to stand alone as a basis for discussion with children, parents or carers or the dyad. At the start of the game, you choose a character with lots of armour to keep you safe. But then later in the game, that armour begins to get in the way and stops you moving forward. The game acknowledges how hard it is if you are stuck playing life on 'hard' mode. I think this could be a useful analogy if you are working with gamers. Whether you invest in this game or not, these are all good teaching points for children, as they explain:

- What the brain does, how it works and the effect of neglect and abuse on the development of the brain in infancy.
- How the brain develops in the womb and is affected by environmental influences such as alcohol and drug misuse as well as violence. The animation compares an 'easy' start in life with a 'hard' one.
- How the brain develops after birth, again looking at 'easy' and 'hard' starts in life, and how they have a different impact on the baby's developing brain.
- How the triune brain is constructed, and how trauma in infancy predisposes the primitive brain to respond in 'fight, flight or freeze' survival mode. The triune brain theory is the theory of brain development that describes three distinct regions, consisting of the brainstem, the limbic system and the cortex, which are relevant in managing stress through the fight or flight response, emotion and cognition, respectively.
- How the brain is 'plastic' and can be changed, and what you can do to help it change for the better.

Finally, if you are looking for a resource for 8- to 12-year-olds to help them understand the complexities of trauma, I love Sally Donovan's illustrated book *The Strange and Curious Guide to Trauma* (2022). There is a range of characters, including Courtney Cortisol and Amy Amygdala, to guide you through the world of trauma. Facts about the impact of trauma are

3 See www.familyfutures.co.uk/product/brain-game-download/0

woven into a therapeutic story to explore the incredibly clever ways our bodies keep us safe, and what the different parts of our brain do to help us when we are afraid.

Flipping your lid: your brain in the palm of your hand

We know that traumatised children can swing quickly between their survival modes of fight, flight, freeze and collapse. When children are in these incredibly anxious states of mind, they will need help to access their calmer 'thinking brain'. Siegel's simple hand model of the brain can help you explain what is happening to the child and their parent or carer (2010). It allows us to picture the brain structure and understand why it can be tricky to control our responses when we feel overwhelmed with strong emotions. You can also find lots of videos on YouTube explaining the principles visually, including from Siegel himself.

During early brain development, beginning in utero, the brain develops from the bottom up. First to develop is the brainstem (wrist), and this part of the brain controls survival functions such as heart rate, breathing, digestion and blood pressure. This part of the brain functions 'automatically', controlling all those essential functions that you don't want to have to focus on because it would literally take up all of your time, and if you forgot just for a second, you would die.

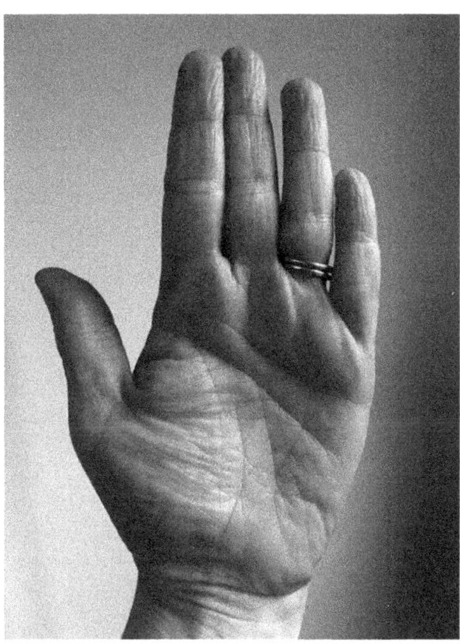

The next part of the brain to develop is the limbic or emotional brain. If you tuck your thumb into the palm of your hand, you will form the limbic system in the deep structures of the brain. This part of the brain helps us survive. The hippocampus helps us form and save new memories, linking them to specific emotions. The little almond-shaped amygdala is the safety radar, responsible for spotting danger and sending a message to our autonomic nervous system to respond to keep us safe. The limbic system is therefore responsible for our emotions and memories, and activating our unconscious survival reactions (fight, flight, freeze and flop/collapse).

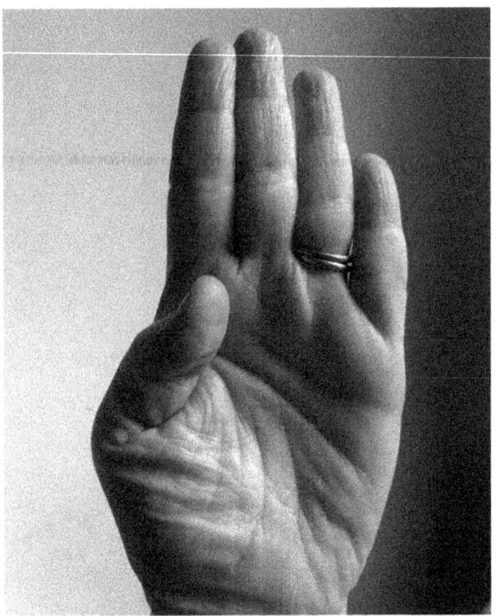

The final area of the brain to develop is the thinking brain located in the cortex, which is the top covering of the brain. Your fingers represent your cerebral cortex, and the knuckle area is your prefrontal cortex, an especially important part of the human brain. Your thinking brain is responsible for judgement, reason, thinking, sustained attention, working memory and time management – the vital stuff that is also known as executive functions or skills. If you close your fingers on top of your palm and thumb, then you have the simple hand model of the brain, divided into the *upstairs brain* (cerebral cortex) and *downstairs brain* (brainstem and limbic system).

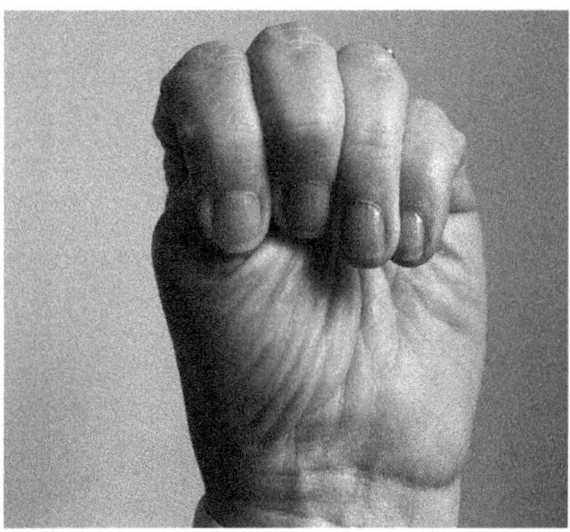

When someone feels tired, hungry, overwhelmed or anxious, for example, the connections between the thinking and emotional brain are not working so well. Show the child how when they lift their fingers (or flip their lid), their thinking brain is no longer connected to their feelings, and they might become upset or hit out and hurt someone, or even run away and hide. But if they curl their fingers over their thumb, now their upstairs and downstairs brain are connected again. They can accept their feelings as well as listening to what their brain has to say about them. The closed fist represents an emotionally regulated brain (adapted from Building Better Brains 2019).

You can explore what is happening in the downstairs and upstairs brain when someone becomes overwhelmed or triggered to zip outside of their window of tolerance. If, like me, you were once stung by a wasp while eating an ice cream at a children's farm, the hippocampus in the limbic brain will have saved this memory, linking it to the fear and pain I experienced when I was stung. Next time I see a wasp, the amygdala (or guard dog) will identify it as a potential threat, and I will instinctively feel afraid again. At the same time, cortisol, a stress hormone, will be released. It will get my heart racing and increase my rate of breathing – the brainstem controls both these functions. High levels of energy will be sent to my muscles so that I can get away from the threat of that annoying wasp as soon as possible.

There is nothing wrong with this response, because normally in these situations the upstairs brain can help us out. It helps us imagine, create and problem solve our way out of a challenge. The prefrontal cortex (wise owl) helps us evaluate the situation detected by the amygdala and control our emotional response before our feelings escalate to the point that we are no longer in control. So going back to the wasp analogy, I can think my way out of the problem without getting overwhelmed. I tell myself I can calmly move away, and I am unlikely to be stung again. I do not become overwhelmed.

However, if you have experienced developmental trauma, especially when you were very young, this can affect the development of the pathway between the amygdala (guard dog) and the prefrontal cortex (wise owl). When we are in a survival state managing a scary situation, we are more likely to flip our lid so that the downstairs brain quickly takes over. Going back to the hand model of the brain to visualise this, lift your fingers to release your fist and you will see that the connection between your upstairs and downstairs brain is lost. When this happens, we can no longer effectively verbally communicate with others, control our emotions or respond to reasoning.

Children do not have to be in real danger to flip their lid, and any situation that is perceived to be stressful can cause their cortisol levels to rise and shut down the thinking brain. This could be something as simple as a transition from playtime to dinnertime, or a seemingly minor change of plan. Since the prefrontal cortex is not fully developed until we are 25, even typically developing children and young people inevitably find it much harder to respond rationally to stressful situations and regulate their emotions.

> A colleague found this a really useful tool when working with an adolescent with additional needs. They valued the visual aspect of the explanation and combined it with their love of popcorn to describe how their brain could become overwhelmed and 'foggy', meaning they had much less control over their emotions and behaviour. They likened their thumb to the mechanism that kept the popcorn at just the right level, and if the thumb was lifted for too long it would push the lid wide open – and out the popcorn would fly, scattering everywhere. They were able to keep coming back to this idea by checking in on their popcorn levels and noticing if some had sneaked out! This in itself allowed for a non-shaming and light-hearted way of communicating when things were starting to feel too much.

WHAT HELPS CHILDREN FEEL SAFER IN THEIR BRAINS, BODIES AND RELATIONSHIPS?

One of the most helpful ways to achieve this connection with a sense of safety in the brain, body and relationships is through patterned, repetitive, rhythmic activity offered alongside supportive relationships. Over time, these kinds of activities can help a child to learn to feel safer in their brain, body and relationships, but this cannot be achieved solely during direct work sessions once a week or fortnight. The most impactful way to use these activities is for a parent or carer to weave them into the child's daily routine so that they have opportunities repeatedly throughout the day to soothe the nervous system and eventually calm the survival response. Please hold in your mind that every child will need different support at different times, but to be most effective in healing, these activities need to be:

- Relational – offered by a safe adult
- Relevant – developmentally matched to the child rather than matched to their chronological age
- Repetitive – patterned
- Rewarding – pleasurable, even fun
- Rhythmic – resonant with neural patterns
- Respectful – of the child and family (adapted from Beacon House 2019).

As with any activities within life story work, it is important to explore what works for each child you support. This experimentation can be really good fun, both in your sessions and at home or school, but must also be approached with caution. The aim is to help someone who feels unsafe to feel safe again.

> And any particular technique may achieve that aim – but equally it may also counter that aim. Asking a trauma survivor to focus on their body might heighten their distress, not lessen it. Asking someone, whose breath was crushed out of them during the abuse, to focus on their breath is risky: it might trigger a trauma memory, not soothe and reassure. The technique has to be tuned to the individual. The individual has to know what works for them. (Spring 2021)

Some ideas include:

- Walking: to do a job at school or to grab resources during a session from a cupboard in the room; a mindful nature walk before you meet; or a fast march with the dog.
- Dancing: at a dance class; in PE; at a kitchen disco while you wait for a cake to bake; to a song on YouTube – I am a fan of *Animal Boogie* for pre-schoolers (Barefoot Books 2021); or learning the latest TikTok dance craze.
- Running: on the spot for a minute; with a running club; in PE; at the park; back to the car.
- Drumming: lessons or informally, with or without a drum...you can tap a rhythm on your knee or on the table alone or with a parent or carer – can you mirror each other? Can you guess what song is being 'played'?
- Tapping: EFT (emotional freedom technique) is an evidence-based, self-help therapeutic method that can also be accessed through a qualified EFT therapist (Craig 2011). As the stress response is experienced not only as a pattern of thinking and feeling, but also as physiological symptoms in our body, tapping works to regulate the nervous system by stimulating acupoints. Try self-tapping your left and right knee, left and right collarbone (like a butterfly hug) or a tapping round – either for relaxation, or it can be accompanied by a positive affirmation.

There are readily available images of tapping points for EFT online, but you can also use a tapping teddy, like the one shown in this image. I have simply sewn large buttons onto the tapping points.

1. Top of the head
2. Eyebrow
3. Side of the eye
4. Under the eye
5. Under the nose
6. Chin
7. Collarbone
8. Under the arm
9. Hand

- Breathing: with a trusted adult. The child matches the adult's breathing using an agreed non-verbal cue; sucking and blowing games like blow football; body scan meditation; techniques that encourage slower breathing from the diaphragm.
- Music: singing (individually or as part of a choir); listening to music in the session or privately with headphones; singing songs or rhymes with actions.

These strategies can be invaluable in the longer term for stretching the child's window of tolerance, but also be mindful of what you might do if the child tips outside of their window of tolerance during a session. When you begin to introduce traumatic material in a session later in the work, there might be multiple perceived threats for children that could cause them to shift into dysregulation.

Other common triggers for traumatised children include:

- Changes of plan or any unpredictability where they struggle to tolerate not knowing what is coming next.
- Transitions – into and out of the sessions and between activities in the session.
- Feeling a loss of control, for example if you introduce a directive activity.

- Feeling rejected or vulnerable, perhaps if a parent cannot join a session or if you have to cancel a session for a holiday or illness.
- When an adult sets limits around behaviour or expectations.
- Sensory overload – be mindful of noise, lighting, smell, excessive decoration/visual stimuli or toys in the room.

Depending on whether a child is experiencing hyper- or hypoarousal, you will need to adjust your support to suit their need in the moment. It is worth remembering that having the child's trusted adult (preferably their parent or carer) in the session with you can be your short cut to safety – provided they understand how to help a defensive child to feel safe alongside them. There is growing evidence that just being with a safe adult can decrease reactivity in the amygdala of a traumatised child (which is more sensitive to social threat and more likely to activate defence responses than the amygdala of a typically developing child) and extinguish the stress response, simply by transmitting signs of safety through facial expression, tone of voice and gesture alone (Tottenham and Gabard-Durnam 2017).

HYPERAROUSAL

When a child begins to move into a *fight* response, you might see any of the following:

- oppositional or defiant behaviour
- verbal/physical aggression towards you or the parent or carer or self
- hyperactivity/bouncing off the walls/'silliness'
- testing boundaries
- trouble concentrating or maintaining focus on a task, even when the child has instigated it, or they enjoy it.

When a child begins to move into a *flight* response, you might see any of the following:

- withdrawal

- escaping – leaving the room repeatedly to go to the toilet, for example
- running away or hiding
- avoidance – sitting alone in class or separating themselves from you in a session
- self-isolation – staying in their bedroom, not doing any activities (adapted from Blaustein and Kinneburgh 2010, p.27).

There are many effective strategies to help children manage hyperarousal, but I stress again that there is no one-size-fits-all approach, and what is experienced as helpful one day might not be the next.

Ways to support children move from hyperarousal to calm

Diaphragmatic or belly breathing. Explain how sometimes when we feel upset, we might forget to breathe, or we take short, shallow breaths (like a puppy dog panting) that don't give our bodies the oxygen we really need. To feel more relaxed and to calm down, you can practice deep breathing. Depending on the age of the child you can use a teddy bear or a little toy animal to help, and always begin by showing the child what to do by doing it yourself. Lie down on your back and put one of the teddies on your tummy. Using the belly breathing technique, demonstrate how you can make the teddy on your belly go up and down for a ride by only using your breath.

Place one hand on your chest and the other on your belly. This will help you to gain an awareness of the movements of your chest and abdomen. Start by taking a slow, deep breath in through your nose, imagining that you are sucking in all the air in the room. Hold this breath for about 5–7 seconds – if you are new to breathwork, this might feel too tricky or uncomfortable, so hold for less time if needed. As you breathe in, the hand on your tummy should rise higher than the one on your chest. This makes sure your diaphragm is pulling air into the base of your lungs. Now slowly breathe out for a count of about 5–7 seconds. As you release the air from your lungs, gently tighten your tummy muscles to completely clear out the remaining air from your lungs. As you do this, you should feel the hand on your tummy moving downwards. It is important to remember to take a deep breath – we need to focus on breathing in, and then make sure we have breathed out fully.

Then guide the child to lie down, perhaps with their parent or carer, and put a teddy bear on their tummy. Encourage the child to try and make their teddy move gently up and down on their tummy by taking deep breaths. As they breathe *in* their tummy is moving *upwards* and *outwards* – so they are lifting their teddy up with their tummy and taking it for a ride. Then as they breathe *out* their tummy moves *inwards* and *downwards* – so letting their teddy fall. Do three or four breaths in a row, and then take a rest.

Breathing in this way has an almost immediate effect on the body – it might make everyone feel sleepy! By breathing deeply from the diaphragm, the body's parasympathetic nervous system is activated. This counteracts the stress response by slowing the heart rate, lowering blood pressure and quietening the mind. It activates the body's relaxation response to encourage the child back into a state of calm.

For older children or adolescents, you might want to introduce slow, relaxing music. Encourage them to listen to the beat (they can close their eyes if it feels safe to do so), and make sure they are sitting or lying down somewhere comfortable. Then ask them to take a deep breath in for 3–5 beats of the music, to hold their breath for 3–5 beats, and then to breathe out slowly for 3–5 beats. They should then repeat this, matching their breathing with the music.

Drinking through a straw, especially if it is a lovely thick milkshake or smoothie that will take some effort to suck, gives good proprioceptive feedback for the jaw, which can play an important role in calming and modulating the central nervous system, and helps with the processing of sensory information.

Yoga is like a short brain break. It empties the mind and can give children renewed focus and attention in the session. There are even lots of poses that can be done sitting in a chair. You might want to look at the *Sitting Still Like a Frog Activity Book* for younger children, which has lots of ideas for mindfulness and yoga games (Snel 2019). You can also find yoga activities on YouTube that may be more suitable for adolescents. Little ones often practice Cosmic Yoga in school, so it might feel familiar to them, and Cosmic Kids also has an app and a YouTube channel.[4]

Strategies for releasing anger, energy or tension – for example, tearing up newspaper, popping bubble wrap, squishing Play-Doh or clay, wrapping

4 https://cosmickids.com

your arms around yourself and squeezing tightly, doing some wall presses, push ups or star jumps – shake, stomp or dance it out of the body.

Use a *self-soothe or calm box*. I make things available to young people to use for self-regulation without them having to ask by having a filled calm box on the table. I am often fiddling with something during the session too. But I also sometimes support children to make their own individual box to use in the sessions, and maybe a separate one for home and/or school too. It can be helpful to have a range of objects that can support regulation as well as something to focus the mind on or act as a distraction if needed. You could include something to smell, something to touch, something to look at and even something to taste. Each child will need something a little different, and it can be such fun experimenting with what works for them. I tend to include fiddle toys, essential oils in a rollerball, hand cream, a mini art therapy colouring book and crayons, a card game, and a lolly to suck. Here are some ideas of how to connect with the senses. Just be aware that what is regulating for one child might be triggering for another:

- Touch: something to fiddle with and a great distraction for the hands. This could be a fiddle toy, fidget cube, a bit of Blu-Tack or Play-Doh or a piece of soft fabric to stroke. You can also use touch and parental presence for regulation. Sometimes it will be enough for a parent or carer to just be close by or in the room, whereas at other times the child will need physical connection and affection or firm pressure on the shoulders, back or upper arms.
- Smell: this could be a parent's fragrance or an essential oil – lavender can be relaxing, and peppermint oil is grounding, for example.
- Taste: a lolly to suck, a crunchy snack like pretzels or a carrot stick, or a chocolate button to melt on the tongue.
- Sound: music, or noise-cancelling headphones or ear plugs to block out external stimuli that might feel overwhelming.

Engage in an activity – this could be a word search, a colouring book, threading beads or making a collage, for example.

Memories – photographs of people, pets or places that have only positive memories attached to them, which serve as a reminder that there are people to turn to in difficult times. It could also be an item like a teddy bear or other soft toy.

You can also buy *Grounding and Soothing Cards* (Treisman 2018) with ideas of how to explore feelings, and to develop effective coping, regulating, soothing and grounding strategies through a range of games and activities. However, I would also encourage you to make your own with the child that are individualised to their needs.

> I worked with a 13-year-old child who was really struggling with anxiety, especially in social situations and at school. This young person was the most beautiful artist, and using watercolours painted some little cards to remind themself when they were out and about of what they could do to feel calmer in the moment. I colour-copied and laminated them, so they were more durable. They were small enough to fit in their school blazer pocket, and the young person would regularly nip into the restroom at school to look at them in privacy when needed. They also used them in the sessions and at home as visual prompts.

HYPOAROUSAL

When a child is in *freeze state* or having the shutting down response of *hypoarousal*, you are likely to see children who describe or experience:

- feelings of numbness or emptiness
- depression or extreme sadness
- brain fog – an inability to retrieve words or make decisions
- extreme tiredness – the child may fall asleep in the session
- struggles with focus and concentration
- dissociation or daydreaming
- headaches and feeling sick
- shallow breathing or a low respiratory rate.

When dealing with hypoarousal (collapse or flop), find ways to signal an increase in energy in the room. So think about the rhythm of your speech, tone of voice and posture. Consider breathing. Breathing can become shallow in this state, so support the child to pay attention as they breathe in and out. Take deep, long breaths in, and exhale slowly, focusing on each breath. Try to slow the breathing down to five or six breaths per minute, so combined inhalations and exhalations should last about ten to twelve seconds. Some children find that using a timer, watching a YouTube clip or an app is helpful to support breathing exercises (others have been described earlier in this chapter).

It can also be useful to introduce some *physical movement*. It doesn't have to be anything too energetic – sometimes just getting up from sitting and having a walk around the room is enough. Depending on where you meet, it can sometimes help to step outside, get some fresh air and connect with nature. You might also sit on the floor and roll a ball to each other to reconnect, or throw bean bags at a target – make sure that the target is big, like a sofa or big plastic tub, because it is important the child experiences success. It is not a throwing or catching competition.

Engaging with sensory material is the next top tip. Focus on mentally engaging the child's senses when they begin to shut down. Connecting with what they can see, touch, hear, smell and taste can bring them closer to the present moment and reduce the intensity of anxiety. Try asking them to describe the room in detail, including five things they can see, four things they can touch, three things they can hear, two things they can smell and one thing they can taste. You could make a paint handprint and write a sense on each finger to be used as a prompt.

Or *anchor to the present* by asking the child to spot three red things in the room or tell you when five black cars have passed by on the road outside. Depending on the setting you are in, the child might be able to stroke a pet, spray an alerting aromatherapy oil or chew/crunch/suck a regulating snack.

Play a categories game together and think of names, animals or fruits that begin with a certain letter of the alphabet. Or sing to lively and stimulating music to *increase arousal*. This is important because where there is a sense of disconnection from the body and feelings in a hypoaroused state, the goal is to increase arousal, which should enable the child to return to their window of tolerance.

Finally consider using *creative arts*. Creative arts, like drawing and painting, can be stimulating depending on the art materials you provide, which can also increase the child's arousal level and help move them out of a frozen or shutdown state.

EMOTIONAL LITERACY

Simply put, emotional literacy is the ability to understand and express feelings. Typically developing children between the ages of three and five are learning how to get along with each other, share and understand their feelings. Learning to recognise and name their own feelings and how to react to other people's feelings is a critical aspect of a child's social and emotional development. But even before they can talk, typically developing children are beginning to learn a feelings vocabulary. This happens through attuned, responsive and sensitive caregiving.

Parents and carers name feelings for their child and talk about their own emotions. They might read stories about feelings and talk to their child about how others might be feeling. Over time, this helps promote empathic responses from the child. Parents and carers work to create an environment where children can share their feelings freely and show curiosity to understand their big feelings. They model good emotional literacy and use statements such as, 'I can see that you are sad/happy/cross', to help children link the vocabulary of emotion to what they are experiencing. They model the safe expression of their own feelings. They also help young children to make sense of the messages they receive from their bodies in order to recognise and name physical sensations, just like feelings detectives.

So, in this early part of the life story work, think about understanding the child's level of emotional literacy because as well as hoping to eventually support the child to develop a coherent narrative account of their story, we also want them to be able to express their feelings about it to a trusted adult. When thinking about emotional literacy I am interested in:

- Whether the child has words for feelings.
- Recognition of facial expressions in other people.
- Connecting feelings with things that might have happened to someone else.
- Connecting feelings with things that have happened to them.
- Knowing where in their body their feelings are located.

Unsurprisingly, emotional literacy is often an area of challenge for children who have experienced developmental trauma. Several language areas in the brain are affected by trauma, which makes finding words for experiences and translating emotions into words very difficult at times. Van der Kolk's research identified that when traumatised individuals experience a traumatic flashback, Broca's area, for example, one of the speech centres of the brain, goes offline, meaning it is impossible in that moment to put thoughts and feelings into words. Even years after a traumatic event,

> traumatized people often have enormous difficulty telling other people what happened to them. Their bodies re-experience terror, rage, and helplessness, as well as the impulse to fight or flee, but these feelings are almost impossible to articulate. Trauma by nature drives us to the edge of comprehension, cutting us off from language based on common experience or an imaginable past. (van der Kolk 2015, p.43)

Even where individuals do eventually find the words to talk about what happened to them, the narrative rarely captures 'the inner truth of the experience' (van der Kolk 2015, p.43). Therefore, it makes sense that it is essential at the beginning of life story work to help children and young people to express, illuminate and learn about their emotions. We must support children to develop their skills in coping with how they feel, but also to express and explore their emotions within the safety of a relationship with a containing adult. It is not unusual for children who have experienced developmental trauma to struggle to articulate their emotional experience verbally and to name different feeling states. This is often particularly noticeable if a child has been traumatised at a pre-verbal stage of their development. We must also remember, of course, that some children will have experienced a restriction of communication during their trauma, having been threatened with a horrible or terrifying consequence if they 'tell', and so talking about it can feel impossible or even life threatening.

In this situation, using image-making to explore the child's emotions can feel safer. I often ask, 'Can you show me what that looks or feels like?' When you resolve to work creatively through art-making or play, you begin a conversation. As soon as a child shares their artwork or plays with you, they invite you to join that conversation, and understanding can grow. Don't try to interpret what the child has drawn. Always let them explain what the image means for them rather than imposing what you think. Your role as facilitator of life story work is to create an environment in which the child feels safe and able to share both positive and negative emotions.

If it becomes clear that a child needs some additional support in this area, the best way to do this is through the day-to-day interactions they have with parents or carers and educators to replicate as far as possible the early childhood experiences they have missed – once a fortnight in a session with you is nowhere near enough. You can introduce ideas in your work about how to develop these skills, but then encourage playing games and practice at home. As these skills grow, it will be important for parents or carers to feel confident in validating and bearing witness to their child's emerging feelings, and how this connects with their core beliefs about themselves, others and the world. I find it helpful to think of feelings as signals, messages from our body that help bring our attention to something important. We are not our feelings; our feelings are our feelings. So I am not an angry person, but I sometimes feel anger. I am not miserable, but I feel miserable at times.

IDEAS FOR BUILDING EMOTIONAL LITERACY

FEELINGS PEEKABOO

Hide behind your hands or a floaty scarf, and every time you show your face, use a different facial expression, and say the feeling word aloud. Work towards the child being able to name the feeling without your prompt, and swap roles where appropriate.

PAPER PLATES

Use paper plates to create masks or puppets, with different feelings faces – these can become a useful resource to aid emotional expression during the life story work, and can be photographed and used later as illustrations in your life story book.

WORD STORM

Word Storms can be played anywhere – in the car, in your session, while the child is in the bath or on a walk. All try to come up with as many feelings words as you can. You could start with a generic 'feelings' storm and then become more specific – how many alternatives can you find for 'happy' or 'sad' in your Word Storm?

SIMON SAYS

Try a version of Simon Says that focuses on understanding different emotions. For example:

> Simon says 'Look disappointed.'
> Simon says 'Show me how you feel when you score a goal.'
> Simon says 'Jump for joy.'

FEELINGS CHARADES

You will need a series of cards depicting different feeling states – you can prepare these beforehand or make them during the session. They can be written ('happy', 'confused', 'excited', 'lonely') or drawn as feelings faces or emojis. You and the parent or carer takes a card and acts out the feeling state for the child to guess the feeling. You can then reverse this so that the child takes a turn acting while you or the parent or carer guesses. I always encourage the use of the whole body rather than just facial expressions because the embodiment of the feeling helps children connect in a more meaningful way with their bodily sensations. A safe way to do this is to encourage showing the feeling while doing something, for example, pretending to open a gift, take a bite of something or opening the front door to somebody and then showing the feeling.

This is a great game to play with children with poor interoception, who might not tune into messages from inside their body about hunger, thirst, tiredness or toileting.

CREATE MOOD BOARDS

For this activity you will need craft paper, magazines or catalogues, scissors and glue. First identify core emotions such as happy, sad, excited, angry or confused, and write each one across different A3 sheets. Then encourage the child to choose images from the magazines or catalogues to represent those feelings. The images might be of people or places, but could equally be symbolic representations of emotions using colours, lines or shapes.

Work with the child's selections to make mood boards to represent a range of emotions.

You will learn very quickly if the child can recognise facial expressions in others, and as you are cutting and sticking, you can explore why they think the person is feeling happy, for example. What might have happened to lead them to feel this way? If they can imagine into the other person's experience, then can they think of a time when they felt this way themself? And where did they feel it in their body?

Again, these boards can become a useful tool during the work where children find it difficult to articulate how they are feeling, or where they might be experiencing complex or ambivalent and conflicting feelings.

MIRROR, MIRROR

In this simple game, sit opposite each other while one person makes a feeling face and the other person copies it. You can extend the game by asking the child to identify the emotion they are copying. If sitting directly opposite each other in this way feels too intense, or eye contact is uncomfortable, it might be easier to both face a mirror and watch each other's reflection to play the game.

MAKE A BIG LIST OF FEELINGS

Sit with the child to imagine all the feelings you can and make a big list or image, with all the feelings recorded. As you do this you can both make the face that goes with the feeling and explore diverse situations where that feeling may arise. You can extend this to add sounds or actions to your feelings list. Some children may not be able to identify a feeling verbally, but might know, for example, that a cheer is connected to a feeling of success, or they might not know the word 'anxious' or 'worried', but they may know that 'uh-oh' goes with that same feeling.

HOW LONG WILL YOU NEED TO FOCUS ON STAGE ONE OF THE WORK?

This all depends on how well resourced the child is at the start of the work. Sometimes, when we begin to focus on relational healing and supporting children to understand their trauma responses, we might see small shifts quickly, but the real change only occurs when the child's view of themself and their relationship with the world fundamentally shifts. When children begin to feel safer, we see them start to understand that adults can be trusted to meet their needs, including for co-regulation. It becomes possible for them to ask for help and to admit when they make a mistake without becoming immediately saturated in toxic shame. They might find it easier to engage their thinking brain before acting, and become better able to manage more complex cause-and-effect thinking. This can take a long time to achieve, even with consistent therapeutic re-parenting. You might even need to take a further step back and access support for the child with sensory integration or bodily regulation before you can effectively focus on emotional regulation. Where children experience disruption to their early motor development and relationships it is common to see tremendous challenges in relation to bodily regulation. Lloyd has written about the impact of developmental trauma on the growth of a child's foundation sensorimotor systems (2016, 2020), and you can find more information about her model for building bodily regulation as a foundation for access to psychological therapies on her website.[5] You are more likely to be able to move on to the next phase of the work if you have mobilised the systemic network to support this work.

You will need to judge, alongside the child's parent or carer, whether enough building blocks are in place for you to have a level of confidence in the child's ability to cope with exploration of their family story without them fragmenting or becoming overwhelmed. They need to able to access a safe adult for co-regulation, and to be developing a toolkit for self-regulation. Be mindful of setting your expectations so that they are entirely consistent with the child's developmental age and capacity. It can be incredibly unhelpful to make assumptions about what a child, young person or young adult *should* be able to manage or do independently based solely on their chronological age.

5 www.bussmodel.org

5

STAGE TWO OF LIFE STORY WORK

NURTURING CONNECTEDNESS, BELONGING AND IDENTITY

The concept of *identity* embraces all the memories, encounters, relationships and values that create our sense of self over time. When all goes well, this eventually creates a robust awareness of who we are, even as new aspects of our character grow. Identity also incorporates the myriad relationships people nurture as a child, friend, colleague, intimate partner and parent or carer, and involves external factors that we have little or no control over, such as our height, ethnic origin and socioeconomic class. As we mature, identity also integrates our political opinions, values, ethics, and cultural and religious beliefs. Ultimately, 'achievement of identity requires knowledge about social and genetic antecedents and the ability to incorporate personal history into a continuing narrative, as self-awareness is mediated through new experiences, relationships, and social contexts' (Smith and Logan 2004, p.12).

Critical to building a sense of identity is the idea of *belonging*, which relates to a human, emotional need to be connected to and accepted by others. Our need to belong is what drives us to seek out stable, long-lasting relationships with other people, be that within a family system, a peer group, through participation in social activities like clubs or sports teams or by being part of a religious group or community organisation. Lyons (2022) compares the landscape of a child's relationships throughout their life to a blanket or a quilt, which wraps around the child and subsequently both nourishes and buffers them from the inevitable challenges they encounter as they grow. This begins with the child's primary caregiver tenderly stitching the first patches of the quilt, but then, over time, extends to siblings, other family members, friends and teachers, with each new relationship adding another patch to the quilt. The relational context will continue to grow in richness over time for a typically developing child. If you then observe the patchwork of a child's life, you will see that those patches will vary in size, colour and significance over time. Some relationships will remain vibrant and nourishing; some will fade or disappear as time passes. If raised within a birth family system with consistent, attuned caregiving, even where little gaps appear, the quilt of a child's life will not fall apart – it is tough enough to withstand a tiny hole or patches that are beginning to fray at the edges.

In writing this chapter, I am reminded of the nights my younger brother and I spent sitting with our mum when she was dying, not wanting her to be alone. Anticipating what would become the greatest loss of our lives, we spent hours together by her bedside, through the dark hours of the night until the sun rose, revisiting the past, sharing stories, unearthing memories, and realising we each remembered details of our early lives the other had forgotten. When I look back at this incredibly traumatic time, in the days before her death, I treasure those hours. I realise how fortunate I am to still be able to use my family to develop a sense of who I am and to make sense of my story. Enough of my childhood patchwork quilt remains intact, which means my sense of self can continue to develop in the context of enduring familial relationships.

The Children's Commissioner's *Family Review* highlighted the power of these relationships and how a family can have a protective impact on its members, with four constituent parts:

- A strong emotional connection, with an emphasis on love and joy.
- The importance of shared experiences (both the regular and the exceptional).
- Mutual support to one another, both practical and emotional.
- The enduring nature of the relationships, and the sense this provides of unconditional support (Children's Commissioner 2023, p.4).

But many children in care and adoption are denied these opportunities. Even at a very young age, where there have been experiences of relational poverty and disruption, their quilt may already be threadbare and tattered by loss. It may never have been well sewn in the first place. These children lose so much when they come into the care of the state: friendships, much-loved pets, community and connections with their extended birth family and siblings. They haven't always had the opportunity to make sense of these losses. No one has mended their quilt, or even noticed the frayed edges. Allan Jenkins came into care as a young boy in the 1960s, and was eventually separated from his brother Christopher. In his memoir *Plot 29* he describes the impact of these gaps:

> I invented my father once. There was a man who regularly used to watch us as we played on the roundabout in the park at the back of the Plymouth home. I told everyone he was my dad. (I didn't say he was Christopher's; maybe my brother wasn't there. My memories are sketchy and episodic, pixelated like worn VHS tape. No one likes to top them up.) (Jenkins 2017, p.30)

In a similar way, by severing legal and other connections with birth family, the finality of the adoption process has been described as drawing 'a veil between the past and the present lives of adopted persons and [making] it as opaque and impenetrable as possible; like the veil which God has placed between the living and the dead' (*Lawson v. Registrar General*, 106 L J 204, 1956, quoted in Cohen and Winter 2005, p.44). Although there is thankfully an increasing understanding of the importance of maintaining and preserving these important familial connections, this is always balanced with a need for protection for the child now and in the future, and for some, gaping chasms of missing information remain.

Lost information and confused or conflicting stories about a birth family or a journey to care can make it difficult for any child to make sense of what has happened to them without support, reassurance and containment from someone they trust. In research conducted with adult adoptees by the University of East Anglia, respondents repeatedly emphasised the importance of knowing their heritage and life story prior to adoption in relation to identity formation and belonging, and how contact with birth family members was a vital component of achieving this. Many spoke of not knowing their heritage when growing up, and the harm they experienced because of this. In her blog, adult adoptee and therapist Lesli Johnson poignantly writes:

> ...adoptees are in reunion whether they are formally searching or not... I recently presented at an adoption conference and had the members attending my session participate in a quick exercise before they took their seats. I asked them to walk around the room and find the person they thought they most closely looked like. After a few minutes and some nervous laughter, I had them take their seats and we talked about what that experience was like. I explained that this is what adoptees often do. They walk through the world looking for their lost 'twin' or for someone they resemble. The author Betty Jean Lifton calls this living in the 'Ghost Kingdom'. It's the place where adoptees can go and 'hang out' with their birth relatives and imagine life if they hadn't been adopted. (Johnson 2019)

It is an incredibly complex task to belong to, identify with, and be loved by two families, even though love is not finite, and children should never feel like they must choose. For some, the loss inherent in adoption is compounded by a lack of contact and exacerbated by a lack of truth and transparency. It is important to acknowledge that although the child's identity is complex and may include birth family, experiences in foster care and for some, adoption, the child has one life, and we need to do our best to support them to integrate all these parts of themselves. As these children become adults, their early experiences will continue to be a significant part of who they are:

> I'm 30 years old now and my care experience is still a massive part of my identity. It illustrates my life. Conversations about family, Christmas traditions, money, just about everything is interpreted by my care experience. (Carter and Maclean 2022, p.79)

Activities that allow children to explore the idea of family can be helpful, such as a genogram or family tree.

GENOGRAM OR FAMILY TREE

You only need pens and paper (preferably A3 size or larger), but if you have photographs of family members you could print, together with a selection of feelings faces or emojis, that can be useful. We are aiming for a graphic representation of family members and their relationships, preferably over at least three generations. There are conventions for drawing genograms that you must follow for court reports, but in a direct work activity, especially with a child, there is no need to be so prescriptive.

You would usually begin with adding the child first. If you have photographs of any family members, feel free to use them rather than symbols, or the child could draw them. Then move to their parents' names, health, age or date of birth, and date or cause of death, if applicable, and then grandparents. If either parent has been married more than once, get information about those relationships too. Then ask for siblings' details, beginning with the eldest on the left. Finally, ask if there are any non-relatives who are particularly important or 'like family'. Remember that you should be concerned with perceptions of who represents 'family' for the child as much as who is family by birth: 'We don't care about whose DNA has recombined with whose. When everything goes to hell, the people who stand by you without flinching – they are your family. Family is about who is willing to hold your hand when you need it the most' (J. Butcher, quoted in Carter and Maclean 2022, p.33).

I always ask if there is someone who used to be part of the family but who is not yet on the family tree. Conversely, is there someone who is in the picture who the child would prefer not to be? It can be useful to extend this activity to understand a child's emotional connection to people on the family tree. You can have feelings faces or emojis ready to attach to individuals, and then ask the child to connect feelings with people.

Don't just record the facts; as you construct the image, take the opportunity to have a conversation about family relationships. Who would the child have gone to if they were upset? Who gets on best with whom? Can they think of three words to describe their mum, grandad, brother, cousin, etc.? You can also ask hypothetical questions and write on speech bubbles to give the imagined replies – for example, 'What do you think X likes most about you?'

This is a relatively simple way to elicit information about family composition and relationships, and offers a visual picture of the complexity of a family system. In fostering and adoption, of course, a family tree may become far more complex. Children may choose to make separate images to represent birth, foster and adoptive families. They may equally prefer to represent their family in its broadest sense. Sometimes people use the analogy of a tree, where the birth family is represented by the roots, the foster family is the trunk, and the adoptive family the leaves and branches. This supports children to present a more integrated self.

Another alternative, if you wanted to focus on the family the child is living in now, is to have a large art canvas, paint a tree trunk and then have each family member choose an acrylic paint colour and add their handprint to the image. For adoptees and children in care, it can be a visual and tactile experience of family belonging. You can write family members' names onto the canvas with a permanent marker when the paint has dried (Tait and Wosu 2015, pp.120–121).

FAMILY SCULPT

Another way to explore family relationships with children is through a Sculpt activity. You will need a selection of diverse objects for this, which could include small figures of people and animals, or buttons, pebbles, shells or pinecones – anything you can carry in a small bag or box to a session – together with a large piece of paper and pens. Think carefully about the number of objects you present to a child for this exercise. It is easy to overwhelm very young or easily distracted children with too much choice. Similarly, if the toys are too engaging or exciting, it might be hard for the child to focus on the task. This exercise is a more creative version of an ecomap where you support the child to create a 3D representation of their family and systemic network, noticing both space and distance as the objects are placed. It can reveal feelings, bonds, conflicts, hostility and isolation or scapegoating as the family structure is revealed.

First, ask the child to choose an object to represent themself. Try to avoid giving too much direction so that you invite creativity and initiative. Then explore why they chose a certain item; they may have a clear reason, or something may just have caught their eye. Place it on a large piece of paper and then suggest they create their own world around it, choosing objects for important people in their life. This might include family, friends, pets, people they live with, people they don't see or people who have died. Leave any omissions of people you might consider significant, which are certainly common when working this way with children and young people, until the end of the Sculpt, as they are rarely 'forgotten'. You can then be curious about whether anyone is missing, or whether there is someone else they would like to add. In some instances, it might be appropriate to offer a more direct prompt: 'I notice you haven't added X yet. Would you want to do that?'

Encourage the child to place each object in relation to themself on the Sculpt, considering how close or connected or not they feel to the person.

Consider the way you explain the process carefully as children will assume that by *close* you mean physically close in distance rather than emotionally close. Suggest that they think of people who are important to them. Then explore which person each object represents, and the reasons it was chosen. You could then ask the child to describe the person to you using a couple of adjectives.

As an extension to this activity, encourage the child to reconfigure the Sculpt to show how they would prefer it to be. Or an alternative to total reconfiguration is to experiment with moving the objects on the Sculpt either closer to the child – 'What would X need to do to move closer?' – or further away – 'Are there any times when X feels more distant or disconnected?' You can represent these movements with arrows on the Sculpt drawing. Then investigate what it feels like to have X closer, etc. For example, if you move a figure closer to the child's object on the Sculpt, you might ask, 'How does it feel to have X close by?'

I find it helpful to draw around each object on the paper and write down words the child uses to describe people, so that the picture is not lost when the physical Sculpt is dismantled. Children often like you to do the writing for them but ask first, and do not assume. You can photograph the Sculpt as an aide-mémoire before it is deconstructed at the end of the session. This image can then be integrated into the life story book (see Wrench 2018, pp.123–125). Finally, think carefully about how the Sculpt is taken apart at the end, to be respectful of those people and the relationships that matter to the child that have been shared with you.

IDENTITY FORMATION

Most of us will have a notion of what identity means: 'Identity could be described as a strange and intangible phenomenon. Difficult to define and taken for granted when we have it and yet desperately sought after when we are denied it' (Nicholls 2005, p.6). Our identity makes us unique. If I was asked the question 'Who are you?', I would draw on many aspects of myself: my name (unchanged after marriage, despite my promises); where I'm from (Manchester) or where I live (West Yorkshire); my footballing allegiances (City, not United); my family (wife, mum, sister, daughter, aunt); my friendships (small in number but of long standing and incredibly precious to me); my love of gardening and growing and the impact this has on my wellbeing... I could go on. Each of you will have a different story to tell reflecting on all aspects of yourself: from gender to sexuality; accent to ethnicity; who you look like and who you take after; education and experiences in life. What matters most to us is likely to change over time and in different contexts as we all show different 'parts' of ourselves depending on who we are with and what we are doing. I am a quite different Katie when I am in the stands at a football match to the Katie who delivers training to social workers.

Our sense of self grows and becomes increasingly more complex from childhood through adolescence and into adulthood, but it is shaped by experiences, and changes as our brains develop the capacity to reflect on ourselves and our lives. This identity formation reaches its peak in adolescence when young people evaluate and revise their identities. They might experiment with different selves in terms of their physical appearance (hair colour, make-up, clothing) as well as beliefs and values. At this stage in development, young people are still influenced most by family values: often adolescents are challenging these values, as the process of individuation or separation from parents or carers happens around puberty.

It is common to show uncertainty in terms of identity formation at this time in your life, but how young people navigate this transition is influenced strongly by their closest relationships, usually with siblings and parents or carers. Peer relationships are also an important factor because of the acute sensitivity adolescents have in relation to social signals from others. If we return to the analogy of the quilt, the adult patches begin to fade and the peer patches begin to sparkle. We contemplate who we think we are, how we are like others, as well as what makes us unique and special.

Where children have not benefited from the relational experiences they needed to help a sense of self grow, they may subsequently:

- not feel deserving of love and nurture or of wonderful things happening to them – you may see self-sabotage
- become terribly upset at seemingly minor corrections, like someone pointing out that their shoes are on the wrong feet, or that they missed a word out when reading aloud
- feel jealous when their parent or carer pays someone or something

else attention – a sibling, a pet, or even being on the phone to the bank

- verbalise self-critical thoughts like 'I'm stupid' or 'everyone hates me'
- become easily defeated or upset by failure (or even the thought of failure), which often means they feel they cannot even try in the first place – they have so much self-doubt and a lack of self-efficacy.

THE ROLE OF PARENTS OR CARERS IN IDENTITY FORMATION AND NURTURING BELONGING

As we explored in Chapter 2, the child's carers or adoptive parents are often in a good position to be alongside their children during life story work and, through this, deepen the child's understanding of themself. They are there when the tough questions arise unexpectedly at bedtime, driving in the car or in the supermarket queue, as children endeavour to make sense of their stories. And importantly, research by Howe and Feast, based on a study of almost 500 adopted people, concluded that love and affection between an adopted person and their parents does not, for the vast majority, falter when there is openness about adoption or where contact has been re-established with a birth parent or other birth relatives (2000, p.93).

Parents and carers are also there to safeguard special memories and stories that are unique to the child, which are so important in ensuring that children in care or adoption are not defined solely by their difficult histories. Parents and carers can add to the richness of the story and to their child's 'quilt', both directly and indirectly. Children will only share their stories if there is an audience to share them with – this audience (the parent or carer) 'plays a pivotal role in the construction and production of and reflections upon these stories' (Hammond and Cooper 2013, p.10). The response, acceptance and availability of the parent or carer for this is critical to identity formation, because our past is such a big part of our identity, of who we are. Without support, these children may feel like parts of their story (and identity) have been lost or cannot be spoken of. This can have a catastrophic impact on self-concept, self-esteem and therefore on belonging.

It is important for adopters and foster carers to be mindful of the way in which they talk about a child's birth family, and this can be a tricky balance to get right. While not wanting to sanitise a story or romanticise the idea of birth parents, nor should they be spoken about in a way that locates everything that is bad in them. Brodzinsky (2005) termed this 'communicative openness', which encompasses thoughtfulness, reflective capacity and openness to the child and their birth family from the foster carer or adoptive parent. Conversations about the birth family should happen and be carefully managed, 'so that the child does not have to make sense of negative, contradictory or idealised ideas about the birth family' (Schofield and Beek 2018, p.269). It is important that the adults in the child's life show their own flexibility about a child's family memberships and what that means for each individual. There are, of course, benefits and challenges inherent in having more than one family, but 'to feel worthy as human beings, children need to believe they came from worthwhile beginnings' (Brodzinsky 2011, p.204).

> I recently heard of a safety plan written around family time for a child in care. One of the actions was that the birth parent and foster carer should not directly meet on the day of contact. The child would be collected from the carer's car by a family time supervisor, and returned there at the end.
>
> The birth parent has no history of violence and is not known to be a threat. They have never behaved inappropriately towards the carer. But the carer had decided for some reason that they would prefer not to have direct contact.
>
> During life story work the child asked if their parent should be included in the life story book, because the foster carer was 'scared' to see them. They wondered, 'Does that mean they're bad?'
>
> It made me question the narrative this child is hearing from the carer about their birth family, and what this will mean for their identity formation.

THE ROLE OF LIFE STORY WORK IN GATHERING STORIES ABOUT OURSELVES

Traditionally, the family has been the source of all knowledge about its children: 'Healthy children develop their sense of self within the reciprocal interactions with their parents' (Hughes 2016, p.10). Where this process has been derailed by experiences of trauma and loss, or separation from birth family and community, it is incredibly challenging for children to develop a coherent and positive sense of who they are: 'Their sense of self tends to be weak and in pieces' (Hughes 2016, p.10). Where children have been separated from family by multiple moves from birth family to foster placement, for example, with each transition their personal history splinters further. With each disruption to relationships, access to priceless, irreplaceable information about the child is potentially lost, unless someone in their world makes an active choice to safeguard it.

Therefore if, through life story work, we are to support children to develop a coherent sense of self, a belief that they belong and high self-esteem, we must include everything that makes a human life: family legacies, the funny anecdotes, the stories that are special just to that child, the idiosyncrasies of family life, the things, for example, my brother and I spoke of in the dark of a summer's night: '"Do you remember when?" is how our story is shared, the way we learn to become ourselves through knowing where we belong' (Jenkins 2017, p.119). We must ensure that fundamental messages are woven throughout the story and our work: that this child is loved and loveable, that the trauma was not their fault, that they deserved better parenting. However, the notion that building self-esteem and a sense of identity that acknowledges the trauma, the losses and the separations, *and* focuses on the strengths, resilience and positive attributes held by the child and within their birth family system can happen with a therapist or social worker for an hour a week is an unhelpful one.

NURTURING COUNTER-NARRATIVES AND A SENSE OF BELONGING

Warmth and trust in the relationship between a child and their parent or carer 'is associated with greater commitment to self-identity and optimal exploration and ultimately robust mental health and wellbeing' (Hohnen, Gilmour and Murphy 2020, p.215). However, where children have grown up without consistent access to safe, nurturing relationships within which their needs are met unconditionally, their sense of self, of the world, and of adults is significantly altered; this is often described as an internal working model (Bowlby 1969/1982; Craik 1943). The stories they may tell about themselves are different to other children *because* they have experienced attachment trauma:

> They can carry around feelings of shame, worthlessness, rejection, and loneliness which are often accompanied by beliefs such as: 'I'm useless'; 'No one really wants to know me'; 'If you come close to me, you'll soon reject me anyway so I may as well reject you now to save us all disappointment.' (de Thierry 2019, p.108)

Sadly, children who experience harm in the context of relationships have often been repeatedly exposed to 'criticism, humiliation and negative attributions, often from the people who were supposed to have been their biggest supporters and cheerleaders in life' (Treisman 2017a, p.171). The stories these people tell stick like glue to their child and can be hard to shake off. Harmful self-beliefs can subsequently be compounded by the systems, services and contexts around the child, and by the language and labels commonly used to shape and define them: 'They can feel like they're inked tattoos or scars etched onto one's body' (Treisman 2017a, p.175).

Just scan a social work chronology, read a school report or school behaviour log for a child in care, or peruse a child's fostering pen picture. Reflect on how the media reports on children in the care of the state or on the furore surrounding planning applications to open a new children's home in a residential area. You are likely to encounter similar negative discourses and harmful language describing children who are: controlling, manipulative, out of control, disengaged, anti-social and disrespectful. A recent survey asked 2000 adults in the UK which words first came to mind when thinking about the term 'children in care', and the most frequently used words were 'vulnerable', 'sad', 'disadvantaged' and 'abuse' (Coram 2021). Although this was considered a 'sympathetic' response within the survey, it also emphasises the focus on challenges rather than strengths.

Where these negative messages come from people the child values most, like a parent or an older sibling, they are likely to place even more importance on them. They hit harder. In his memoir *My Name is Why*, Lemn Sissay reflects on the day he had to leave the foster carers who had taken care of him since he was a baby: 'My mum told me they would never visit me because it was my choice to leave them because I didn't love them' (2019, p.71). It was not, and he did. He says to his social worker as they drive to a children's home, 'I know this is my fault and I will ask for forgiveness' (2019, p.72). The case notes report that his mum described him as a 'naughty boy and that she sometimes thinks he is amoral. She told me that he smokes, swears, steals and he seems to harbour a grudge about being black...he would have to go' (2019, p.62).

Care-experienced adults have written about the devastating impact of reading their own case files after making a subject access request (SAR). Rebekah Pierre published an open letter to her social worker on social media after discovering her name had been misspelt over a hundred times, and the social worker had referred to allegations of abuse in a way that blamed Pierre, the child victim, and minimised the harm caused.[1] Similarly, Sissay reflects on reading 'eighteen years of records written by strangers'. In a quest to understand himself and his journey through care, he acknowledges, 'I feared what they'd reveal about me or what they'd reveal about the people who were entrusted with my care. What truths or untruths?... Maybe my mother didn't want me. Maybe it was all my fault' (2019, p.3).

So I encourage you to bring conscious awareness to the language you use, and the way in which children in care and adoption are storied. I implore you to look for the counter-narratives and to support children to begin to hear and to integrate alternative stories about themselves and the world:

> The identity of an individual should be treated as if it were a treasure trove comprised of a myriad of stones, each representing a different facet to that identity, be it physical, social, or genealogical. Each part, though different, belongs to the whole... The job of the practitioner, therefore, is to recognise the potential value of identity to the beholder, to collect as many of the different stones as possible and to make these available when/if requested. (Cohen and Winter 2005, p.50)

But I have also learned the hard way that children cannot shift their world view or alter their sense of themselves just because we say it is so. These children 'will not have had the same opportunities to develop positive internal cheerleaders or a chain of built in memories of people who were there for them – unconditionally and consistently rooting for them, believing in them and supporting them' (Treisman 2017a, p.171). We must therefore find ways to support these children to feel loved and loveable, to trust the care they receive now and to understand their losses

1 https://twitter.com/RebekahPierre92/status/1548967226316816386

were not their fault – that they deserved better parenting. Self-concept only shifts through experiences and through relationships. Children in care need support to feel loved and accepted, and as if they belong *from the inside*.

An ex-colleague, clinical psychologist Martha Pearson, has recently written about her strengths-based work with two care-experienced young women. Both were finding it hard to access therapy. Both had found other ways to manage their losses and pain through self-harm and drug use. Martha wrote 'a document of strengths and resources', saved it in their social care file, and shared it with them. Neither young person was able to answer questions directly about their strengths, so she went to the systemic network and, with their consent, gathered those stories for them. These were the kinds of questions she asked:

> Give me a bit of background on your relationship with Emily. When did you first meet Emily?
>
> Do you have any guesses about what has made your relationship work? Do you have a favourite memory of spending time with Emily?
>
> What qualities do you most admire in Emily? How do these qualities help Emily keep going when things are difficult?
>
> What is your sense of what Emily values, hopes for, and is committed to?
>
> Can you describe ways in which Emily may be taking steps to protect, care for, and assist other people?
>
> What have you most enjoyed about working with Emily? What have you learned from working with Emily? What has your relationship with Emily given you?
>
> What do you think it is about Emily that means you will remember her in particular in the future?

Feedback from young people suggests these documents have real significance (as seen in the words of Emily and Gina below):

> 'That's the nicest thing I have ever read – it made me cry. I will definitely keep it, thank you.'
>
> 'Thank you so much. I'm reading it in parts because it makes me cry. I will never forget what you have all done for me.'(Pearson 2023, p.11)

SHIFTING SELF-CONCEPT – PATCHING THE QUILT

While not wanting to minimise any child's experience of trauma, once we support a child to experience external and internal safety, we can often begin to help them make significant developmental gains and to grasp the wonderful opportunities and relationships life has to offer. This is only possible once the child can set aside thinking about their trauma for long enough to discover the 'personal qualities and strengths that were not seen and valued when he was living in his traumatic past' (Hughes 2016, p.35). A child needs to develop the capacity to be in the present, rather than anticipating a recurrence of traumatic experience long after the immediate danger has passed (see Chapter 4).

So how do we shift this self-concept and collectively and individually patch this quilt? Bearing in mind the only way to do this is through repetition, consistency and predictability, this places adoptive parents and carers at the heart of change, with those 'in-the-moment' opportunities to really have influence through their relationship with the child:

- Validate the child's feelings and lived experience of separation and loss – their feelings matter, and they deserve to be heard. It is not necessary to work towards forgetting the past and living only in the present, but we must support children to understand their complex stories and integrate the past, rather than denying it or being bound by it, unable to move forwards. The life of an adoptee or a child in care can be negatively impacted by a lack of validation for what they have been through. They can easily be made to feel something is wrong with them when people dismiss their belief that a lost or severed connection to their birth family matters. This can lead to them feeling as if they don't have permission to speak their truth, which can further compound the trauma (adapted from Dolfi 2022).
- Support children to explore and begin to tell stories about themselves that acknowledge the trauma but also value the positive relationships they have in their lives, together with stories about their qualities and spirit in the face of adversity. The child must play an active role in this process, as opposed to having a story constructed for them, wherever this is possible.
- Work to increase the amount and quality of positive relational

experiences the child enjoys – with their parents, foster carer, friends, neighbours, teachers, social workers, siblings and birth family too, where we safely can. Where there have been significant ruptures to relationships, seek to repair: 'The repair, if speedy and genuine, is usually full of an oxytocin release and can actually build a healthy attachment' (de Thierry 2019, p.44).

- Look for confidence-boosting opportunities – seeking out activities the child enjoys and can experience success in – whether that is knitting, sport, drama, baking or dog walking.
- Provide opportunities for the child to experience mastery and control, both of which are critical where they have experienced powerlessness in their abuse or history of care. Depending on their developmental age and stage, this might be teaching you something they are good at – Minecraft or plaiting hair – or just day-to-day allowing them developmentally appropriate choices and responsibility for decision making that affects them.
- Notice the child's strengths and qualities like courage, honesty, persistence, loyalty and hopefulness, and together bring them into the light through gentle noticing, praise and encouragement.
- Recognising ourselves as unique and different from other people is important, as is membership of social groups, especially for children in care and adoption. Like everyone else, they strive to find connection and acceptance. So find ways in which to nurture a child's sense of social connectedness and belonging, not only to a family system, but also to social groups like a choir, a sports team, their school community or religious organisation. The more a child identifies or connects with a particular group, be that swim club or orchestra, the more significant a role that group plays in shaping how they feel about themself.

  Gaining status or acceptance within a group can help build confidence, satisfaction and efficacy. Our self-esteem grows when we feel like we belong. Children in care, young adults with care experience and adoptees can also find connection through peer support groups and interactions with others who share a similar story or experience of separation from their birth family.

- Safeguard a child's memories, new and old, as if they are the most precious treasure, and proactively seek to do so. Identity formation and self-concept is dependent on the contributions of others who have access to shared memories. History is linked to identity. If you don't know your history, if you don't know your birth *and* foster family stories, for example, who are you?
- Work to strengthen and support the relationship between the child and their parent or carer – this is at the heart of recovery from relational trauma: 'The magic is in the relationship, the interactions and the human connections' (Treisman 2017a, p.233).

A combination of these ideas, applied consistently, can be impactful in terms of building a child's sense of themselves, their identity and belief they belong. They can all positively impact on self-esteem and resilience.

ACTIVITIES TO BUILD SELF-ESTEEM AND RESILIENCE

ACHIEVEMENT JAR

Create an Achievement Jar. Encourage the child to write down one thing they have achieved, enjoyed or experienced success with every day. Foster carers or parents can do this if the child is still young. The easiest way to do this is to write or draw the achievement on a piece of paper and add it to an empty glass jar, then you can all see the achievements growing. The child can decorate the jar with glass paints or stickers if they'd like too.

3 GOOD THINGS

Encourage the child to journal daily and to record 3 Good Things that happened to them each day. If that feels too much, make it an end of the week task.

THINGS I LIKE ABOUT ME

This can be a list, image or piece of prose that explores all the things that make this child beautiful and unique, both on the inside as well as on the outside. Encourage the child to think about their personality, what they do well, and how they treat other people, as well as things that they like when they look in the mirror.

ALL ABOUT ME

Use sentence prompts to encourage the child to make an image, collage or an All About Me wallpaper outline of their own body that explores their strengths. For example:

- 'My friends think I'm cool because...'
- 'My teacher says I'm brilliant at...'
- 'I feel happy when I...'
- 'Something that I'm really proud of is...'
- 'One special thing about me is...'
- 'My best quality is...'

PHOTO ALBUM

Make a special Photo Album and fill it with the child's passions, comforts, interests, biggest loves and most important people.

THE A-TO-Z CHALLENGE

Challenge the child to write or draw something amazing about themself, working their way through the alphabet. For example,

Katie is:

A for artistic
B for a brilliant baker
C for courageous
D for a dreamer
E for energetic...

And so on. You don't have do this all in one go – use it as an opener in a session or ask the child and their parent or carer to add a new letter every day at home in between your sessions and bring them to share with you.

BUTTONS AND BEADS

This is lovely activity for celebrating people in the child's life who have had, or continue to have, a positive impact on their life. They may have cared for them, encouraged or protected them. They could be friends, carers, relatives, teachers or sports coaches. They may or may not still be in the child's life.

You'll need a selection of beads or buttons and something to thread them onto – this could be yarn or string, or if you are making jewellery you will need nylon, leather or beading thread. You can buy beads and bags of buttons from craft stores, but I have a spare button box at home, as I'm sure many of you do, and you can often find cheap costume jewellery in charity shops or at car boot sales to dismantle, which then makes this a much cheaper option.

Ask the child if they would prefer buttons or beads (if you have both on offer), and then whether they prefer to make a bracelet, necklace or a simple chain. Spend some time looking through the beads or buttons, seeing which ones they are drawn to and wondering why. The child can thread as many as they like, but for each bead or button they have to name someone that is important to them. With a good selection on offer, you and the child should be able to think about the reasons why a particular bead or button is chosen for a particular person. You might need to offer gentle prompts, for example: 'Which bead could you choose for your dad/teacher/childminder/neighbour?'

Once it is made, you can celebrate how wonderful it looks and how special the child is to have so many connections and important people in their life. Make sure you keep a note of who was put on the chain and the associations with that person if they emerge, and this can be added to the life story book (see Wrench 2018, pp.104–105).

You can do a similar activity with gems, or layering different coloured sand in a jar. Each gem or layer helps in thinking about and celebrating a positive connection in the child's life.

MAGAZINE SELF OR FAMILY PORTRAIT

This is one of my all-time favourite activities to do with children of all ages – the child can make a self-portrait or, if you are working with parents or carers and the child together, they could make a family portrait. Magazines can be used for this. I have become expert at tracking down free ones in shops, travel agents and supermarkets, and in begging from friends and family with magazine subscriptions. I only buy them if I know a child has a very particular interest they will want to include on their self-portrait, but it's just as easy to print some images from the internet ahead of the session. You should aim to source magazines or images that will represent the child's cultural and ethnic background, as well as being appropriate in relation to their developmental stage.

Ask the child to browse through the magazines and choose pictures that they feel represent who they are, describe their personality or how they feel about their life. This can be likes and dislikes, things they aspire to or things they just find funny. They can cut out as many things as they want and then stick them on a piece of paper to create a collage. It's important to say that they can add their own drawings or words too, because children can sometimes get a little stuck if they can't find the exact image they need, or become preoccupied with finding accurate visual representations of someone with the same eye colour, hair, etc. Older children are usually better able to find more abstract or symbolic images to represent themselves. As always, while you are searching for the appropriate images you will be chatting about what is being included and why – all rich material for the here and now parts of the life story book.

STARS OF PRIDE

For this you'll either need to cut out some gold stars, or I buy packs of fluorescent stars from bargain high street shops to use. You can do this as an opening exercise in a session where you invite the child to write or draw on the star something that they feel proud of that has happened since you last saw them. You can also use it as an ending ritual to write something on a star the child is proud of that has happened during the session. Or, have a massive pile of stars and use it as a longer activity when you all write as many things as possible that you are proud of about the child. I save all the stars, put them together in a collage, and photograph it for their story.

This is a great way of identifying and celebrating the child's successes in a range of situations and with different people. You may have to work harder to find examples of successes with some children who do not feel they have very much to feel proud about, so make sure you and their parent or carer are prepared with plentiful examples.

6

STAGE THREE OF LIFE STORY WORK

INFORMATION SHARING AND INTEGRATION

TRAUMATIC MEMORY

There is a growing consensus among professionals working in fostering and adoption that the resolution of early traumatic experiences requires a child to have developed a coherent narrative account of their story (Hughes 2003, 2004; Perry and Hambrick 2000; Solomon and Siegel 2003; van der Kolk 2005). Saltzman *et al.* (2013) contest that humans are innately meaning-making creatures who strive to organise their experiences to make sense of events in their lives. This need to actively categorise and understand life experiences is evident in even very young children and infants in the form of social referencing. They primarily rely on their parents or carers to make sense of the world, and to support them to organise their feelings and reactions. As they grow, pre-verbal forms of meaning-making give way to verbal forms that explicitly require the co-construction of a narrative. This is how we make an experience knowable, integrate it into our conscious life, and then eventually access it as a memory.

This process is at the core of life story work where we develop a coherent narrative together. Yet this can also be one of the most challenging aspects of the process, and so in this chapter we will explore the basics of information sharing and supporting children to integrate their story. In this stage of the work, *we* first must find the words that are developmentally appropriate for the child, to talk about the most distressing and traumatic events. Sometimes these are experiences about which children have no verbal memory. Our words matter – this might be the first time a child has been supported to put words onto unconscious or implicit memories.

Therapists in recent years are increasingly understanding the need for body-based interventions, which help people process the trauma by making what is held in the body implicitly, explicit (Levine and Frederick 1997; Perry and Szalavitz 2017; van der Kolk 2015). This is because traumatic memories are stored as associated feelings and sensory experiences that are not accessible through language alone. It is important therefore to be able to translate these sensory experiences or traumatic reminders (smells, sounds, tastes, etc.) into a verbal narrative to support the child to be able to understand their experience on a conscious level. Until those experiences are understood, resolved and healed, the trauma will continue to play out, triggered by sensory input in the environment and from within the body. It simply cannot be accessed without support from somebody to help put words onto those experiences.

As a care-experienced adult, Allan Jenkins writes:

> I crave hugs. I long to be held. I have felt incomplete without it much of my life. I can do cuddles and massage. I have worked on this. But don't come quietly up behind me. Never stroke my neck. It is instant, the reaction, like a trip wire or the emergency cord on a train... I go into lockdown. My emergency shutters crash. I cannot connect to kindness or loving intent. All I get is a body memory that my brain no longer holds. Something bad happened. My mind is amnesiac but my body less so. (2017, p.163)

When babies experience traumatic events (including in utero), these are imprinted on the brain and body, even though the infant cannot retrieve the experiences verbally. As implicit memory is present at birth, and because it involves parts of the brain that do not require conscious processing when we are retrieving it, we cannot fully know the influence of what we have experienced in the past on how we act in the present. In the first year of life, we only have implicit memory. Autobiographical memory does not start until babies reach 18–24 months of age, and refers to the memories of our first-hand experiences and events in our lives, as well as our relationship to events happening around us. This type of memory allows us to recall specific details of what we did, what we felt and what happened at a certain moment in time. Autobiographical memory can also be shaped by the way we encode or store information. For example, if we focus on the emotional aspects of an event, it is likely we will recall the experience differently than if we focus on the factual details.

One of the challenges for children and young people who have experienced early trauma is that safe adults around them may be offering reassurances that all is well, but their body is telling them something altogether different. The evidence before them is therefore conflicting. Although in most cases they *are* safe, the body and brain are remembering that something very scary or unsafe happened when they, for example, heard a siren approaching, smelt alcohol on a parent's breath or heard the theme tune to a particular TV programme. Data stored in their implicit memory warns them danger is approaching or is present. The list of potential sensory triggers is endless and must at times be terrifying.

Explaining to children why it can be helpful to explore traumatic memories

There are a number of analogies to support children to understand why it can be helpful to explore traumatic memories, even if it feels like a very scary thing to do.

The wardrobe or cupboard

One simple idea is of a disorganised wardrobe or cupboard whose contents are forever spilling out and need to be organised (Ehlers and Clark 2000). In a well-organised wardrobe, everything will be stored neatly, and you will know where to find something when you want to wear it. It might be colour-coordinated or sorted into trousers, shirts, skirts, etc. You can wear an item, wash it, iron or fold it, pop it back where it belongs, and simply close the wardrobe door to get on with your day. Memories of everyday occurrences work in a comparable way in that each memory is stored alongside other similar memories. We can straightforwardly recall an event by bringing the memory to our mind. When we don't need it anymore we can put the memory neatly and simply back in its cupboard, close the door, and get on with our life.

Traumatic memories are very different. They're much more painful and difficult to deal with, so we might try to just shove them back in the drawer or cupboard rather than think them through and come to some resolution. It's as if someone has thrown a bulky duvet at you, which is covered in thorns, and then they expect you to put it effortlessly away in the wardrobe. You could try to squeeze it in, in but handling it would hurt. You would struggle to put it away anyway, because there isn't enough space, and the wardrobe door probably wouldn't close properly. If you tried to leave it there, half in and half out, to focus on doing something else, before you knew it the duvet would probably have fallen out, scattering thorns onto your bedroom floor. Traumatic memories do the same – you're trying to get on with your day or trying not to think about them but they fall into your mind with their prickly thorns, uninvited.

> I worked with an older adolescent who was brave enough to tell me about intrusive thoughts and images of past abuse that had been a feature of their life for as long as they could remember. They described this as 'popping' – an image would pop into their mind when they were least expecting it...at college, when they were trying to fall asleep, when they were travelling on the bus. They had no control over when this might happen. They often couldn't make sense of the images. They thought there was something 'wrong' with them because they didn't know anyone else who was experiencing something like this. They also described how incapacitating it could be because the experience often left them feeling 'frozen'.

The chocolate factory

Another analogy is to think about the creation of a bar of chocolate – all the individual ingredients are combined in the chocolate factory, and then the bar is wrapped in packaging that has all the ingredients listed on the side. This means that Wispa bars won't get muddled up with Twix bars or Yorkie bars, which is very important! Compare this to how our mind organises sensory input connected with an experience – what we could see, hear, smell, taste and touch at the time of an event. This information is processed and bundled up into memories that are wrapped up in the words of a story. The wrappers stop the component parts from spilling out unexpectedly. We understand the content of each memory from the words on the *outside*.

But some events are so awful and terrifying that the mind struggles to translate the information into memories. This means that the sensory information remains unprocessed, often then coming into our awareness when it's uninvited, perhaps at school, at bedtime, or even when trying to have fun with friends. Every time this happens it can be painful to think about, and so it remains unprocessed with a life of its own. Similar issues can arise in a chocolate factory if a machine malfunctions and the ingredients aren't mixed properly. Someone might re-start the machine, but if the mixture is too lumpy, it'll probably break again. They will need to call an engineer to come and fix it, or those lumps will need to be made smaller, before the machinery can start to work again.

This is just like the mind. Sometimes children are better able to process the difficult memories if someone is helping them. Sometimes it's about waiting for the right time. Sometimes they need to be supported to take the memory piece by piece to develop a story – this is how you wrap the memory in words, so it will stop having a life of its own (adapted from Richards and Lovell 1999).

> Another adolescent explored the idea of files being organised on the hard drive of their computer; no one had organised them into folders, and some were corrupted and repeatedly caused the system to crash. They realised they needed to deal with the corrupted files first to create more storage and allow the computer to run more efficiently.

HOW TO DECIDE WHAT TO SHARE

In my view, if you are working with a child who is old enough and cognitively able to participate in life story work, it is never sufficient to write a life story book and hand it over to the child to make sense of themselves. Work through the history *with* the child, preferably with their parent or carer alongside: 'Explaining to children is not enough – they deserve a collaboratively developed account that gives them a record of these events' (Devlin 2012). The rationale for this (as explored in Chapter 4) is that children can only approach these difficult memories when they feel safe: 'The presence of the parent or carer enables the child to feel that they and their past are accepted, and they are not "bad" or unlovable because of the things that have happened to them' (Burnell and Vaughan 2008, p.229).

Children *always* have a right to understand why they are not living with their birth parents together with why and how big decisions about their lives and families were made, whatever the circumstances. It is important that we ensure that wherever possible we do not lose any part of the child's own story, and that they can take it with them, wherever they go. They know it already, remember – it is stored in their brains and bodies. By putting words onto these experiences, we are confirming the child's intrinsic data. By withholding those words or information that would help a child make sense of how they experience the world, we risk increasing their confusion and sense of shame. They may conclude that their story is too awful to bear or to share. They will potentially miss opportunities to safely review events in their lives, come to some understanding and then update their view of themselves and the world: 'I know the who. But when, where and why is harder to tell. I have lived with my lack of an early narrative, found strength in it, trusting my instincts. It has fashioned who and how I am. But it is not enough now. And I'm not sure I understand why' (Jenkins 2017, p.135).

If you are anxious about this phase of the work, that's understandable, but please make sure you prepare thoroughly, get advice from colleagues and your supervisor, and speak to the child's parents or carers about what they think before getting started. Never make unilateral decisions about what to share and how to share it. The day I feel blasé about talking about highly traumatic and distressing information with children should be the day I stop. It is such a responsibility and a privilege to be supporting children in this way. It is right we take time to ensure that we share information sensitively by being truthful and yet compassionate.

If children later discover that information has been withheld without good reason, or there has been a degree of dishonesty in the sharing of information, this can have a catastrophic impact on trust. Any other information that has been shared with the child, no matter how accurate, could then be brought into question. At times you will need to negotiate this with parents or carers who may feel certain information should be withheld or vice versa. You will need to be able to justify your decision making, either to share or not to share. This always needs to be in the child's best interests and not because the grown-ups are unable to face the truth or find the right words.

Children and young people often have an ability to deal with the facts of their lives that adults underestimate, and having unclear, only partial or even inaccurate information can be a frightening and confusing experience for them, often worse than the truth. What they don't know they often make up. Hold in your minds that even where children were very young when they experienced trauma, or when older children tell you they remember nothing, they have lived through it once and so, as a rule, should be able to bear knowing it on a conscious level. Talking about what this means for them, about thoughts and feelings associated with these events, can be a vital part of processing and integrating these experiences. Not knowing can be an invisible load that the child is carrying, and opportunities to share it are created within a sensitive piece of life story work.

> I worked with a care-experienced young adult who had been traumatised as a small child. I could see no evidence of anyone speaking with them about these events throughout childhood. I worried what the impact of this information would be given their incredibly stable context. However, their initial response to hearing the information was not what I anticipated. Primarily, there was a sense of relief. After experiencing intrusive thoughts and images related to the abuse over many years (and never speaking of them), they were relieved to know weren't 'going mad'. They were having a 'normal' response to an abnormal set of terrifying circumstances they'd experienced as a young child.

BASIC PRINCIPLES OF INFORMATION SHARING

1. Take age and developmental stage into account

Think of information sharing as being like peeling off the layers of an onion. It is always easier to peel additional layers away than to try to stick them back on again. Children do not need to hear or know every detail all at once. You wouldn't give a 1000-piece jigsaw to a four-year-old any more than you would give a simple 10-piece jigsaw to a to a typically developing 16-year-old. Sharing information in smaller, digestible chunks means that over time you are constantly building on previous knowledge and understanding at the child's pace, but you also provide enough breaks and pauses for the child to assimilate the information and work out what it means for them.

There should not be any big surprises as the child reaches adolescence or as they mature – you will simply be offering more detail and facilitating a deeper understanding of their story. This work should be ongoing throughout the lifespan, not a one-off event. At the time of your work, they might not be ready or able to integrate this new information or knowledge. They may choose not to hear more, even if their parent or carer or the system thinks they should.

A child in foster care had some explicit memories that we thought about together, and we shared information about some implicit memories. However, they then started to not be waiting when we arrived at school to meet for the session. They sometimes decided they'd prefer to continue doing whatever they had been doing in class. They began to withdraw at home. We talked about this together and decided to take a break – it coincided with the build-up to exams, and we weren't sure what was most unsettling.

When we came back together after a couple of months the child was given the option of stopping, even though we hadn't completed the work, or carrying on. They opted to stop. There was another significant piece of information that was highly relevant to the decision for them to come into care that I hadn't shared yet. But they had done enough for now. When I wrote up the story, I explained how there was more to share when they were ready. I wrote a letter to the child, given to the foster carer for safe keeping, which explained this missing piece of the puzzle.

2. Ditch the jargon and acronyms

'Because the language of the social care world is so deeply entrenched, we don't think about the true meaning or impact of the words we use, or question why we continue to use them' (Shannon 2019). However, a life story book filled with acronyms is the antithesis of a child-centred approach; it is as if we are speaking another language. Children should not need a social work degree to understand the words used to describe them or their experiences. If there is any doubt about whether the child will understand what you are saying, think again and find an alternative. For example, rather than writing about an *ICPC* (initial child protection conference), you could describe 'a big meeting where everyone came together to think about how to keep you safe'. Rather than saying a child was in a *parent–child placement*, could you talk about 'living with a foster carer who is there to help parents with their babies'? Aren't *siblings* simply 'brothers and sisters', and *peers* just 'friends'? You might find it useful to look at the dictionary of terms developed by representatives from Children in Care Councils and groups across the country (TACT 2019).[1]

1 See also bettercarenetwork.org

Adoption language can be particularly tricky. Avoid words like 'chosen' and 'special' because they can be loaded with meaning. Similarly, the phrase 'Your birth mum loved you so much she wanted you to have a better life' is difficult for a child to understand. Instead, use language like, 'Adoption was a decision the adults made.' Emphasise that the child had nothing to do with the decision and, more importantly, they did nothing to create the situation. Be clear about what got in the way of their needs being met within the birth family (adapted from Johnson 2019).

3. Be prepared

Many professionals, parents and carers worry that one question will lead to another, and they may then feel ill equipped to provide the answers that children need. It is important to know that you don't have to have all the answers or understand everything that has happened yourself, but you must be well prepared. Practice what you want to say beforehand. Test the words out on a colleague or in supervision. Agree how you are going to frame events with the child's parent or carer. Then, when a child asks a direct or clarifying question, please don't try to change the subject. It is important to give the child a clear message that it is okay to talk about any part of their story, and that you will try and answer their questions as honestly as you can. If you close a conversation down, the child may never feel confident in your capacity to respond in the future.

> Working with an adopted child and their adoptive parents, we were talking about the reasons they were never able to live with their birth parents, going straight from the hospital to foster care from birth.
>
> We were talking about drug use and what it can mean for parenting capacity. The child then asked if their birth mother was using drugs during pregnancy. We hadn't planned for that question. But nor did it feel appropriate to close the question down. A quick non-verbal consultation with the child's parents gave agreement to go ahead and answer, meaning we were able to follow this child's lead, even though it led to great anger and disappointment being expressed. These were valid feelings. We were able to show the child we could contain them. The child understood that asking questions is okay. The adoptive parents would survive talking about birth parents and be available for co-regulation and validation of the child's feelings.

There may be times when you do not know the answer to a question or where, in the moment, you are not sure how to respond, and the same might be true for parents and carers. I find the use of a simple *question box* essential in these cases. This is usually just an empty shoe box that we decorate. Children can be encouraged to draw or write their question and pop it into the box. The question is thereby validated and remembered. Tell the child that it is a great question, and that you will do your best to find out the answer and help them understand things better. At home, a carer or parent can suggest the question is added to the box and then it can be thought about together at the next session when you are together again. By the end of a good piece of life story work, the child should be able to answer any question they popped into the box independently and if not, they should know the lengths you have gone to in a bid to find out missing information.

4. Pace the process

This is complex work, potentially of great depth, depending on the child. It cannot be rushed or completed within a very tight time limit simply to suit the needs of an organisation. It is impossible to say how many sessions or how much time it will take, although I am aware of others who do offer session-by-session guides to life story work (Shotton 2020), or who set out a prescribed number of sessions (Rose 2012, 2017). Progress and pace will depend on many elements, including the child's age and developmental stage, factors that may affect their processing speed, the capacity of the child to engage in focused work, the period of time you're covering, what the child knows already, how they respond to new information, and whether further disclosures emerge during the process: 'Providing information should be an ongoing process that unfolds over time, one that is geared toward their children's readiness – cognitively and emotionally – to assimilate what they are learning and to make appropriate use of it' (Brodzinsky 2011, p.204). The child needs to feel they have some control over the process, and that the memories and feelings can be contained.

> On trauma-focused cognitive behavioural therapy (CBT) training several years ago, the facilitator shared a story that has stuck with me about a 14-year-old child who was exploring some incredibly traumatic events in therapy. The child filled a waste bin with scrunched-up paper

> until it was overflowing. This represented all the awful things that had happened to them. They described how it felt walking to school when these memories fell out of the bin into their eyes. When they slept the memories fell into their dreams. Their experience of therapy was being able to take a piece of paper out of the bin, un-scrunch it, and then read it with the therapist. Then the piece of paper could be folded neatly and put in the bottom of the bin, where it was safely contained. The memories no longer fell out of the top any more, and the young person was therefore left with more capacity to think about other things.

5. Choose your approach carefully

Life story work will look different for different children, and so it should. It is often useful to use non-verbal techniques like art and play to support processing and understanding. Art-making is a form of non-verbal communication. For children who, for whatever reason, are unable to articulate their thoughts, feelings or experiences verbally, it is an alternative way of conveying or sharing what cannot be spoken about. For those who have experienced abuse, or who may have been silenced by the perpetrator, it can be a way of 'telling' more safely. As a sensory approach, it also allows individuals to experience themselves and communicate on multiple levels: visual, tactile and kinaesthetic.

With a tangible product like an image or 3D model, children can not only be *heard* but also *seen*. Certain sensory aspects of art-making also help with regulation, calming both the mind and the body, which is crucial, for maintaining traumatised individuals within the 'window of tolerance' during sessions (adapted from Wrench 2018, p.48). If a child or young person is still feeling overwhelmed by their trauma, or is very young, also consider techniques that involve metaphor or a one step removed or 'arm's length' approach. This could be the use of therapeutic stories, miniatures, sand tray play or puppetry.

6. Forget the idea that there is one story or one truth

In a blog post, educational psychologist Emma Birch (2023) discusses the idea that professionals love a single, clear narrative, especially when working with complexity: 'As humans, we seek the safety of a clear and certain narrative. As Psychologists, we need to hold these narratives lightly and retain our curiosity and reflectiveness about our own biases and preferred stories.' It is normal for us to seek *the truth*, but we must hold in our minds that children's stories will hold multiple truths and perspectives, and our job is to present them, not to judge or filter them. When dealing with contradictory information you should always include all perspectives, highlighting which the child believes to be true, and creating space for some curious thinking. Remember that younger children will still be egocentric in their thinking and might struggle to integrate different perspectives or more complex, ambiguous information until they reach eight or nine years old.

> I worked with a child of six who had been injured as a toddler in the care of their parents. They gave several different explanations of how the injury was caused at the hospital and to the social worker. The medic who looked at the X-ray of the child was of the belief that the injury was non-accidental. The child was convinced that their parents loved them and would never hurt them deliberately. The judge made a finding of fact that one or both parents was responsible. This is what I wrote in their story, even though I knew at this age they would hold fast to their own version of events. They would not, however, be six forever.

When you are sharing information from your research with the child, they will also hopefully have information to add or revisions to make. This is how you co-construct a story and it becomes a more collaborative process. They may sometimes say things that you definitively know not to be true or that may veer into greyer areas, but this doesn't matter. If they are the child's memories of the time, it is important they are recorded as such. You simply need to state different perspectives on the story.

EXPLAINING THE 'WHY'

Answers that gloss over the challenges that lead to a child coming into care rarely satisfy their curiosity, but sometimes practitioners do sanitise stories or worry about saying negative things about birth families that might cause distress. However, in many cases

> we can differentiate between birth parents' intent and desire, and their actions. It is probably safe to assume that virtually all birth parents

> wanted the best for their children, and if they could have, to have been good parents to them. Nevertheless, intent and desire are not always translated into loving and competent behavior. (Brodzinsky 2011, p.206)

Nicholls (2005) talks about five primary reasons why children do not always receive the care they need, and sometimes therefore cannot live safely within their birth family. It can be helpful to explore with children whether they think any of these explanations fits with their family's experience. They can choose more than one. In generalising in this way, you also support children to know they are not alone in their experience:

1. Parents might have big problems of their own that make it tricky to care for themselves and others, and especially to do all the jobs parents need to do to help their children grow to be happy, healthy and safe. (Experiencing domestic abuse, addiction and mental health fit this category.)
2. Parents might not have been shown how to care for children – perhaps they didn't have good care when they were little, so they're not sure what they need to do or how to parent their children safely. (Parents with their own childhood trauma or care experience, or who might parent without adequate support or guidance.)
3. They may be too unwell to be a parent or to care for other people. (Chronic physical health conditions, terminal illness or disability without adequate support *or* addiction/mental ill health.)
4. They might not be able to learn how to be a safe parent or care for other people. This might be because they have a learning disability, head injury or some other reason why they can't remember to do all the things a parent needs to do every day. Alternatively, they might be capable of learning, but they find it hard to let people help or teach them a different way.
5. They might have been shown the wrong way to be a parent or to care for other people. It might be hard to accept they should do things differently for their child. Maybe they were hit by their parents when they were growing up and don't see a problem with it if they feel it did them no harm (adapted from Nicholls 2005, p.156).

In this chapter and the next, I am simply offering some starting points for thinking about and explaining difficult things to children and young people. Remember to adapt and personalise your explanation for every child. When you begin to explain or explore the reasons why children can't be cared for safely by their parents, you will need to help them understand why. It is helpful to hold in your mind the work of Brodzinsky and colleagues writing about children's understanding of adoption (1984). They interviewed about 250 adopted children in the USA between the ages of 4 and 13 together with about 180 non-adopted young people, as well as adoptive parents and teachers of adopted children. As a result of this research, they outlined six levels of understanding of adoption, and in a much later paper (2011) Brodzinsky provided a developmental framework for helping us to understand the way children comprehend adoption. I think we can also draw some parallels for children in care.

Pre-school years

At this stage, perceptions develop before an understanding of complex concepts like adoption, which means children can recognise and classify simple differences like gender, age and ethnicity, and different personal qualities. The notion of being adopted is another difference: 'For the most part, they learn the language of adoption; in other words, they learn to talk about being adopted, without really understanding what that means' (Brodzinsky 2011, p.200). If very young children become aware that their adoptive parents are uncomfortable or cautious in discussing adoption, or if they are exposed to views about adoption that lack positivity, there is a risk that on one level they will perceive that there is something inherently bad about being adopted and therefore about themselves. Therefore, it is critical that parents create 'a family atmosphere that makes it comfortable for children to ask relevant questions about their backgrounds and current family status' (Brodzinsky 2011, p.200).

Middle childhood (4–13 years)

Between the ages of four and six, it's not possible for children to distinguish between adoption and birth. It is common to imagine that all children are born to one set of parents and then move to live with different parents. Even when adopters are giving clear explanations about the child having a birth family before adoption, the child is likely to be able to repeat the story, without really understanding it or connecting with what this means for them. They may, however, ask lots of spontaneous questions about how babies are made, pregnancy and birth.

By six to eight years old, the differentiation between adoption and birth becomes clearer. Children can assimilate basic and sometimes bleak justifications for why they couldn't live safely within their birth family. They are likely to have a firm belief in the permanence of the new adoptive parent–child relationship, based on the developing trust in their adoptive parents, but the way in which information is shared about their birth family and the process of adoption is key.

As a child truly begins to understand the difference between adoption and birth around the age of eight to ten, they might also begin to doubt the stability and permanence of their relationship with their adopters. It is common to see the emergence of anxieties in the child that they might be abandoned or 'given back', especially if there is any disruption or unsettled times in the adoptive family. They may believe their birth family is able to come and reclaim them. Because the child is capable of more complex thinking, they may wonder what life would be like if they did return to their birth parents. If their birth mum has stopped using heroin, could she care for them now, safely? If their adoptive parent becomes unwell, will they have to leave?

Children are beginning to reflect on their own feelings and the feelings of others, so might begin to imagine how their birth parents felt when they were adopted. They sometimes like to envision what life would have been like if they had never been removed or if they hadn't been 'stolen'. Some magical thinking can emerge about how life could have been. Some adoptees will grieve for all they have been separated from – birth parents and siblings – even where they acknowledge their care wasn't good enough or might have been abusive. They need permission to mourn those important losses, even though this can lead to distressed behaviour and feelings that can be hard to manage. This is even more likely if they subsequently avoid any discussion of adoption, or alternatively become preoccupied and furious about their own adoption.

By the age of 10–13, children can comprehend the legal basis for adoption as well as the importance of the relationship with their adopters. They can cognitively separate out and understand the differences between unsafe parenting that resulted in removal from their birth family and the experiences of being parented they have now. They begin to fathom the concepts of safeguarding and parents meeting basic care and emotional needs. As their sense of permanence becomes more secure, this allows them to explore some of the more complex or traumatic details of their own story. This is a common time for children to access life story work as a result:

> As children develop a more realistic understanding of adoption, they naturally begin to examine what it means to them, as well as to others. Psychologists and other professionals need to emphasize the normality of children's curiosity about their origins, and their emotional reactions in response to better understanding their families, as well as help adoptive parents validate and support their children's efforts to find connections with and more knowledge about their pasts. (Brodzinsky 2011, p.202)

Adolescence

As children enter adolescence, their 'capacity for understanding the meaning and implications of adoption deepens' (Brodzinsky 2011, p.202). Their ability to understand other people's thoughts and feelings also matures during adolescence, which allows them to become more curious and empathic in relation to their birth parents' lives and decisions. Like all adolescents, adolescent adoptees are trying to work out their place in the world, and to define themselves and their identity. This is, of course, a much more complex undertaking if you are connected to two families: 'In their search for self, adoptees must find ways of integrating aspects of both families into their emerging identities' (Brodzinsky 2011, p.202).

In relation to life story work, Brodzinsky found that

> parents who are more open, supportive, and empathic in their communication about adoption are more likely to have children who are able to integrate this aspect of their lives into a positive sense of self. Access to information about one's birth family and the circumstances surrounding the adoption, as well as contact with birth family, generally facilitates positive adoptive identity development. (Brodzinsky 2011, p.202)

DIRECT WORK TOOLS

BUILDING STRONG WALLS

When explaining why children can't live safely with their birth parents, it is important to comprehensively break down what parenting is and should be, to establish what 'good enough' care looks like. I like to do an activity called Building Strong Walls – you just need paper and pens, or building blocks if you have them. Avoid DUPLO® or LEGO® bricks that stick together – wooden blocks are best for this activity. This is an exercise adapted from Rees (2009) that we also describe in our first book (Wrench and Naylor 2013, pp.89–92). I do this exercise with most children of all ages, so it's worth repeating here.

Explain that bringing up children is a bit like building a wall, and to build a strong wall, all the bricks must be in just the right place. Describe the foundations and the cement as being the love that the parent or carer has for the child, but also explore what else children need from their parents or carers. Ask the child to think about all the different things that parents or carers need to do to look after their children and keep them safe. If you are using paper, post-it notes can be useful to write a child's needs on, and they have the advantage of looking like little bricks. Then stick them together to form a wall, with the foundations (the parent or carer's love for their child) at the bottom. If you are using building blocks, you can represent each 'need' with a brick and build a wall together. Again, if you have mini post-its, you can write the need on the note and pop it on the brick. Otherwise, I tend to draw out the wall alongside the one made of bricks to help me remember which brick represents which need. You can then photograph the finished walls to eventually add to the life story book.

The idea is to explore what *all children* need – broadening out the idea of care needs being unique to this child, unless they have needs specific to health for example, beyond what most children might need. The wall should include functional and non-functional care – providing nurture and physical affection, meeting the child's health and physical needs, providing rules, supervision and boundaries and a safe environment – together with the need for fun, play and laughter.

It can be helpful first to sometimes ground the child in the here and now if they are receiving good enough care – so encourage them first to think about all the things their parent or carer does for them now, every day. Sometimes this is where you need to stay focused for some time, and the exercise of reinforcing that the child now has safe care needs to be repeated. You may need to provide prompts if they find it hard to produce ideas themselves. Dr Karen Treisman has developed a versatile deck of cards, *The Parenting Patchwork Treasure Deck* (2020), which comes with a detailed manual to help you have these conversations and explore child–parent or carer relationships, parenting experiences and capacity and child development. Even if the child is resistant to thinking about their birth family in relation to this exercise, you are nonetheless giving them important messages about being worthy of loving care.

> This exercise became a ritual for a seven-year-old child living in kinship care for weeks throughout the life story work. At the beginning of the session, they would build the wall with their relative. We would then ask 'Does X just do this for you on a Monday?' And the child would reply, 'NO! On a Monday, Tuesday, Wednesday, Thursday, Friday, Saturday AND Sunday.' The repetition provided a sense of safety in the work as they knew what we would start with each week. But the repetition was also important in reinforcing the idea that this child's needs can now be met consistently and unconditionally by their current carer.

Sometimes when you have finished constructing the wall, be curious about what might happen if some bricks were missing from it. If you have used actual bricks, encourage the child to push a brick or two out to see what happens, for example if there is not always food, boundaries or safety. The important message here is that parents or carers consistently need to do all these things for the child, or the wall becomes too wobbly and can fall. If the parent or carer cannot build a strong enough wall, then no child can grow up to be safe, healthy and happy.

If you think the child can manage such a direct discussion, extend the exercise by making links with their own situation and the reasons they are not able to live with their birth parents. Reflect that even with strong foundations of love, parents or carers sometimes struggle to do all the things children need. Using the analogy of having a wobbly wall can build safety into the discussions you may have with children when caregiving was not good enough to meet a child's needs. If their wall is built on poor foundations, even if they subsequently have good enough care and their needs are consistently being met, those earlier developmental gaps will not easily be filled. If nothing changes, as the child grows, the wall will become more unstable because its foundation was too weak. In most instances, this does not mean the child's birth parents did not love them, and it is imperative, where we can, that we acknowledge the times when parents have loved and cared for their children as best they could under the circumstances.

By using a creative method that begins in a more general way to discuss all children's needs, over time it can become as specific as you feel is appropriate for the child you are supporting. This can help them understand and integrate the reasons why they were unable to remain with birth parents, or begin conversations about why the child was removed from their birth family. This can be a powerful exercise, whether you make direct links with the child's own experience or not. Many children will make their own links with the past irrespective of what you do and say, so be prepared for this. It is important to emphasise that *all* children need the right sort of care from parents, and it is the parent's job to provide it. There was nothing the child could have done to change things or enable their parents to be better able to care for them.

An alternative to this activity is to bring a baby doll or soft toy and have a conversation with the child about what this baby doll needs. Ask the child to imagine what they might need to do if the baby was crying, and role-play meeting their needs together. Consider the baby's changing needs as they get older and start to crawl and walk. Children's needs inevitably change over time: 'They will always need food, safety and nurturing, yet each will be fulfilled differently depending on the age of the child' (Oakwater 2012, p.25). This is an opportunity to talk about what a parent's job is, in whatever detail is appropriate. For the child who carries a sense of blame that they were responsible for not being cared for, this activity can help to reinforce the universal needs of small children. As Herman writes:

> Self-blame is congruent with the normal forms of thought of early childhood, in which the self is taken as the reference point for all events. It is congruent with the thought processes of traumatized people of all ages, who search for faults in their own behaviour to make sense out of what has happened to them. (1997, p.103)

If I have done this exercise with a child during life story work, I will write about it in their life story book. This is an effective way of reinforcing the fact that the child was loved by their birth parents, but that love in itself was not enough. The idea that love is a mixture of what is said and what is done by the parent is important. It is critical to be honest in your explanations of what went wrong in the child's parenting without using too many euphemisms or oversimplifications that can leave the child confused: 'Your mummy wasn't very well' when she was addicted to heroin, for example or 'Your daddy was working away for a while' when he was in prison. I have seen and heard both these examples, many times – one parent was 'indefinitely staying in a holiday cottage' when they were, in fact, detained in a secure hospital after committing a serious offence. Sanitising a child's story in this way will not be helpful to them in understanding their experiences.

You can use this analogy of a wall to think with children about having a 'wobbly wall'. So if the wall is built on poor foundations, even if they subsequently have good enough care, and their needs are met consistently, those earlier developmental gaps will not easily be filled. If nothing changes, as the child grows, the wall will become more unstable because its foundation was weak. In most instances, this does not mean the child's birth parents did not love them, and it is imperative, where you can, to acknowledge where parents have loved and cared for their children as best they could when you consider the circumstances they were in.

LOVING HEARTS

This a lovely activity to highlight to children the practical things that parents or carers do to demonstrate love and care (adapted from Tait and Wosu 2015, pp.129–133). You'll need some heart shapes cut out of cardboard, glue and craft materials to decorate the hearts. Then think together with the child about all the ways people show that they love each other – you might want to begin with thinking about the care they receive from their parent or carer now, as a starting point, or give some examples yourself:

> 'I care for my dog by stroking him, taking him for exciting walks in the woods and giving him treats when we get home.'
>
> 'I show my friends I love them by being there to support them when they have things to celebrate but also when life is tough.'

You can also share what you've noticed happening in the sessions:

> 'I see mummy's love for you when she gives you a hug if things feel tricky and always remembers to bring your favourite drink and snack.'
>
> 'I notice how Nanna always holds your hand when you come through the car park to meet me – she is making sure you are safe and showing you how much she loves and cares for you.'

Then encourage the child and their parent or carer to start to write some of what they notice happening in their family on the hearts – use as many as possible, because you really want to emphasise how important each action is – making sure the child has a clean uniform, helping with homework, making a packed lunch, etc. The final step is to put all the hearts in the middle, maybe in a bowl, and mix them up. Invite the child and their parent or carer to pick a heart and either read it or describe the drawing. This should be accompanied by extravagant whoops, high fives and applause, where appropriate, topped off with a family hug.

THE PARENTING GAME

Another activity that can be helpful in thinking about parenting needs is the Parenting Game. Fahlberg (1994) was the first to write about the three-part parenting model, and others, like Ryan and Walker (2016) and Nicholls (2005), have followed. Nicholls has developed a game that can help children understand the complexities of parenting. It can be adapted (by you) for all ages, but will need a little more planning and preparation than most activities I suggest.

You will need four boxes, making sure one of them is big enough to fit the other three inside, with a letterbox opening in each one. Label the largest box 'The Parent Thing' and the remaining boxes 'Born to Part', 'Parenting Part' and 'Legal Part'. It is fine to adapt these names if you think of something more suitable for the child you are working with. Then write out different tasks for the different jobs on cards, or use the cards from Treisman's *Parenting Patchwork Treasure Deck* (2020) and pop them into the relevant box.

BORN TO PART

- The colour of your eyes, hair, skin.
- The way you look – the shape of your face, mouth and nose.
- Your build, shape and height.
- How clever you are.
- The size of your feet, hands and ears.
- The sort of person you are – shy, loud, chatty.
- Your talents – art, music, sport.
- Hereditary illnesses that might affect you in life.

PARENTING PART

- keeps you safe from harm
- makes you feel good about yourself
- helps with homework and supports your education
- takes you out to different places
- makes sure you have age-appropriate clothes, toys and books
- provides a safe, clean, warm home to live in
- loves you no matter what
- takes you to school or nursery when you are old enough
- takes you to the doctor or dentist when needed
- gives you nutritious food to help you grow
- teaches you what is wrong and right
- gives you hugs or cuddles
- helps you learn new things.

LEGAL PART

- decides on your name and registers your birth
- decides what immunisations you should have
- gives permission for medical treatment
- chooses what religion or cultural practices you follow
- chooses your school and makes sure you go regularly
- gives permission for you to go on school trips
- gives permission for you to stay overnight or go on holiday with family or friends.

Explain to the child that being a parent is a complicated job because there are so many things to remember to do to make sure any child is safe, happy and healthy. Parents cannot just do these things for some of the time; they must do them until the child is grown up and able to take care of themself. Then describe how there are three interconnected parts to being a parent: the *born to* part that makes us what we are; the *parenting* part that looks after us and makes sure we are safe and well; and the *legal* part that makes big decisions for us now and in the future. All these things make up being a parent, and parents must do them all at once and all the time (Nicholls 2005, p.146). Think together about how hard it would be to juggle all these jobs if you also had troubles of your own as a parent.

Encourage the child to take each of the cards out of the smaller boxes, look at them and think about them together, one at a time. As each card is considered, ask the child to post it back into the large box. When all the cards have been posted, give the box a good shake and make the connection with how parents must juggle all these tasks at once. Then, if appropriate, open the large box back up to review all the things a parent must remember to do. This is another way of supporting a child to understand the complexities of parenting, laying the foundations for a fuller explanation of the reasons why a child may be separated from their birth family.

You can reverse this game to ascertain whether the child has understood the concepts and to reinforce initial understanding. Do this by jumbling up the cards and spreading them out face up. Ask the child to read the individual cards and post them into the appropriate box. As with Building Strong Walls, this can be repeated multiple times to assist the process of understanding and integration.

LIFE GRAPH OR LIFE MAP

Once you have established an understanding of what 'good enough' parenting looks like, it is time to begin to pull the narrative together with the child. I find an effective way to do this is to create a simple timeline. This is sometimes known as a Life Graph or Life Map, but ultimately is a helpful way of mapping a child's journey over time, which is a common tool in contemporary life story work practice (Wrench and Naylor 2013, pp.64–65). The purpose of the timeline is not simply to share facts; it is a tool to develop both sequential event coherence *and* emotional and psychological coherence. To achieve this, it must be an interactive process. The child should be supported to express their feelings, no matter what they might be, and preferably to also be comforted and contained in the moment by their parents or carers. It is unlikely they would have had this opportunity at the time of the events when they would have needed a safe, calm-brained grown-up to soothe them. Indeed, the source of potential comfort was likely to have also been the source of or connected to their fear.

I tend to use a roll of good quality lining paper for this activity, so we don't feel constrained by the amount of space there is to write or draw.

Some children prefer to begin in the present and then work gradually back towards their birth family experiences. However, life rarely follows a linear process, and if you begin with the child's memories and narrative, you might find yourselves flitting around much more, which is also fine. You can then carefully expand on this as and when the child is ready and able to do so, or add in new information from the chronology or the trauma-nurture timeline (see p.57), gently and slowly dripping this in at a pace the child can tolerate. It is so important that this is not rushed. Remember that it is not just about sharing or recording information; just as critical is creating space for the child to process their feelings about this new information – this is where having a parent or carer present for co-regulation is vital. You should be tracking the child's regulatory state – are they in their 'window of tolerance'? If not, how can we help them make a U-turn, back into the calm? Notice whether the child is still connected to the material and processing it, or has been pushed beyond their window.

It is also important to record any positive memories the child has or that you have noted in the chronology. They may have been times of relative stability or signs of progress in a birth family. There may have been other protective factors or people in the child's life or times when things were going well. Gilligan discusses the important, protective role of non-parental adults 'with a strong and ideally partisan commitment to the child' such as extended family, a friend's parents, teachers or sports coaches and community leaders (2010, pp.178–179). This gains more significance when relationships with primary caregivers are compromised; children have more need of other compensatory relationships.

Some children find a big piece of paper or roll of lining paper too overwhelming, so consider other options. You could try making a *washing line or bunting*. Still start with the safest information that the child can manage or remember, which probably means starting in the here and now, and write or draw each event on a separate smaller piece of paper, which can then be hung on a washing line with pegs. If you make triangular shapes from card, the memories could be stapled onto a ribbon instead, to make bunting. As further information is added, the narrative slowly grows, but it will not be linear. You will achieve coherence when all the pieces are in place.

Younger children might prefer an activity that is more tangible – so you could use a train track or car mat to represent their journey and play their story out. You can also draw a road map – this way you can show 'bumps in the road', a hill to climb, a fork in the road or deep, dark tunnels to navigate your way through.

You can also step out of working on the timeline if need be. You will need to be monitoring whether the child seems able to process information at an age-appropriate level and respond in a reciprocal way. Are their responses focused and topic-related, or are they going off on tangents? It is common for children to dip in and out of this activity – if you use a roll of lining paper, it is easy to roll it back up and do something else when they have done enough – that might be 5 minutes or 50 minutes, and both are perfectly acceptable.

> I worked with a 15-year-old in residential care who dipped in and out of their 'road map' over about eight weeks. They slowly added the more traumatic events in their life, but understandably didn't necessarily want to be reminded of these things every time we rolled out the map. They came up with a genius idea (I thought) to cover the difficult parts of the story with post-it notes on which we drew 'no entry' signs. That way, each time we met we could peek underneath to decide if that was something they wanted to come back to think about that day or not. For a young person who had felt so powerless during their abuse, it felt incredibly powerful when they were supported to take back some control.

POTENTIAL BLOCKS WHEN INFORMATION SHARING

1. Overwhelm

The child may become overwhelmed and pushed too far outside of their window of tolerance, in which case slow the pace and use the tools you thought about in the earlier stages of the work for co-regulation. Take breaks where necessary, and allow the focus of the work to be elsewhere for a time, to stay at the child's pace of processing.

Similarly, the practitioner might become overwhelmed. If you are inexperienced in this work, make sure you adequately prepare and have a supervisor who can support you through the process. You might feel anxious if the child is saying the work is boring or if they refuse to do an activity you have prepared, and this can lead quickly to feelings of incompetence or inadequacy. At these times, the pressure can be high to give up and to think it is not the right time for the child, or you are not the right person. Always try to troubleshoot collaboratively. I often say things like, 'I feel like I'm not quite getting it right for you – can you help me with that?' Or have a review with the parent or carer to ask for their perspective.

2. The child struggles to hear any negative stories about their birth family

Respect the child's loyalties: they might find it unbearable to think about their birth mother with their adoptive mother in the room, for example. They may struggle to hear examples of when a birth parent was not able to meet their needs or caused them harm. I have supported many children who have been adamant that an injury deemed to be non-accidental must have been an accident because the idea that their birth parent might deliberately harm them is so unbearable. Similarly, you will hear fantasies about how wonderful life might have been had they been able to remain with their birth parents.

Children may need to revisit this work repeatedly to internalise the narrative or to process feelings further. They may need to revisit a particular theme multiple times or return to look at different aspects of their journey at different ages and stages. Healing occurs with the repetition of a story, especially for children, because repetition allows the experience to become integrated into their system as a whole. This is supported when young adoptees and children in care have adoptive parents or carers who are comfortable with their story and repeat it to them so they can know it and tell it with ease. However, sometimes children may need more specialist trauma-focused therapy to achieve this, and it is important only to work within the boundaries of your skill and experience. If you feel a child may need more, and you are not qualified to deliver, it is important to have this discussion with the systemic network. If you do have the training to integrate trauma processing into the life story work, I have always found this an incredibly impactful approach using a combination of creative therapies, emotional freedom technique (EFT) and eye movement desensitisation and reprocessing (EMDR).

3. Children who do not want to talk

Sometimes this happens when you scrimp on the preparation. If you have not taken the time to get to know the child, and help them to feel more at ease with you and the work you are going to do, you may struggle to encourage them to think and talk with you about more difficult things. Consider whether you have planned activities that are appropriate for the child's age and stage, and whether what you are offering is varied and interesting enough. Perhaps you are not yet pitching it right. Have you encouraged the child's participation enough, or focused too much on the parent or carer? Did you push too far and cover too much material in too short a time?

Sometimes the problem might look like apathy – the child might seem disinterested and not want to focus on their story. A more likely explanation is that the avoidance is a protective mechanism because you are asking them to talk about painful and personal things. When children have been masking their pain for a long time, the idea of talking about it can make them feel like they will lose control. Other children will have been silenced in their abuse and are therefore terrified about what might happen if they talk. Make sure you offer reassurance that it is normal to be a little apprehensive. Think about how you help the child take some control of the pace, what you discuss, and when. Give them explicit permission to pause, stop or do something different for a little while. Sometimes having more of a gap between sessions can help – moving from weekly to fortnightly, for example. Sometimes children find it easier to engage non-verbally through creative communication – if they cannot or prefer not to speak, I often ask 'Can you show me what that looks like?' You can use art, play, puppets or dramatic techniques to help facilitate the conversation.

4. When things feel 'stuck'

Where there is trauma there can often be 'stuckness', because trauma survivors often find themselves in a 'freeze' state. Carolyn Spring suggests questions that can be used as a prompt in therapy with older young people or as journal prompts to think about in between sessions, to help put words to the feeling of being stuck:[2]

- What would it look like to not be stuck?
- What patterns of 'stuckness' are there, of repeating dynamics in your life?
- What do people who aren't stuck do?

2 www.carolynspring.com/shop/a-stuckness-checklist

- What does the 'stuckness' look and feel like?
- What are the consequences of remaining stuck?

Another activity that I find useful with older adolescents in this situation is What's Your Anchor? This is an exploration of what is keeping them from moving forwards. What is weighing them down? Explore how long this anchor has been in their life. What does it look like? What is its size, shape and colour? You could encourage the child to show you and draw it. What purpose does it serve? What would life (or life story work) look like if the anchor were raised?

5. Information about the child is lost or missing

Sometimes, no matter how hard you try to find missing information, it remains lost or inaccessible. This can be incredibly frustrating and disappointing for children who yearn so desperately for answers. We all find it hard to deal with losses in our lives, and in life story work we must attend to the gaps in knowledge as much as we attend to the facts. Give space to the gaps or the missing information, and don't avoid them. It may be that the child needs to grieve for what is not known or what has been lost.

You could bring some blank leaves and have the child draw or write their loss on the leaf and then stick them on to a Loss Tree.

Children sometimes talk about there being missing pieces of a puzzle so it can help to use a blank *jigsaw* template to visually represent what is known and what is not (by leaving blank pieces).

Mandalas are also an effective way of bringing feelings about loss and the pain associated with those losses into the open. Looking at the centre of a mandala is like looking into our heart. Mandalas have been used for many years for meditation, prayer and healing and have a circular design with repeating colours, simple shapes and patterns. The child can either create their own mandala or you can print one for them to colour in, like the one below (Jay 2014, pp.44–45).

MANAGING DISCLOSURES

It is possible that children may feel able to share memories of abuse or trauma they have not previously disclosed during life story work. It is important that you are transparent and clear from the outset about the procedure you will follow should this happen. You can discuss this when you talk about confidentiality in your working agreement. When disclosures occur, give the child the message that any information they have shared or any memories that have been triggered will always be taken seriously.

Here are some suggestions that might help both you and the child feel safer in the moment in the light of a disclosure (adapted from Martin 2007, p.28):

- Try your best to stay calm, or at least appear calm.
- As your default position, always believe the child. Children very rarely lie about abuse, and some will have been discouraged from disclosing by being told no one will believe them.
- Do your utmost to reassure the child the abuse was not their fault. You might say things like, 'You are so brave and so right to tell me about this.' 'I'm sorry this happened to you, and it isn't your fault.' 'How clever of you to remember to tell someone you trust.' This is a message that will need repeating multiple times before the child will begin to be able to integrate it, but this is a starting point for removing any sense of blame or shame from the child.

- Do not pressure the child for more details or information – if a police investigation ensues, for example, they will have to re-tell this story. In my experience it is common for children to drip-feed parts of their story – testing out your response before sharing the full story. Can you tolerate it? Do you still like them even though you know this new information about them? Will you believe them?

CONTACT OR FAMILY TIME IN RELATION TO INFORMATION SHARING

Contact in fostering and adoption has always been complex, and the reasons for seeking to reconnect with a birth family encompass grief, loss, a search for identity or curiosity. Interestingly, a study of young people who entered care as infants in Northern Ireland by Fargas-Malet and McSherry (2020) identified that the 'Type of placement, that is, whether the young people had been adopted, lived with kinship foster carers or non-relative foster parents, did not determine their emotional reactions to their birth family' (2020, p.2263).

The process of information sharing and integration can be supported through *facilitated contact or family time*, particularly for children in care. Where face-to-face contact or letterbox exchange is a feature in adoption, this is also a possibility with good planning and preparation. The child, with the support of the adoptive parents or foster carers, should be prepared by reviewing what is known already about their life in the birth family, and preparing a list of any questions that they would like to ask. This is really important in being able to fill in the gaps that are most meaningful to the child rather than the adults making assumptions or a best guess. It is vital that the child feels able to ask whatever they need to in a safe environment. It is important that they feel empowered and supported to say things they would wish to say to their birth parents. This can be done directly, with the facilitator speaking on the child's behalf, or through a letter.

The next step is a meeting coordinated by the facilitator of the life story work or the most suitable adult, with the birth parent or family member to consider the questions, feelings and issues the child has raised in their session. It is important that they, too, have time to prepare in advance and have support to process both how they feel about their child's questions and to generate an appropriate response.

> I worked with a six-year-old and their foster carer who still had family time once every six weeks with a parent. Through a combination of role-play, art-making and talking they were working so hard to understand why they were in care. Unbeknownst to me and the carer, they had also been privately practising questions to ask their parent at the next contact. They then directly asked 'Why didn't you give me any food?' The family time supervisor hadn't been prepared for the direct question, and nor had the parent. The parent answered, 'Because I only had £5.' At six years of age this answer was enough... they accepted there simply hadn't been enough money to provide for the family. However, had they been given this answer at age 11, they might have had a different response and felt £5 was plenty to be buying food for their child.

It may be that there is then a carefully managed meeting between the child and birth relative, which is facilitated within the context of psychological and physiological safety for the child. An alternative is to exchange video messages through an intermediary, or for a social worker or therapist to visit the birth parent to ask the child's questions on their behalf, providing it is assessed as safe to do so. I know, for example, of an adoptive family where the letter exchange coordinator played a helpful role in supporting a birth mother to answer questions from her children and their adoptive mum.

In the ideal scenario, the child's questions are asked and the birth parent is supported with a script to share helpful answers. Ideally the child will hear:

- Their parent is sorry that they could not care for the child safely when they were living at home.
- It was not the child's fault that things went wrong.
- They are still loved.
- They think about their child often, and want them to have the happiness they deserve.

- Where appropriate, that they would love their child to be happy in their new family, and trust their new parents to care for them.

After the meeting, the birth parents and child should have separate debriefing meetings. If the contact is successful, questions are answered and helpful messages are communicated, this may then be a protective factor for the child's psychological life in the future, as well as providing a more positive basis for meaningful interaction between the child and their new parent or carer. In the age of social media, where contacting birth relatives is now relatively straightforward, it is more critical than ever that contact between children and their birth families is managed and mediated proactively. Otherwise it can be physically and psychologically dangerous for some children who proceed to make contact in unsupported, unplanned ways.

There are some brilliant projects around the country that support birth parents who have lost children to adoption or who are living apart from their children, and it is worth considering if any are operating in your area. For example, Threads of Connection[3] is a project that recognises that adoption connects two families indelibly. An exchange of letters between those families, complex as it is, can give children access to information from before and after their adoption. An exchange about small details like milestones, shoe size and whether the child still loves to dance can build bridges between the child's past, present and future. Letters can help nurture the bond between the two families. Both parties can be curious, ask questions and share updates and stories, as in a verbal conversation.

3 https://womencentre.org.uk/threads-of-connection-2

7

TALKING TO CHILDREN ABOUT TRAUMATIC EXPERIENCES

As the question of trying to find the right words to say to a child or to write in a life story book is one of the most common requests in training, I wanted to offer some 'starters' in this book. I'm sure they're not perfect, and they will need to be adapted depending on the child's experiences, developmental age and stage, family's use of language, etc. Do not copy the suggestions verbatim, but they will at least give you some idea of where to start, and for many of us, this is often the hardest part. I have focused on the most common issues facing children in care and adoption, but this isn't a definitive list, of course – that would be a book in itself. Because of the nature of developmental trauma, and the abuse and neglect experienced by children in care and adoptees, it is inevitable that some readers may find the content of this chapter distressing, so please be mindful of this as you begin to read.

It's critical that we don't rely on social work jargon or terminology in our explanations, and that we try to make challenging material accessible for children and young people. Think about how to adapt the detail for much younger pre-school children and for older adolescents. I've pitched the explanations in this chapter for a child of about eight to eleven years old, as that is often the time developmentally when children begin to ask more questions and need to know more about their early lives: 'Middle childhood also is a time when logical thought emerges, leading children to recognize that gaining a new family through adoption also means having been separated from a previous one' (Brodzinsky 2011, p.201).

There is often an overriding instinct to protect children from knowing or hearing things that will hurt them. But generally speaking, children of all ages often know more than adults realise – they might overhear conversations, be told something by others, or intuitively pick up that you are worried about telling them something – and partial or inaccurate information can be more worrying than the truth. What you tell children about their stories will depend on many factors, one of which will be their level of understanding.

We cannot prevent children from feeling sad, angry or distressed, but if we give them information openly and honestly, we can then support them with those feelings. Adult adoptee research supports this principle by highlighting the necessity of more open discussion about birth family links that focuses on 'consistency, reliability and the importance of open discussion within the adopted family on this topic (neutral and supportive with the adoptee's needs in mind)' (Rawcliffe *et al.* 2022, p.5). More direct and transparent discussions about birth family links can then inform future decision making around the reality of making and maintaining contact with birth families.

In supporting thinking about how to talk and write about difficult experiences, I share ideas in italics for how you might talk about each subject with children and young people, as script prompts to be adapted to fit the child's individual experiences and the context.

EMOTIONAL HARM

Emotional harm often, but not always, goes along with other kinds of harm. Here are some of the ways a child or young person might experience emotional harm. You will need to describe only what is relevant and relatable to any individual child:

- Being criticised or told off all the time when you've done nothing wrong.
- Being threatened, shouted at or called mean names.
- Being laughed at to hurt your feelings or to humiliate you.
- Being blamed no matter what goes wrong and when it isn't your fault, or made to feel different to others in the family.

- Not being allowed to be your own unique and special self.
- Being put under too much pressure or expected to have too much responsibility for a child of your age.
- Having to hear or watch very upsetting things, like parents arguing or taking drugs.
- Not being allowed to have friends.
- Being ignored all the time.
- Never hearing anyone say anything kind to you or showing you they're proud of your successes.
- Never having any hugs, kisses or care when you need comfort or are unwell (adapted from NSPCC n.d. b).

It can be just as painful to have your feelings hurt like this as it is when someone physically hurts you. We don't always understand why parents say or do these things, which mean children feel unloved, that they are unimportant or that they don't matter. Sometimes this happens when parents don't feel happy or good about themselves, but this is still not okay and is very unfair. All children deserve to have parents who can help them feel loved and special, and not sad or scared.

NEGLECT

Use the Building Strong Walls activity (pp.136–140) to help explain neglect.

All children need to be looked after by grown-ups, especially when they're little. A baby can't change their own nappy or get themself dressed. A toddler can't make their own lunch or get themself to nursery. A seven-year-old can't buy their own school uniform, and probably shouldn't be walking to school on their own, crossing over busy roads. Even teenagers need adults to make sure they're safe, that they have a warm, clean home, clothes that fit and cuddles when they need them.

But some children don't have safe grown-ups to do these things for them. Or perhaps sometimes they do and sometimes they don't. They might not have a warm, clean and safe home or a bed to sleep in. Maybe there isn't always enough food for everyone. They may not have someone watching to make sure they're safe from harm. They might not be taken to see the doctor when they're sick. They might not go to school as often as they should. They could be left at home on their own or have to look after their brothers and sisters when there are no grown-ups around. Perhaps they are left for too long in their cot or buggy without anyone to cuddle or play with them. They might not be kept safe from people or things that might hurt them. Sometimes people call this neglect, and it could affect lots of parts of a child's life if it goes on for too long.

Then ask yourself, how is this relevant to the child? What fits with their lived experience. Consider whether poverty was a factor – did the parents not have enough money to pay for fuel or food? Did they spend their money on other things to make themselves happier – drugs or alcohol? Was mental health an issue if care was inconsistent? Can you imagine into the child's experiences if they're not old enough to have a verbal memory? 'It must have been scary for such a tiny baby to be left all alone. I wonder if you sometimes had a hurting, empty tummy?'

Sometimes, it's not clear why parents neglect their children, and it is difficult to establish what was getting in the way of them caring for and meeting all their needs. Be curious about the 'why' if you're not sure.

PHYSICAL HARM OR ABUSE (NON-ACCIDENTAL INJURY) – HURTING CHILDREN ON PURPOSE

Sometimes the people who should be taking good care of children hurt them on purpose. If someone hurts a child on purpose, this is called physical abuse. They might hurt them with their hands or feet or with an object like a stick or a belt. The abuse could be:

- *hitting, smacking or slapping*
- *punching and kicking*
- *pinching, scratching or biting*
- *shaking them or making it hard for them to breathe by covering their mouth*
- *scalding or burning*
- *hair pulling*
- *spitting or throwing things at them*

- *making them swallow something that hurts or makes them feel ill, including giving medicine when they're not ill or don't need it.*[1]

Children are likely to wonder why this is happening to them. This is such a tricky question to answer. People who hurt children give different reasons as to why. They might be struggling with different problems of their own, or they might be more likely to hurt their child if they've been drinking alcohol or taking drugs. Sometimes they feel that this is the right thing to do to teach their child right from wrong. They may have been hit when they were children as punishment, and so they think it must be okay. They might be feeling angry about other things that have nothing to do with their child or under lots of stress, and this leads to them losing their temper with their child.

No matter what a parent or carer is going through, it doesn't ever make it okay for them to hurt someone else, especially their child, whether it was done on purpose or because it was meant to be a punishment. It doesn't matter if it's a one-off thing or something that happens over and over. It's not okay. Even if hurting a child doesn't leave a mark or injury you can see, it's still not okay. In fact, it is against the law to hurt a child like this.

Some children might feel they must have done something wrong if their parents want to hurt them, but that is never the case. Even if a child has hit out at their brother, broken something deliberately or said something unkind, it's never okay for a grown-up to hurt them. There is never an excuse for hurting a child.

SEXUAL HARM OR ABUSE – UNSAFE TOUCHING

When thinking about sexual harm with children it is a helpful starting point to think with them about safe and unsafe touch – psychoeducation about what's okay and what's not okay. When a child or young person is sexually abused, they are forced or tricked into sexual activity. They might not understand that what is happening is abuse or that it's wrong.

> I worked with a five-year-old child who had been sexually abused since infancy by their father. Sexual abuse was so 'normal' for them and was experienced in the context of a 'loving' relationship with a parent, that when social workers were telling them that this sexual contact

1 Adapted from www.childline.org.uk/info-advice/bullying-abuse-safety/abuse-safety/physical-abuse

> was not okay, it made no sense at all. In foster care, all they knew was that they were missing their daddy and missing the time they spent together, including the sexual contact. This was how they showed and were shown love all their life until coming into care.

Similarly, they might be afraid to tell someone or have been threatened to stay silent. However, it is important to remember that in the UK, the law says that anyone under the age of 13 can never consent to any form of sexual activity. This is the same regardless of the person's gender identity, sexual orientation and whether sexual activity is between people of the same or different genders. In the UK, the age of consent is 16 (the legal age when people can engage in sexual activity). The law is there to protect children from abuse or exploitation rather than to prosecute under-16s who take part in sexual activity that everyone has agreed to.

Although children over the age of 16 can legally consent to sexual activity, they may still be vulnerable to harm through an abusive sexual relationship. The law gives extra protection to all under-18-year-olds, regardless of whether they are over the age of consent. For instance, it is illegal:

- to take, show or distribute indecent photographs of a child under the age of 18 (this includes images shared through sexting or sharing nudes)
- to sexually exploit a child under the age of 18
- for a person in a position of trust (for example teachers or care staff) to engage in sexual activity with anyone under the age of 18 who is in the care of their organisation.

For reference, the key legislation relating to child sexual abuse in England and Wales is the Sexual Offences Act 2003. In Northern Ireland it is the Sexual Offences (Northern Ireland) Order 2008. In Scotland it is the Sexual Offences (Scotland) Act 2009 and the Protection of Children and Prevention of Sexual Offences (Scotland) Act 2005.

In establishing what the child understands about sexual abuse, first teach them the correct names of all their different body parts, including their private body parts, if they don't know already. It can be hard for a child to talk to adults about sexual abuse if they don't know the words to use, and it's important to develop a shared language and understanding.

Learning the anatomical words for private body parts gives children the vocabulary they need, and helps them know it's okay to talk about those body parts.

Let children know that they are in control of who touches their bodies and how. Encourage parents or carers to model this day to day, enforcing their own privacy boundaries and personal space. Likewise, immediately respect the child's wishes not to be touched in certain ways: 'It looks like you don't want a cuddle right now. That's okay. I'm here if you need me.' If they're playing with friends or siblings, be clear that they need to stop tickling or playfighting if someone says 'stop'. It's also important not to insist that children give or receive hugs or kisses from people, even relatives, if they don't want to. This teaches children that it's okay to say no to touches from people in their family.

You can then explore the idea of three kinds of touch:

- *Safe touch:* This is touch that keeps children safe and helps them feel cared for and important. Safe touch can include hugging, pats on the back, a high five or a kiss. Safe touch can sometimes include touch that might hurt, like if a parent or carer is removing a splinter or washing a muddy graze because it's done to keep them healthy, which makes it a 'safe' touch.
- *Unsafe touch:* This is touch that hurts children's bodies or feelings, like hitting, hair pulling, pinching and kicking. It can also include touch on a child's private body parts. It is critical to teach children that this kind of touch is not okay.
- *Unwanted touch:* This touch might be safe, but a child doesn't want it from that person or at that time. It's okay for a child to say no to an unwanted touch, even if it's from someone they know well. Sometimes children need help to practice saying 'no' in a strong, assertive voice, to set personal boundaries.

Of course, it is never a child's responsibility to protect themselves from abuse, but learning to say no to unwanted touch or activity is an important part of children being able to understand their own body boundaries. There are many ideas for how to build protective behaviours for children who have experienced complex developmental or relational trauma in my second book, *Helping Vulnerable Children and Adolescents to Stay Safe: Creative Ideas and Activities for Building Protective Behaviours* (2016).

Sexual abuse can happen anywhere to anyone – and it can happen in-person or online. There are two types of sexual abuse, known as contact and non-contact abuse. In contact abuse, the perpetrator makes direct physical contact with a child. This includes:

- sexual touching of any part of a child's body, whether they're clothed or not
- using a body part or object to rape or penetrate a child
- forcing a child to take part in any sexual activities, like touching, kissing or oral sex
- making a child undress or touch someone else, a child or adult.

Non-contact abuse is where a child is abused without being touched by the abuser. This can be in-person or online, and is no more or less harmful than contact abuse. It could include:

- exposure or flashing
- showing a child pornographic material
- exposing a child to sexual acts in person
- making a child masturbate in front of others
- forcing a child to make, view or share child abuse images or videos
- forcing a child to take part in sexual activities or conversations online or through a smartphone (adapted from NSPCC n.d. a).

Sometimes adults touch children in ways they shouldn't in their private places, and this is not allowed. This is called sexual abuse. It is fine for parents and sometimes other grown-ups who look after children to give them a hug, get them dressed and, when they are very little, to wash their bodies for them or change their nappy. Sometimes doctors or nurses might also need to touch a child's body, even in their private places, if they're unwell or sore. It is not alright to touch children's private parts when adults are not washing them, changing nappies, or putting cream on them if they are sore. It is not okay for adults to get good feelings from touching children's private parts or to make children touch their private parts. They are breaking the law and, if the police and a judge in court are certain that the adult has done this to a child, they may be sent to prison.

Sometimes it can be very scary for children who are touched like this by adults. They might feel ashamed about what has happened, even though they had no choice. This is because some adults who touch children in this way threaten them that something bad will happen if they say no or tell. Others are good at making it feel 'nice' for the children. They work hard to get to know the child or young person, and have special, fun times together, so they can abuse them. This is called 'grooming' and makes it much harder for the child to tell. They might even make friends with the child's parents or family to get closer to the child and make their parents trust them. Sometimes they might give children sweets, money, drugs or special treats for doing what they ask, or in return, for staying quiet. Adults who do this are using the fact they are bigger, stronger and more powerful than children to control them, which is not okay.

These adults sometimes think what they are doing is alright. They might even say they do these things because they love the child so much and they are so special. But they want it to be kept secret because they know that other adults would **not** *think it was alright and they would be in trouble with the police if anyone found out. Children who have been touched like this, have touched an adult, or have been forced to touch another child have done nothing wrong.*

SEXUAL OFFENDING

One of the most common queries I come across in training and consultation is how to explain to a child that a parent or someone close to them has been convicted of sexual offences or that a parent has allowed a known sex offender to have contact with their child, even though they were warned that this person posed a risk to children. It is usually unnecessary to go into detail about the nature of the offences for a child; it should be sufficient to use the descriptions above to explain how sexual abuse occurs and why. It is important that the information is then adapted to reflect the child's lived experience and that you use language relating to genitalia that the child understands. Not all sex offenders have convictions against children, as the term refers to anyone who has committed a sex crime, but I will focus the following example on offences against children.

People who sexually abuse children are sometimes called sex offenders. They hurt children in lots of different ways – for example, they might touch them on their private parts or take photographs of the child naked to share with other people. They try to keep it secret to make no one finds out what they are doing. But if they are found out, the police will get involved and they might go to court. If they are found guilty of hurting a child in this way they will be punished, usually by going to prison. They will also be put on the Sex Offenders Register and then have to follow lots of rules to keep children safe. For example, they must tell the police if they want to travel abroad, or they are living with or staying with a person under the age of 18 for more than 12 hours.

The rules are different for different people, but if the police are very worried about the risk from a sex offender, they might say they are not allowed go near a place where it is likely there will be lots of children, for example a playground or school. They might not be able to have any unsupervised contact with children under the age of 18. They might not be able to use the internet without having special computer monitoring software installed. They won't ever be allowed to work with children.

Social workers will become involved if someone is being investigated for sexual offences against children and they have contact with children under the age of 18 in their family or social circles (this might be their own child/niece/nephew, etc). It is important that parents understand whether people they know might be a risk to their children, so they can make sure they keep them safe. Often this means not letting them have any contact with their children or making sure they are never on their own with a child.

You might want to include something here about grooming and why it is the parent/carer's job to protect their child from harm.

Sex offenders can be very clever. They often don't make it obvious straight away that they want to abuse a child and first they try to get the child to trust them. They might even work hard to get the whole family to trust them, so they can be on their own with the child. There are lots of ways they might do this. They might buy presents or give the child lots of lovely attention. They might offer to babysit, to take them on exciting days out or holidays. Then, once they've built that trust, they use their power to make the child think they have to do exactly what they're told. Parents can be tricked like this too, just like children. But if a parent knows a person has been convicted of sex offences and that they might be a risk to their child, it is always the parent's job to take action to keep their child safe.

INCEST

Use the general explanation for sexual abuse, and then be more specific about the nature of relationships.

If sexual abuse happens in a child's close family by a grandparent or parent to their grandchild or child or between siblings, this is called incest. It is against the law. If a child is hurt like this by someone in their family, it can lead to complicated feelings. Children will know they have to keep the abuse secret, and this might mean they feel ashamed or that they have done something wrong. It is especially hard when the person who should keep you safe is the one who is hurting you.

RAPE

Sometimes a child may be separated from or not have contact with their father because he was convicted of rape, or they themselves may be a product of rape. It may also be that the issue of not knowing the identity of a child's father becomes bound up in their conception where a stranger has raped their mother.

To explore the concept of rape, it is important that the child understands how babies are made and what sex is. The nature of this explanation will differ widely in families and between children depending on how interested the child is in learning about sex; if they are the oldest or youngest in the family; their level of understanding and developmental stage; whether the child has had any sex education in school; and cultural norms.

The legal definition of rape in the UK is when a man intentionally penetrates another person's vagina, anus or mouth with a penis, without the other person's consent. Assault by penetration is when a person penetrates another person's vagina or anus with any part of the body other than a penis, or by using an object, without the person's consent. To understand rape, it is also important to understand the idea of consent in terms of sexual contact. Consent is when someone agrees to do something sexual and both people involved want it to happen. If you don't ask first before you touch, kiss or do anything sexual with someone, or they don't say yes, then you don't have that person's consent, and what you're doing to them may be rape or sexual assault. That is why consent matters.

It's not okay to pressure, trick or threaten someone into saying yes. It's okay to say yes and then change your mind – at any time. You can only agree to something if you have all the facts about what is going to happen, and there are also laws around consent to protect people. If a person is drunk or has taken drugs, is asleep or has passed out, is below the legal age of consent (16 in the UK) or has a disability that affects their ability to understand what they're being asked to do, then they cannot consent.

Children need to understand the circumstances of their conception, but this knowledge may negatively impact their sense of self. Where they remain in the care of their birth mother, there will be the possibility that this child may represent a reminder of an event that was traumatic and agonising, and this might impact the care they receive. Work with rape survivors and their children of the Rwandan genocide is chronicled in *Rwandan Daughters* (2019), a book of photographs by German photographer Olaf Heine, and supports this position. Many mothers admitted to resenting their children, who were constant reminders of the horror they had experienced – and a source of ongoing stigma in a conservative society. Some found a way to process their grief and love their children. For other mothers, keeping their child was too unbearable a thought and so they came into care and then adoption.

Daisy's story – an adopted adult

Birthdays really weighed heavily on me because that just marks the day I came into the world... No one was celebrating my arrival – I arrived in the world as evidence of a rape and a child that needed to go into the care system because of that. I was only 18 when I found out what had happened. And that is a lot to carry. I remember thinking: Do I look like him? Do I look like my birth father? Do I have the face of my birth mother's rapist? I represent the worst thing that's happened to her. (Cross 2022)

Usually when people have sex with each other, they do it because they enjoy it, and love or care for each other. But, when a man forces a person to have sex with him when they don't want to, perhaps by threatening them and making them feel scared, this is called rape. This is a serious crime and is against the law, which means the man could go to prison. When a man and woman have sex, sometimes babies are made, and then they are born about nine months later. Sometimes a baby is made and is then born after a man rapes a woman.

These babies grow just the same as any other baby. It is never the mother's or the baby's fault that the baby was made this way.

MENTAL ILLNESS

Mental illness is like any other physical illness, like chicken pox or the flu, except it's the mind that gets ill rather than a part of the body. Mental and physical illnesses are similar in the sense that a person can become unwell through no fault of their own, they may have to see a doctor, and sometimes need help to feel better. But because you can't see an injury to the mind, and nothing looks painful on the outside, it can be hard to understand. Mental illness is not something a child or their loved one with the condition should feel guilty or embarrassed about. Children cannot cause a parent or someone they love to develop a mental illness. It's not always clear why some people get ill, but one thing is certain – it's no one's fault. After all, it's not the child's fault if their mum or dad gets a bad cold.

Depending on the experiences of the child you may need to go into more detail about specific mental health difficulties. There are many books that can help explain too, which I've listed under each subheading, and it's important, of course, not to generalise and to adapt what you say or write to the child's lived experience.

ANXIETY OR BIG WORRIES

Think with the child about what it can feel like when they're filled with big worries or feeling anxious. Map it out. Maybe draw around their body and ask them to write on the image what happens when they are worried about something. They might feel sick or dizzy. They might get sweaty palms and butterflies in their tummy. They might feel tension in their shoulders or get horrid headaches. They might find it hard to sleep. Normalise these feelings...anxiety is a feeling we all experience from time to time. But for some people their worries are so big they get in the way of living life, taking care of themself and being a parent. Anxiety affects how you think and how your body feels. *Listening to My Body* (Garcia 2017) is a terrific book that helps children (aged 4–10) make a connection between their emotions and body sensations.

Anxiety is a feeling of worry or fear that can be a mixture of physical sensations you notice in your body, as well as thoughts and feelings. Everyone feels anxious sometimes, but these feelings will usually fade away when the thing you're worrying about has passed – like a test at school, or meeting someone new. It only becomes a problem when the feelings don't go away. This can leave people feeling anxious, overwhelmed and upset for most of the time. Sometimes even doing things they used to love can start to make someone feel anxious, so this can really limit what they feel able to do.

When people feel anxious, it can sometimes be a real struggle to do the things they need to do every day for themselves and sometimes for their children. They might find it hard to:

- *leave the house to go to work, to the supermarket or take their children to school or nursery*
- *talk to other people*
- *have fun or play*

- *find the energy to look after themselves, their home or their family.*

Stories for children

Don't Worry, Murray by David Ezra Stein (2022) is for children aged 4–8 who love dogs! And worry a lot.

What If, Pig? by Linzie Hunter (2021) goes over the different 'what ifs' and solutions for easing an anxious mind. With the help of his mouse friend, Pig learns how to turn his 'what if' worries from anxiety to optimism (for ages 3–7).

The Huge Bag of Worries by Virginia Ironside (2011) is a reassuring picture book encouraging children to open up about their fears and anxieties to help manage their feelings (ages 4–8).

DEPRESSION OR DEEP SADNESS

Everyone feels sad or fed up sometimes, but depressed people feel like this often and for a long time, not just for a few days. The sad feelings just won't go away. Someone who has depression often feels tired, sad and hopeless. They might not want to eat or make food for others. They can find it hard to fall asleep or to get up in the morning.

This might mean for some people it's hard to show when they're happy or for them to enjoy doing things they used to love. It might mean sometimes they are quiet and don't want to talk, even to their family. They might not be able to go to the park with their children, help with homework or have friends visit. They might not have the energy to keep the house clean and tidy, to walk their children to school or make dinner. Depression can make people not see the point in doing anything – they sometimes just want to stay in bed or lie on the sofa.

Some people develop depression, and some people don't. There are many different reasons why. Sometimes depression is unavoidable, but there are things we can do to protect ourselves against it, as well as things to manage and treat it. Depression is an illness that can be treated with medication or therapy, but getting better will take time. In the meantime, depression can cause a person to say or do things they wouldn't say or do when they are well.

Stories for children

The Very Cranky Bear by Nick Bland (2010) is about helping people to cheer up when they're not feeling so happy.

Can I Catch It Like a Cold? by CAMH (2009) discusses what depression is and how it is treated, and can help ease a child's anxiety about being around others who are mentally ill (ages 5–8).

Michael Rosen's Sad Book (2005) is a heartbreakingly honest account of a father's grief for his son after his death from meningitis at the age of 19. It acknowledges that sadness is not always avoidable or unreasonable, and makes complicated feelings seem easy to understand (ages 5–9).

SCHIZOPHRENIA

Schizophrenia is a mental illness that can be very serious. People with schizophrenia can think and act in ways that don't make sense to other people. They might see, hear or believe things that aren't real or true that no one else can see, hear or believe to be true. This is called psychosis. It can be very frightening hearing voices telling you to do things that might not feel safe.

Many people with schizophrenia think that someone or something is reading their mind or trying to hurt them. These beliefs that aren't true are called paranoid delusions. They might also see things that aren't there, which are called hallucinations. Sometimes when people have this illness, they think they have special powers, and this can make them dangerous to themselves and other people, especially children.

The voices they hear might make them think they can never be hurt so they might do very risky and dangerous things, like try to walk across a busy road or motorway, or tell others to do risky things, and if you're only a child, it might feel hard to say no. The voices might tell them people are out to get them and they need to protect themselves. The voices might tell them to hurt themselves or someone else, even if that is someone they love. They don't realise that what the voices say is not the truth. It can be really scary for children when their parent has this illness – they might also end up believing that the things their parent is telling them are true.

Medicine helps with managing these scary things, but the illness will never go away. Sometimes the side effects of the medicine are not very nice. They can make people feel very sleepy, put on weight or feel they have lost the spark that makes them who they are, and this means they might stop taking it. Unfortunately, if this happens, they will probably get very unwell again. Sometimes it's the illness that might tell them they don't need the medicine after all, which can make it tricky to stay well and to be the parent their child needs them to be.

Stories for children

Helicopter Man by Elizabeth Fensham (2005) is a story based on the real-life experience of an adolescent whose father is a paranoid schizophrenic, afraid of helicopters, police and life itself. Themes include foster care.

Please Stop Smiling: A Story about Schizophrenia and Mental Illness for Children by Richard Carlson Jr. (2012) tells the story of a 10-year-old whose big brother has schizophrenia.

SELF-HARM

People hurt themselves for lots of different reasons that they might find hard to put into words. Some people have described self-harm as a way to:

- *express something they cannot say*
- *turn invisible thoughts or feelings into something visible*
- *change emotional pain into physical pain*
- *lessen overwhelming emotions or thoughts*
- *have a sense of being in control*
- *escape traumatic memories.*

Ensure that you only write about what is relevant to the child's story here.

Sometimes it can feel like life is just too hard, and problems can seem overwhelming or too much to manage. Sometimes when people are feeling pain and upset or have bad feelings, thoughts or memories, they might think about hurting themselves to manage or make these feelings go away. For others it's a way to punish themselves because they feel guilty or ashamed about something they have done or something that has happened to them. Some people might think that if they feel physical pain, they won't feel so much emotional pain inside.

There are lots of different forms of self-harming. Some people use the same one all the time; other people hurt themselves in different ways at different times. People can self-harm by:

- *cutting or burning their skin*
- *poisoning themselves*

- *eating too much or not eating enough*
- *doing way too much exercise*
- *biting, picking or scratching at their skin*
- *hitting themself or walls or deliberately getting into fights where they know they will get hurt*
- *drinking too much alcohol, or taking too many prescription and recreational drugs*
- *pulling hair or eyelashes out.*

Ensure that you only write about what is relevant to the child's story here and leave out this detail if necessary.

Sometimes people hurt themselves in secret and on parts of their body that other people won't easily notice, but sometimes the injuries are more obvious and can be upsetting for others, especially children, to see. Self-harm can be something that someone tries once, or it can become something that in the moment helps them feel better, and so they keep on doing it. The problem is that they usually only feel better for a short while, and the things that made them feel this way usually stick around.

It can be hard to stop hurting yourself when you get into the habit of doing it. It can also be very upsetting to see someone you love hurting themself. It might feel like you should be able to help or make them feel better. It might feel like it's your job to keep them safe, but it's not. They might need some help to learn ways to manage how they are feeling in a different way, as well as help with the things that are making them feel these big feelings too.

BEREAVEMENT

Sadly, it's not unusual for children in care or adoption to have a birth parent or close relative who has died. It is important to be aware of the child/family's belief system or religious beliefs about death and dying as this will also dictate how you respond to questions about what happens after death. It is hard to be prescriptive about what to say. Ideas that might be a comfort to children include seeing death as an end to suffering; that the person who has died lives on in their hearts; or that the person who died would want to be remembered, but would also want the child to be happy too.

When exploring death, dying or bereavement with children it is important to have an appreciation that what a child understands and how they react will vary at different stages of their development and depending on whether they have any conscious or verbal memories of the person. There are some generalisations to be made, but ultimately, just like adults, children will all respond to grief in their own unique ways.

When supporting much younger, *pre-school* children, they are unlikely to understand the finality of death, thinking that it's reversible and that a loved one can come back. It's important to use clear and simple language, such as 'dead' and 'died', rather than euphemisms, because at this age, children have a very literal understanding of language. For example, if you say, 'You sadly lost your daddy when you were a baby', children under five will think 'Well let's go and find him then!' It can sound harsh, brutal even, but it's important to have clarity of language so there is less scope for misunderstanding. Explain what 'dead' and 'alive' means – you can help the child feel their own pulse or heartbeat, feel the breath come in and out of their lungs and explain that when someone dies their heart can't beat anymore and they will stop breathing forever.

When someone has died their heart stops beating. This means they stop breathing. Their whole body stops working. They can't walk and they can't talk any more. You won't be able to see them again.

Be prepared for repetition. It is not uncommon for young children to need to repeat the story of the death or ask lots of repetitive questions – this doesn't mean they haven't listened or that you haven't explained it well enough; this is just how they work out what's going on and process the information.

Between the *ages of five and eight*, children are starting to understand that death is something that is final, but this can feel scary for them because they will be starting think about themselves and their influence on things that happen in their lives. Exploring the life cycle as a natural thing can be helpful, and there are lots of stories to help with this because 'magical thinking' is common. The child might think that it's their fault that the person has died because of something they said, did, imagined or even wished for, but probably won't have the emotional vocabulary yet to express how they feel.

At *nine to twelve years of age*, children fully understand the finality of death and that the person is never coming back. They are increasingly aware of the impact the death has on them – their special person won't be there for birthdays, celebrations or milestones like moving to secondary school, learning to drive or getting married. They will have developed the capacity to begin to understand how they're thinking or feeling, but they might not want to share this for fear of upsetting other people. It's important to be explicit in giving permission to talk about how they feel about the person who has died.

By *adolescence* there should be an adult understanding of death and dying. As always, it's important to give clear, honest information about the death, and to answer any questions the young person might have as openly as you can.

Although they will feel it just as deeply as adults, the way in which children will experience and express grief is likely to look quite different, dependent on their age and understanding of death as well as their ability to talk about their thoughts and feelings. They are less likely to be able to verbalise those thoughts and feelings if they haven't previously had good opportunities for co-regulation. The range of responses a child might have to someone dying or to thinking about the death of a loved one can vary greatly, from extreme distress, to finding it hard to speak, or appearing indifferent. This is normal and doesn't mean that the child doesn't care or isn't impacted by what has happened. It may take them some time to process events, and they may need some help in finding ways to express how it feels for them. Be mindful that if the person who has died is responsible is some way for harm caused to the child, their response might be even more complex.

When someone close to you dies, it is normal to move between intense grieving and times where it feels more possible to look to the future with some hopefulness. This movement back and forth between two extreme feeling states can happen even more quickly for children than for adults. One useful illustration used by the bereavement charity Winston's Wish[2] to describe the difference between an adult and a child's grief is to compare the feeling of being swept along in a river with jumping in and out of puddles. Adults can often feel overwhelmed by grief, as if they are caught in the current of a river and it is impossible to find a way out, whereas

2 www.winstonswish.org

lady in the park who tells her to look in the mirror to see the face of her mother through her own reflection.

Muddles, Puddles and Sunshine by Diana Crossley (2009) is an activity book that offers invaluable practical and sensitive support for bereaved younger children. It suggests a helpful series of activities and exercises accompanied by the friendly characters of Bee and Bear.

The Garden of Hope by Isabel Otter (2019) is a story about a little girl and her father who rebuild their lives and plant a 'garden of hope' after something sad happens. Whether her mum has died or has left the family is not made clear. The story features a Black, Asian and minority ethnic (BAME) family and is for ages 4+.

The Scar by Charlotte Moundlic (2012) is the story of a boy who wakes up to find that his mother has died, who is overwhelmed with sadness, anger and fear that he will forget her. He shuts all the windows to keep in his mother's familiar smell, and scratches open the cut on his knee to help him recall her comforting voice. He doesn't know how to speak to his dad anymore, and when Grandma visits and throws open the windows, it's more than the boy can take – until she shows him another way to hold on to the feeling of his mother's love.

What Does Dead Mean? A Book for Young Children to Help Explain Death and Dying by Caroline Jay and Jenni Thomas (2012) addresses the 'big' questions children often ask about death and dying. Questions such as 'Is being dead like sleeping?' 'Why do people have to die?' and 'Where do dead people go?' are answered simply, truthfully and clearly to help adults explain to children what happens when someone dies.

Stories for ages 9–12

Lifetimes: The Beautiful Way to Explain Death to Children by Bryan Mellonie and Robert Ingpen (1998) focuses on the life and death of plants, animals and insects, before moving on to people, emphasising that death is part of the life cycle, and is natural and normal whenever it occurs.

Only One of Me: A Love Letter from Mum by Lisa Wells and Michelle Robinson (2018) is a rhyming poem, which is both a love letter to Lisa's own daughters as well as a testament to the unwavering strength of parental love. The author was diagnosed with terminal cancer at the age of 31, and this book grew from her determination to leave a legacy for her daughters and her desire to help other families.

What On Earth Do You Do When Someone Dies? by Trevor Romain (2023) is a factual guide, answering questions such as 'Why do people have to die?' 'Is it okay to cry?' and 'What is a funeral/memorial service?' It is written in a straightforward way, with practical tips, advice and information about different faiths and beliefs. It describes the strong, confusing feelings you might have, and suggests ways to feel better. The author explains it's okay to cry, talk about the death, to grieve, and to go on with your life.

Stories for young people 13+

The Fault in Our Stars by John Green (2013) is a book about a teenage girl who has been diagnosed with lung cancer and attends a cancer support group where she meets Augustus. The couple embark on a rollercoaster of emotions, including love, sadness and romance, while searching for the author of their favourite book.

A Monster Calls by Patrick Ness (2015) is a fantasy novel about a 13-year-old boy who is coping with the diagnosis of his mother's cancer. It is a book about stories and myths, about courage and loss, and the fear of loss.

Straight Talk about Death for Teenagers: How to Cope with Losing Someone You Love by Earl A. Grollman (1993). This book was written after the author spoke to thousands of teenagers and found they often felt forgotten after someone has died. Written in short, clear sentences that are easy to read, it covers feelings, different types of death and dealing with the future. This book gives the reader many options of what can happen, how they may feel, giving advice and reassuring readers that grief is normal.

DEATH BY SUICIDE

The way in which we talk about suicide has changed in recent years. This is because the phrase 'committed suicide' dates from a time when suicide was a criminal act. However, suicide was decriminalised in England and Wales in 1961, and in Ireland in 1993, and is no longer against the law. It's important to be able to talk about suicide with children without shame or stigma, and so our use of language matters. Alternatives to 'committing suicide' include 'died by suicide', 'took their own life' or 'ended their life'.

Children may hear the word 'suicide' being used in relation to loved ones who have made attempts to end their own life, so it's important that they understand what it means.

Suicide is a difficult subject to think and talk about because the child must acknowledge extreme psychological pain and, in the case of a violent death, the physical pain of a person to whom they were close. Not only can it be seen as an act of ultimate despair, but death by suicide can lead loved ones left behind to feel they were not good enough or lovable enough to want to stay with, in life.

Winston's Wish suggests there may be several steps involved in telling a child that someone has died by suicide. First, explain that the person has died and give simple details about how they died. You can say that the person took their own life and provide a more detailed explanation of how the person died if they ask. You might then explore reasons why the person decided to take their life.

Each of these pieces of information may be enough for a child at one time. Give them space to process it at their own speed, until they ask a further question, or you offer a bit more information. If you don't have the answers, it's okay to say, 'I don't know' or 'I wish I knew, I have lots of questions too.' As you build the child's understanding of what happened, the pace between these stages should be led by the child's age and developmental stage, capacity to understand death and how much interest they show in knowing more. Also think about other factors, such as the possibility of the child finding out what happened from other people or searching online. The picture should become clearer to the child over time, like piecing together a jigsaw puzzle to build a fuller picture. Remember that just like sharing any difficult part of a child's story, it's important to be honest, and for the child to know they can ask questions when they're ready for answers (adapted from Winston's Wish 2020).

By avoiding talking about something as important as people dying or the way in which they died with children, we risk increasing their anxiety and confusion. Children may make up a version of events, or have heard more frightening, inaccurate stories about what has happened. But also, when we don't talk openly about a loss, we give children the implicit message that this is something we cannot manage, and therefore we think they can't either.

Sometimes a death by suicide of someone we love comes as an enormous shock and no one sees it coming. Even if someone has said they plan to end their own life or has tried to before, it can be a long time before you can believe it is true. You might be left with lots of questions about whether there was anything you could have done to stop it from happening. You might be struggling to understand why it happened.

> Was it expected? Often I said no. Sometimes I said yes. Yes, it was expected. But not by me. My mother expected it. That's not quite the right verb. She planned it. She planned her own death. And she told us to expect it, but I didn't... I did not expect it. I did not expect my mother to kill herself. (Walter 2023)

The reasons why people choose to take their own life are always complicated, but in the moment, it can be hard for them to remember and think about the part of them that loved other people and once enjoyed life. They sometimes can't see that there are many important things and people to stay alive for. Some people who feel very strong feelings of pain or sadness might see suicide as a way to end the pain, especially if they're dealing with lots of difficult things in their life all at once. Their feelings can become so overwhelming that they feel they can't cope anymore. It can feel like there is no way out, or that there is no escape from the feelings.

Where appropriate you might add contextual details here. While the link between suicide and mental health is well established, many suicides happen impulsively in moments of crisis with a breakdown in the person's ability to deal with chronic life stresses, such as financial difficulties, a relationship break-up, chronic pain or illness.

When someone you love dies by suicide, you might feel lots of complicated and often muddled-up feelings that can be difficult to manage. You might feel angry at the person who died at the same time as feeling sadness and pain. If the person had been suffering for some time you might also feel relief, but with that might come guilt.

Stories for children

The Little Flower Bulb: Helping Children Bereaved by Suicide by Eleanor Gormally (2011) tells the story of Jamie, his mum and twin sisters, and of how he deals with the death of his father by suicide.

Luna's Red Hat: An Illustrated Storybook to Help Children Cope with Loss and

Suicide by Emmi Smid (2015) is a book to be read with children who have experienced the loss of a loved one by suicide. The book approaches the subject sensitively, and includes a guide for parents and professionals.

Someone I Love Died by Suicide: A Story for Child Survivors and Those Who Care for Them by Dorothy Cammarata (2009) is a story that talks through the normal symptoms of grief and identifies various ways to promote healthy ways of coping with the death of a special person.

I Am Here for You! A Story to Support Your Grieving Child Through Death from Suicide by Carla Mitchell (2021) will help you discuss the topic of suicide using nature elements and child-friendly rhymes. There are spaces for the child to capture their favourite memories or photos, or suggestions for remembering their loved one, together with ideas for coping with feelings of grief, and resources for caring adults (ages 4–10).

ADDICTION

When you are talking to children who have grown up around addiction, be mindful of the ways in which they may have adapted to cope with living with uncertainty or lack of parental presence or availability. Social worker Richard Devine talks about minimising his own needs but also anticipating and meeting the needs of other people. Yet these strategies only served to reinforce his sense of shame, inadequacy and worthlessness:

> Shame because my dad was rejected by everyone who should have cared for him
>
> Shame because his drug and alcohol use hurt those around him
>
> Shame because my mum couldn't protect and shield her children from violence and drug abuse
>
> Shame because she couldn't be the parent she knew she could and wanted to be
>
> Shame because when my dad turned to drugs, I thought he didn't love me
>
> Shame because my mum's depression left me feeling rejected and unlovable
>
> Shame... (Devine 2022, p.149)

Alcoholism

People have drunk alcoholic drinks like beer, wine or cider for thousands of years. Some people like the taste. They might drink at parties and other social events with family and friends and have a lovely time. Some people drink because they like the feeling of being drunk. Some people drink alcohol to help them feel calm, or to try and cope with problems, like relationship or money worries.

Drinking alcohol affects the brain and body, so it can quickly change the way people feel and act, even if they've only had a small amount. It can affect people more if they're smaller, weigh less or haven't had anything to eat. Alcohol can also affect memory, meaning people often don't remember silly, embarrassing or unkind things they might have said or done when they've been drinking. Some people are more likely to get into fights or arguments if they've been drinking, or to make bad choices.

People keep on drinking because the good feelings they have at the time feel more important than any horrible effects, such as being sick or feeling ill (hungover) the next day, or upsetting people who care about them. If they're already feeling depressed or incredibly sad before drinking, alcohol can make them feel even worse.

Like any other drug, there is always a risk of getting addicted to alcohol if someone drinks a lot. If it feels too hard to stop drinking, this can be very worrying for the person and for the people in their lives who care about them. Alcoholism is an illness where someone has lost control over their drinking – this is called addiction. They might only mean to have one or two drinks, and always end up drinking much more. They often need professional help to stop drinking.

Sadly, when somebody has become dependent on alcohol, they continue drinking even when it is having a negative effect on their lives, their health and those around them. When people drink too much alcohol for a long time it can sometimes lead to lots of health problems with their liver, stomach, heart and brain. But when someone has a problem with drinking, alcohol becomes their focus in life. They see drinking as the answer to their problems, while others might see it as the cause of those problems. The need to drink becomes so important that they may hurt and upset those they love. If they are a parent, this can leave their children not feeling important or cared for.

Often the person drinking doesn't even see they have a problem. Even if they become aware that something is wrong, they may not think it has anything to do with drinking. They may blame other people, or other problems in their life, like work stresses or not having enough money. Whatever anyone says, a child is never responsible for their parent's drinking, and it's never their fault.

You can't stop someone else from drinking. There is help for people who are drinking too much, but first, they have to accept that they have a problem and want help. Admitting that they have a problem is the first step to getting better. Talking about it can also help them work through the problem and tackle the cause of the drinking (*Nacoa n.d.*).

Drug use

There are lots of different kinds of drugs. Some are medicines that a doctor prescribes or that can be bought from a chemist if someone is ill. The amount taken is controlled by someone who understands how they work so it is safe for everyone. These drugs are legal. That means people won't get into trouble with the police if they take them just as the doctor or chemist asks.

Some drugs are not legal. That means they can't be obtained from the doctor or pharmacy, and it's against the law to buy or sell them. There are lots of drugs that are illegal, and they have different names and nicknames. They also have a different effect on the body. Taking drugs can be a bit like taking the wrong medicine that makes you ill instead of making you better.

You might want to give details that are specific to the child's experience here and describe, for example, the impact of taking heroin or crack.

There is always a risk of getting addicted to drugs if you take too many, too often. If someone feels they can't stop taking drugs, this can be very worrying for the person and for the people in their lives who care about them. If someone has lost control over their drug taking – this is called addiction. They often need professional help to stop using. When people take too many drugs for a long time it can lead to lots of health problems. Sometimes people might accidentally take too much of a drug and it can kill them. This is called an overdose.

Sadly, when somebody has become addicted to drugs they often continue using even when it is having a negative effect on their lives, their health and those around them. When someone has a drug problem, getting hold of drugs and then taking drugs becomes the most important thing in their life. Life seems unbearable without it. The drug may have helped them feel good when they first started to take it, but over time, they might need to take the drug just to feel normal. The need to take drugs becomes so important that they may hurt and upset those they love. If they are a parent, this can leave children not feeling important or cared for. The most important thing is to get more drugs, but they can cost a lot of money. This means sometimes people do things that are illegal to get money for drugs, like stealing.

Sometimes the person taking drugs doesn't see they have a problem. Even if they become aware something is wrong, they may not think it has anything to do with taking drugs. They may blame other people, or other problems in their life, such as not having enough money. Whatever anyone says, a child is never responsible for their parent's drug use, and it's never their fault. No one can stop people taking drugs if they really want to do it. There is help for people who are taking too many drugs, but first, they must accept that they have a problem and want help.

Stories for children

Critters Cry Too: Explaining Addiction to Children by Anthony Curcio (2016). This book is a wonderful resource that explains a difficult topic that so many children are faced with. It tackles difficult feelings and answers questions that often arise in a child's mind who loves someone who is addicted: Is this my fault? Why does _______ act like this? Does ______ love me?

Elephant in the Living Room by Marion H. Typpo (1994) is an illustrated story to help children understand and cope with the problem of alcoholism or other drug addiction in the family.

My Dad Loves Me, My Dad Has a Disease: A Child's View: Living with Addiction by Claudia Black (2018) gives children aged 8–12 the opportunity to work through their feelings of loss, loneliness, fear and frustration, both verbally and through drawing exercises.

I Can Be Me: A Helping Book for Children of Alcoholic Parents by Dianne S. O'Connor (2009). For children ages 4–12, a child can read it alone or work through it with a caring adult. Written from the perspective of children whose parents are addicted to alcohol and other drugs, this book helps children take off the masks that hide their true feelings, and educates them about alcohol or drug abuse in the family.

When a Family is in Trouble: Children Can Cope with Grief from Drug and Alcohol Addiction by Marge Heegaard (1993). This text gives parents and professionals an approach to help children ages 6–12 understand and cope with the problems they might face when someone they love is struggling with addiction.

I Wish Daddy Didn't Drink So Much by Judith Vigna (1993). Lisa's father's drinking problem threatens to ruin the Christmas holidays for Lisa and her family until her mother and a sympathetic neighbour help Lisa gain insight into her father's alcohol abuse (ages 7–9).

DOMESTIC ABUSE

In the research literature, children are often called 'witnesses' to domestic abuse. This term implies a passive role, but children living with conflict and abuse will actively interpret, predict, assess their role in causing a 'fight', worry about the consequences, engage in problem solving and/or take measures to protect themselves or siblings, both physically and emotionally. Even though infants can't understand what is happening between adults, they can still hear the noise and feel the tension. Babies may be distressed or scared if their needs are not met promptly, too frightened to explore and play, or will sense a parent's distress. They can't protect themselves or leave a stressful situation, and depend entirely on adults to keep them safe. The Domestic Abuse Bill 2020 therefore

> provides that a child who sees or hears, or experiences the effects of, domestic abuse and is related to or under parental responsibility of the person being abused or the perpetrator is also to be regarded as a victim of domestic abuse. This means that where the Act imposes a duty in relation to victims of domestic abuse, this will include children.[4]

During abusive incidents children may attempt to 'referee', rescue their parent, deflect the perpetrator's attention onto them, distract them, take care of younger siblings or seek outside help (like calling the police or running to a neighbour's house). Some try hard to stay out of the way – below the radar – to avoid harm and keep themselves small, quiet and safe. Some hope for rescue, or relief. They may hide, wrap pillows around their ears, hug their pets tight, put on their headphones and turn up the music or lose themselves in a computer game or social media, pretending they are somewhere else.

So when you talk to a child about their experience of living with domestic abuse, don't make assumptions about their experience – it's

4 www.gov.uk/government/publications/domestic-abuse-bill-2020-factsheets/statutory-definition-of-domestic-abuse-factsheet

important that what you say or write in their story resonates. An abusive parent, seen as a dangerous parent by most adults, can still be adored and respected by their child.

> I worked with a 12-year-old child whose father had been abusive to their mother for many years. After an afternoon of heavy drinking, he then committed a violent offence and was remanded in prison. We worked through the child's feelings about missing him, yet not feeling they could share those feelings with their mother. The child, of course, remembered the violence, but they also remembered the fun their father had brought to family life. They were understandably conflicted about the statement they had given to the police about what they had witnessed on the day of the offence, which would subsequently be used as evidence against their father at trial. As a witness, they were not allowed to have any direct contact until the case was heard. They worried what their father would think of them, and this became a major preoccupation.

Over time, some children will grow closer to and identify more with the perpetrator than with their protective parent, perhaps believing their stories and justification for the abuse. If that parent must leave the family home, children may grieve their loss. For children too young to understand cause and effect, coming into foster care because of domestic abuse may seem to be caused by the parent who was not able to leave the relationship rather than by the perpetrator whose behaviour made the home unsafe for the child.

Domestic abuse is when one grown-up hurts another grown-up who is or was their partner, or who belongs to the same family. It can happen when people live together or in different houses. Usually (but not always) it is the man who hurts the woman, but both men and woman can abuse and be abused. Although domestic abuse happens between grown-ups, children can be affected by what they see and hear. This could include:

- *Physical abuse – hitting, pushing, kicking or strangling.*
- *Emotional abuse – saying things to frighten the other person or make them feel bad. This can happen face to face but also on the phone, on the internet or social media.*

- *Sexual abuse – making someone do sexual things or acts that they don't want to do.*
- *Financial abuse – like taking away the other person's money, not letting them get a job or spend their money on the things they want or need.*
- *Coercive control – controlling behaviour (like threats, humiliation or intimidation) that is meant to isolate someone, harm them, make them feel very afraid or punish them. This kind of behaviour can make someone feel like they're in prison or trapped because their everyday life has been taken over. They might not be able to choose where to go, what to wear, where to sleep, or who they can meet or speak to.*

Adults sometimes think that children aren't really affected if they don't see all the fighting. But this isn't true. Even if a child doesn't see the shouting or the hitting, they've probably heard it, or maybe they've seen their parent bruised or upset after an argument. They may sometimes get caught in the middle trying to make the violence stop or to protect a parent. They might even sometimes be forced to join in the hurting.

When grown-ups hit or hurt each other it is very frightening for anyone who is there. For children who might love both their parents (even if they don't like what is happening), they might be left feeling muddled up about what is wrong and right. It is wrong for a daddy to hit a mummy or a mummy to hit a daddy. Most grown-ups, mummies and daddies do not hurt each other like this.

Children might wonder why their parent didn't just leave to keep them all safe or ask for help. There are lots of reasons why this might not be possible, even if they really wanted to.

Insert whatever explanation is appropriate for the family context.

- *Sometimes people are terrified about what will happen if they leave. They might have been threatened with more violence towards them or their children if they tried to get away.*
- *An abuser will often try to control the person by cutting them off from contact with family and friends, money and transport, so it will feel impossible to escape.*
- *If a parent is offered help to leave, or to move away to a refuge or safe house, they can feel guilty for moving their children away from their other parent, their home, pets or school. It is normal to worry about leaving behind family and friends who have been supportive.*

- *Sometimes victim-survivors feel embarrassed or ashamed that they have experienced domestic abuse. They might worry that other people will find out, and that they will be treated differently as a result.*
- *Sometimes parents stay because they still love the person who hurts them. Perhaps there are times when their relationship is good and they are happy together, as well as tough times. Love can be a powerful reason why people don't feel they can leave, or why they leave and then go back again. The abuser might promise never to behave like this again.*
- *The abusive person might threaten to end their own life or hurt themself if the other parent leaves. They know this might make their partner feel guilty if they still care about them, so they will be more likely to stay* (adapted from Wiener *et al.* 2022).

Stories for children

How Are You Feeling Today Baby Bear? Exploring Big Feelings After Living in a Stormy Home by Jane Evans (2014) is a story written for children aged 2–6 who have lived with domestic abuse at home to begin to explore and name their feelings. Accompanied by notes for adults on how to use each page of the story to start conversations, it also features fun games and activities to help children to understand and express difficult emotions.

Mommy's Black Eye by William George Bentrim (2012) is a story for preschool children. The children in the story don't witness any violence; they just see the aftermath because their mummy has a black eye.

A Family that Fights by Sharon Chesler Bernstein (1991) explains the difference between family disagreements and family violence. The children depicted in the book show emotions that children reading can easily identify with, like embarrassment, fear and helplessness.

Hear My Roar: A Story of Family Violence by Gillian Watts (2009) tells a story of family violence. A family of bears experiences good times and bad times, often very close together. Alcohol plays a part in the depression and anger of the father, and eventually the mother and child seek help from the family doctor.

8

ENDINGS AND LOOKING TO THE FUTURE

In any work with children who have a history of disruption, fragmentation and unplanned endings, it is imperative that we start planning for the ending from the beginning of the work: 'Beginnings are somehow different, and often full of anticipation and hope. Endings, in contrast, may bring feelings of loss and emptiness' (Mitchell 2018). This starts with clarity within the working agreement about how many sessions we will have together, but also features in our own planning and reviewing process, so the work doesn't drift aimlessly. This includes reflection in supervision but also in consultation with the parent or carer. Ending is a phase of life story work like any other. It should help the child prepare to build on what they have learned and move forward positively.

However, it is highly likely when supporting an adopted or care-experienced child with their life story that they will have experienced complex feelings in relation to previous endings. Many of those endings may have been thoughtless, unplanned or unwanted by the child. Leaving their birth family or previous foster placements may have been traumatic, terrifying or chaotic. There may have been a lack of co-regulation or meaningful explanation. Therefore 'endings, changes, goodbyes and new beginnings can evoke a range of feelings, including resurfacing and re-triggering past experiences of rejection, sadness, being disposed of, being let down, being insecure, deprivation, abandonment, pain, grief, and/or loss of a meaningful relationship' (Treisman, 2017a, p.387).

We have a responsibility in our work therefore to try to re-write the ending script and offer the child an opportunity to experience a 'good goodbye'. To achieve this, we must acknowledge that the ending of a relationship that felt important can be painful – and not just for the child!

But endings can also 'be reparative, hopeful, healing even. Our past is unalterable, our history and relationships may have been destructive, painful and might always carry some anguish for us. However, we can empower ourselves to have a different future and outcome' (Mitchell 2018). Ending life story work is a beautiful opportunity to celebrate the road you've travelled together and to connect with the child's hopes and dreams for the future.

I often find when working with older adolescents and with young people approaching leaving care age that the implications around endings and transitions are amplified. There may be multiple changes and losses on the horizon. They might need to move when they reach the age of 16 or 18. They will be leaving high school or college. They may lose their social worker as they transfer to the leaving care team. They are also grappling with the transition from childhood to adulthood that all adolescents must face, but often without a truly secure base. As we support young people through these transitions it can feel as if the work we do mirrors work around loss, grief and bereavement. The mourning process is about integrating a loss into their life story. Rather than letting go, we are supporting young people to connect with their story differently at this stage in their lives, hopeful they can then go on to create a new connection with what has been lost, but also look to the future with more optimism. It can take a long time for young people to allow the pain they feel about core losses to be expressed, and it is rare in adolescence to find space to address the grief they may hold about those core losses. It is hard to express tangled, complex emotions if the world is shifting under your feet and you feel unsafe or uncontained.

It may also be that adolescents hold fiercely onto positive fantasies about their birth for a long time. This is functional – a safety device if the young person doesn't feel strong and supported enough to face the reality and experience of pain of loss. This denial can also be motivated by loyalty – they may still depend on birth parents and feel drawn to returning home at 18. So many care-experienced young adults talk about feeling as if they drop off a cliff in relation to support services when they reach adulthood, so it is inevitable that birth family connections might exert a strong pull. If they haven't had sufficient support or opportunity to grieve their history, they may not have acquired the proper 'tools' for dealing with feelings of loss. This often means that it's difficult to make room for new losses. Every time they experience a new loss, it is hard to know what they are mourning, because those earlier feelings of loss are triggered: 'New pain about the loss often comes to the surface again (piece by piece) in a new developmental phase' (Wolfs 2015, p.43).

There are many things to think about in planning for the ending with any child or young person, but remember above all that it is a process, and not an event:

1. Clarity about how many sessions are needed, and how many remain. For many children, verbal reminders are not sufficient. With at least six sessions to go, you should be supporting a transparent countdown using a calendar, visual timetable or verbal prompts at the end of each session about how many are remaining. You could create a simple session tracker or chart, like the one shown. The child can colour in the images or choose a sticker each week, as the session is complete.

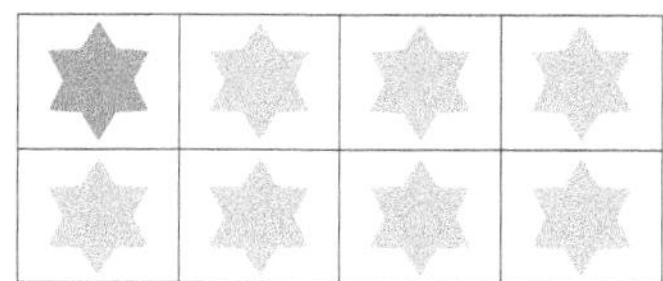

2. Collaborate with the child about what the ending will look like, so they have an element of control. In effect I have two endings – the end of the direct work and then the sharing of the book – which feels like it softens the end of the life story work.

3. Give enough time and space for feelings of rage, sadness, frustration or disappointment as the ending approaches. It's important these tricky feelings are validated, but also that there is time to repair the relationship after they've been expressed. Offer different ways – not simply verbal – for these feelings to be shared. You could think about a Feelings Wheel or Pie or a Bag of Feelings. Or you could simply encourage the child to draw their head and show you what it looks like inside when they think about ending. Similarly print a blank jigsaw puzzle and have them draw their feelings on the puzzle pieces. This is a good time to draw on the child's toolkit of strategies for self- and co-regulation you will have worked on throughout the work, and to remind them of transitions and endings they may have previously managed well.

4. Don't be surprised if children, even those who have attended regularly, miss a session or two as the ending approaches. This may be their way of managing their feelings about saying goodbye, or a strategy to keep in control of the ending. It's also a great way to show you they're cross with you without actually having to say anything.

5. Sometimes a new issue will arise as you approach the ending – occasionally this will be coincidental, but it can also be an attempt to extend the work and delay saying goodbye. In most cases it will be sufficient to remind the child and their parent or carer of the toolkit of strategies they've developed to manage challenges and hold your boundary.

6. Think about how you'll manage your own feelings about the ending, particularly in relation to your personal experiences around loss and how you will support the parent or carer and the child. Similar feelings can be triggered in us as in the child, and this can impact and shape the ending process. It can be helpful to reflect on whether you have a pattern of relating in terms of responding to endings, to change or transitions. Do you have any worries or fears about the work ending? If so, how will you address them?

7. Consider together how you will celebrate the life story journey you have taken together. I usually incorporate a review of the artwork made in the direct work because this helps the child and I to reflect on the process, but also allows us to decide which pieces should be included in the book, what they'd like to take home and whether there are things they'd like to leave with me or dispose of.

8. Think about whether it is appropriate to exchange gifts or do something different to what you might usually do in the final session. Depending on your training, you may have differing views. I sometimes offer the option of making a gift for each other in the final session or two – we paint a pebble or decorate a handmade clay tile to exchange, for example. Or we might create a memory bracelet or keychain together. You can use letter beads to spell out meaningful words or phrases that resonate (such as fearless, hero or hope), or use different-coloured beads to represent different memories you have worked on together. You can each make the

same bracelet and then exchange them at the end. This serves as a transitional object and longer-term tangible reminder of the process and the relationship. Sometimes I also make a certificate for younger children to mark that they have completed life story work (and that I'm very proud of them!).

9. If the child would like to mark the ending with a cake, for example, or a little tea party, I would facilitate this within the usual space in which we meet rather than going somewhere new or different. This is because there is safety in sameness, and you won't necessarily be able to anticipate the child's emotional response to saying goodbye. This is best managed in a safe, familiar space and not in a busy McDonalds.

10. How are you going to share the life story book? Will that be in the final direct work session, or will it come later? My preference is for later – it would be unusual for me to have completed the book before the final session, and for it to have already gone through a robust quality assurance process.

11. Where and when are you going to re-score the goals you set at the beginning of the process (see pp.69–71)? This will depend on who has set them, but it's an opportunity to review the life story work process, looking at what worked and what's still to be gained in the future. Hopefully, you will have supported the child to give some shape and meaning to their life. They will have 'a *coherent narrative* that makes sense and which leaves them with a view of themselves and their history that can be reflected on without being overwhelmed or having to defend against thinking about the past' (Schofield and Beek 2018, p.355; original emphasis).

12. How are you going to encourage parents or carers to continue with the work after you've gone? With younger children in particular, 'it is necessary to check back to the child weeks and months after issues have been raised to see how the child is storing that information *now* and the meaning it has *now*' (Schofield and Beek 2018, p.356; original emphasis). It's hard to think of life story work in terms of resolution as we all continue to make new meanings as we grow, including into adulthood. We can never scrub experiences from our hearts and minds, but we can work towards managing

the feelings about those experiences and about ourselves without being overwhelmed or denying them.

WHAT IF A GOOD GOODBYE ISN'T POSSIBLE?

Sometimes, despite your best efforts, planning and preparation, your ending may not be neat. Sometimes, people who have never experienced a good goodbye before will actively avoid the ending and refuse to come. You might get an email, text or no communication at all. Requests to have an ending session might be ignored or refused: 'Ending a healthy therapeutic relationship might be a way for a client to seize back the dangerous feelings of powerlessness and fear of betrayal that a trusting relationship can bring' (Mitchell 2018). When the ending is approaching it may feel easier to disengage as quickly as they can – the driver can be a sense that they are going to be rejected by you and will therefore get out first. It's about survival, and may feel more comfortable than risking familiar loss and hurt again.

Don't give up too quickly on facilitating an ending even where there are challenges. However, if a formal ending proves impossible, I will always send a card and/or a letter, and in this I will reflect on the process. I will express my sadness that we weren't able to say goodbye, but also my acceptance of their choice to end differently. I will suggest alternative arrangements for sharing the life story book if appropriate:

> Cards can be read over and over again, and you can write a reflective message as well as positive encouragement. Cards are tangible and you can choose one with a subject that you know the person/family is interested in or one that has a meaning connected with the work you have done together. (Tait and Wosu 2015, p.201)

This sends a powerful message of having been held in mind by you.

> As a student social worker, I worked with an 11-year-old on a child protection plan doing some work around feelings in school over about six to eight weeks. This was a child who didn't get a lot of validation, praise or encouragement at home. They had enjoyed this 'special time' where they had been the focus of someone's undivided attention and been able to make some artwork together. At the end of my placement, I went to collect them from home (it was the school holidays). We had

> planned to share some cake and have a walk in the local park. But no one answered the door. I knocked and knocked. I rang the parents. I went and sat for a while in my car in case they were late coming home. That was when I spotted a little face at an upstairs window. I knocked again but still they didn't answer the door. I think saying goodbye to something that had been meaningful, albeit brief, had felt too hard. After trying and failing to rearrange with their parents I sent a card, saying how much I had enjoyed meeting with them, how much I would miss our sessions and what I hoped for them in the future.

IDEAS FOR ACTIVITIES AROUND ENDINGS AND LOOKING TO THE FUTURE

END OF THERAPY LETTER

A letter from the practitioner to the child or young person doesn't have to be limited to when an ending session isn't possible. When life story work ends, it can be helpful to write a letter to remind the child of the journey they have been on, the progress they have made towards understanding their story, together with a reminder of their successes. You might thank the child for the opportunity to have worked together and to get to know each other. You can reflect on the life story journey, both the successes and the challenges. Describe how knowing this child has mattered to you – what you've learned from them or enjoyed doing together. If there have been routines or rituals established, comment on those, and similarly on any funny anecdotes or stories that are special to this child.

WHAT WILL I TAKE WITH ME?

Make an image, collage or list to represent the tools, skills and knowledge the child has gained through the work. Ideas for prompts might include:

- strategies for managing big feelings
- positive affirmations
- reasons to be positive and hopeful
- goals met
- increased understanding of the child's story
- understanding the impact of trauma.

GIFT EXERCISE

Write down or draw something that each person in the session has given you – parent or carer, practitioner and child. Perhaps they made you laugh, gave you hope, helped you understand your own story, brought great biscuits. Below each description, describe an imaginary gift you would give each person – this could be a superpower, an endless supply of pick 'n' mix or a magic mirror to see their true qualities revealed.

A GOODBYE POSTCARD

You and the child each take a blank postcard and on the front draw an image for the recipient. On the back, write a brief message to say goodbye, reflecting on the time you have spent together – if this activity involves a practitioner, parent or carer and child, each has three postcards to write to each other. Remind them of a funny story, of something important you want them to take away from the work, or of the positive impact knowing them has had on you.

TREE OF LIFE

Shotten (2020, pp.47–58) uses this activity in her session-by-session guide to life story work. The idea is that parts of the tree represent different aspects of a child's life. As such I find it a useful tool towards the end of therapy, both to reflect on the journey, but also to look to the future. You can prepare a tree template or draw a simple tree together. Give the child the choice of whether they would like to draw or not.

On the *trunk* draw or write the strengths the child sees in themself, but the child's parent or carer and practitioner could contribute too.

On the *branches* draw or write the child's hopes and dreams to support looking to the future with some optimism, as well as the freedom to aim high and choose things that might even seem impossible just now.

On the *leaves* draw or write people who are most important to the child. Explore the 'why'...do they have fun together? What would this person think to know they were one of the child's leaves?

On the *fruit* draw or write the gifts others have given the child – not just tangible gifts, but also encouragement, love or hope, for example. Explore why the child thinks others gave them this gift. Why did they deserve it?

On the *roots* draw or write the people who have been most influential from the past. Who taught the child the most? What did they learn from them?

On the *ground* draw or write the things the child loves to do. What do they enjoy most? How often do they get the chance to do this?

Throughout the activity, which can be done across a few sessions, use curious questions to expand the depth of the stories.

TEAM OF LIFE

This activity is great for any young person with a love of team sports, having originally been developed for Sudanese children who loved football (Denborough 2008, 2018). Again, it is an activity that could traverse several sessions. This is a great activity for older adolescents, especially those approaching leaving care age and who have a limited support network.

First, identify the things the young person loves about the sport – who introduced them to it? What do they like the most about it? How long have they been playing/watching the sport?

I asked my daughter why she loves Manchester City, and she said:

Then think together about favourite players – why choose them? Is it their speed, skill, humour, loyalty to the club, goals scored? This can lead to discussions about whether these are things that feel important in other areas of the young person's life. How do they know these things are important?

Then, in the second part of the activity, support the young person to identify who is in their Team of Life. Using the following prompts, ask the young person draw it out using a football or hockey pitch, basketball or netball court, etc.

- 'Think about the team members – people who are current members, previous members who have had an influence – even people you'd like to be in the team.'
- 'Goalkeeper – who is the keeper? Who looks after you, stops shots hitting you? Who can you rely on to protect you?'
- 'Defence – who else helps you achieve your hopes and dreams and protects what is most important to you? If you feel under attack, who will take your corner and stand up for you?'
- 'Attack – who helps you to achieve? Who inspires you to take on a challenge? Who supports you most to achieve your hopes and dreams?'
- 'Other teammates – who do you like to spend time with, and why?'
- 'Coach – you can have more than one who you learn from, are inspired by and lean on when times are tough.'
- 'Interchange – are some people a bit hit and miss or unreliable? Do they sometimes look like or pretend to be in your team, but then go missing? Are some people working against you?'
- 'Stadium – where is your home ground? Where do you feel most at home? You could name several places.'
- 'Team song – do you have a theme tune or a song that means a lot to you?'
- 'People watching – who are your supporters? Who wishes you well?'
- 'Goals – one goal you've achieved over the last year – how long did it take you to reach it? What help did you get from your team?'
- 'Training – how did you prepare to achieve your goal? Where did you train? Who with? Who encouraged you with helpful tactics?'
- 'Celebration – how does your team celebrate success? How did you celebrate when you achieved your goal? Who with?'

- 'Future goals – what is your next target? How are you training to achieve the goal? Who will help you out?'

The third stage is to think about challenges or difficulties. Think about areas where the child needed to improve in their chosen sport. How did they approach this problem? Did teammates help? What skills did they need? What tips would they give a player in a similar situation? Stress the idea that if you have a good team around you, obstacles can more easily be overcome. Just like in a game of football, there will be problems to overcome – an injury, a dodgy VAR decision or a sending off. Explore some of the obstacles that might make it harder to achieve goals and, where possible, relate the discussion more directly to challenges the young person has faced in their life.

THE WELCOME MAT

We described this exercise in our first book, but it's such a favourite it's worth repeating here (Wrench and Naylor 2013, pp.96–97). Suggest that the child creates a Welcome Mat, like the one at the front door. They can draw or write things they'd like to have in their future home – this could be people, pets or material belongings, but can also be more abstract ideas, like happiness, safety or financial security. You can offer the alternative of finding images in a selection of magazines to add to the image or offering a selection of objects to make a Welcome Mat Sculpt (see pp.106–107). For example, one young adult selected a purse to represent their financial security and desire to provide for their family to live comfortably and a tiger to represent the courage and bravery they would take forward into their life in the future.

> A seven-year-old drew a chocolate fountain, a bike, a big garden with a football net and lots of footballs, their big sister and a house where their foster carers were living next door.
>
> A 15-year-old drew the stew and dumplings their carer used to make, a guard dog, PlayStation and multiple boxes of Nike trainers. And love.

9

LIFE STORY MATERIALS

The process of undertaking life story work is incredibly important, but it is equally essential for children and young people to have a lasting record, which, where possible, also integrates their perspective, memories and understanding. This can subsequently be used to help the child or young person to share their story with others, or as a tool for parents or carers to think about and talk with their child about their history when the time is right. As such, it is critical that the child (where they are old enough to contribute) and their parent or carer feels that the resources you provide are fit for purpose.

Life story materials can take many forms, from memory boxes brimming with celebratory swimming certificates and event tickets, to photo albums and scrapbooks documenting a child's journey, to later life letters and metaphorical or parallel stories. However, the most common format is the life story book, written for babies and young children usually when placed for adoption or special guardianship, or after undertaking a piece of life story work with an older child. Children ideally benefit from access to a range of these materials because, as Baynes (2008, p.45) commented, 'a pile of messy drawings may represent a piece of high quality, deeply personal work with a child, while a beautifully presented book may have little meaning for the child concerned.' Whatever the content of the life story materials, the quality and nature of those resources should not be dependent on which professional gathers them together, their time or expertise. The story belongs to the child, and should be honoured.

THE LIFE STORY BOOK

The purpose

A life story book is a legal requirement for adopted children, and is considered good practice for children in care and special guardianship arrangements. A thoughtful and sensitively written life story book is essential for children who are not being brought up with their birth family, naturally surrounded by their history. These children do not have the luxury of seeing who they are and where they come from reflected daily through family relationships. A life story book can therefore offer parents or carers an invaluable tool to begin to open the door to communication about the child's birth family and journey to care, to ultimately create a coherent narrative account of their life. Without the support of this 'tool', it is more likely that parents or carers will be reluctant to share information about the past with their child; they may not be able to find the words or may worry about making things worse and causing upset by talking about traumatic losses or experiences.

When preparing life story books for adopted children, children in care or in special guardianship, it is also imperative that we do not allow their history to overshadow the present and deny their opportunities for the future. It is important to get the balance right in allowing these stories to bridge the past and the present. The child's early history is critical to understanding the 'why' of guardianship, fostering or adoption, but should be safely 'contained' and held by the current parents or carers. For this reason, it is critical that there is a significant focus on the present in the story and on offering the child a glimpse into a positive and hopeful future life. For this to happen you must involve adoptive parents and carers in the construction of the book, even where children are newly placed.

The book is a tool or resource to be used by adoptive parents or carers to support their child to develop a sense of identity and an understanding of their story when needed. It should give details of the child's journey to care, and explain why they could not live safely with their birth parents. It should support the child to share their past with their adopters/carers and others by offering a realistic account of early events and dispelling any fantasies or misunderstandings about their birth family, while also acknowledging and giving space to the significant separations and losses the child has lived through. Although the life story book is often the culmination of life story work, or in adoption is the starting point (ideally being delivered shortly after the adoption order is granted), life story work is a lifelong process, never at an end.

Constructing the life story book

Pulling a child's story together can be a daunting task. I find that after completing a lengthy piece of life story work with a child, I have so much rich material that it can feel like an impossible challenge to organise such meaningful work into a coherent narrative. What do you leave out? How do you ensure that you honour the process and the child's journey without overwhelming them? I want the story to be something the child can pick up and carry with them – a neat backpack, rather than an unwieldy burden. It is the job of the lead practitioner or therapist to write the story, and in my experience this can take up to 20 hours to do well.

I hear of practitioners tasked with writing stories for babies and toddlers they have never met, often within ludicrously tight time frames as soon as a plan for adoption is ratified or with the expectation that the book is complete at the point of placement. This makes my heart sink because it allows no opportunity for stories about the child's life with their adoptive parents or special guardians to be integrated into the book at all. When the child is old enough to have the story shared with them, they will see no evidence of the life they are living and of the family they are now part of reflected in the story. As Rees (2017) says, this is simply not a very family-friendly approach *and* runs counter to guidance, which unequivocally states that the completed life story book does not have to be shared with the family until, at the latest, 10 days after the making of the adoption order. Practice like this undoubtedly prioritises the needs of the organisation above the needs of the child, and is inexcusable. Please challenge it if this is something you are asked to do. There is absolutely no reason why the story cannot be shared in two parts – share the child's early history at the point of placement, but then complete the book when they have settled into their family.

The format

All children are unique, and no two books should look identical, but there are undoubtedly some basic premises to follow when constructing the story:

- Write in a child-friendly style, free of social work jargon. It should be a book that a child is not afraid to read or look at.

- Think about the child's developmental age, and ensure that what you write is accessible for them.

- Make certain that the book is colourful, inviting and engaging, including scanned photographs of the child and their family as well as illustrations of any direct work you have completed. At the end of a piece of direct work I like to review the work we have created together, both in 2D and 3D, and decide together with the child which pieces they would like to include in the story, which they'd like to take home and which they'd like me to keep or dispose of. Including photographic evidence of direct work activities can help to synthesise the process and the product in a much more meaningful way, and supports the development of a coherent narrative account of the child's journey. If objects are too big or messy to take home, I take photographs for an album instead.

- Think about the format. I write the story as a Microsoft PowerPoint presentation. This has the benefit of being able to use Design features to bring the story to life and to make it look more engaging, but it is also simple to adapt the layout and to add images. Using the Slide Sorter feature you can also play about with the structure of the story, adding new pages or slides or rearranging the order with ease. Alternatives include using Microsoft Publisher or Canva, a free-to-use online graphic design tool that has thousands of templates to inspire you.[1]

- Avoid too much embellishment. Scrapbooks that are decorated with hearts, flowers and glitter can look incongruous in relation to the traumatic material they contain. Repeat motifs like Disney princesses or Paw Patrol have a very short shelf life, and the book will soon become outdated and irrelevant to the child as they age. Glued-in photographs soon fall off.

- It can be helpful if the record of the life story work is presented in such a way that the child can choose which parts they would be happy to share with people in different contexts and, where appropriate, parents or carers can edit the information, so that it is relevant to the child's age and developmental stage. The

1 www.canva.com/en_gb

importance of flexibility was a key message from research with adoptive parents, who emphasised that the child's life story book needed to change with the child as they grew (Watson, Latter and Bellew 2015). Therefore, do not hard bind the story because this makes it impossible for the family to add new stories or to edit what can be shown to whom and when. You might be tempted to laminate the pages, but this can make the book very heavy. I prefer to use a ring binder with A4 clear punch pockets to contain the pages. Don't forget to number them.

- Add extra blank pages and punch pockets at the end as an invitation to the child and family to continue to add to the story over time.
- Write the book in the third person, using the child's first name, rather than writing it more like a letter, addressed to the child, or even writing it in the first person as if you are the child. Although I appreciate there is a drive in some areas to write care records *to* the child, I believe that in relation to life story work, this represents a more effective and gentler way of sharing difficult information, especially for a young child. Rees (2017, p.50) also suggests it facilitates 'gentle or playful conjecture with regard to the child's emotions. "I expect John may have felt..." rather than writing in the first person. This allows for further discussion between the child and parent. The child can either identify with or reject the suggested feeling.'
- Remember that the book is the child's life story, and not their birth parents'. While acknowledging the challenges, the sadness and the losses, the book should also be a celebration of the child's life. It should leave the child with a positive sense of who they are, highlighting any threads of positive connection with birth family members, and reinforcing the sense of permanence and connection they hold now, with hope for the future. We do not want children to read the story and feel burdened by the birth parents' history, or to become preoccupied with fears or worries for their wellbeing that prevent them from embracing life as it is now.
- Be mindful of your ongoing duty of care to the child when considering how much information to share. You will be balancing identity needs with the need for protection. With the rise of social media, many adoption agencies and local authorities are now exercising

extreme caution in relation to the inclusion of identifying information about birth family members in life story books. Full details are therefore either included in a later life letter or shared with adopters/carers to disclose at their discretion. It is preferable for a young person to learn about their birth family with adoptive parents or carers available to provide guidance, support and protection where required, rather than searching for answers independently on the internet, based on information included in a life story book.

The structure

Historically, stories have been written starting with the child's birth, moving chronologically through their life, and ending with foster or adoptive family stories. However, starting the story with birth parents and the story of the child's journey to care can feel overwhelming for children, so Joy Rees, who was an adoption social worker before her retirement, developed a more family-friendly approach, which has subsequently been adopted by many local authorities across the UK (Rees 2017). The child is invited into the story by first reading about themself in the here and now. This should support them to feel safer, more contained and grounded in the present as a starting point, and from this position, the parent or carer can support the child to go back and begin to make sense of their story (adapted from Rees 2017, p.40).

Present	Past	Present	Future
Fun, grounding information about the child in the here and now. School, pets, parents or carers, friendships, home, holidays, etc.	Back to the child's birth (or before, if there are older siblings). Tell an honest, simple story of life with the birth family, stressing the child was not responsible for their losses.	Bring the child back to the present and family life now. Perhaps mention family rituals and routines – reinforce the child in safe care and love.	The child's plans, hopes and aspirations. End on a positive note and by reminding the child that wherever they go and whatever they do they will always be loved by and part of their family.

Ideally, as well as following this simple structure, you will also organise the contents of the story. The book can be divided into brief chapters, which makes it easier for parents or carers to share the story in more digestible chunks with their child. Children can also choose which parts to read when they are old enough to. Given that the story is written in a developmentally appropriate way, it will not always contain all the details of what happened, but it needs to give children a sufficient platform to ask more questions as they grow older.

The structure of a story for a baby or young child who is to be adopted or subject to a special guardianship order or for an older adoptee or child in care or special guardianship is the same, but clearly the content will differ. I appreciate that when you are writing a story, especially for a young child, it may feel that you have one shot at this, and you therefore want to include as much information as you can. But there is an inherent danger in this approach. By including too much detail into a book for a child of any age, it can become too much for them to 'carry', integrate or comprehend. I always find it useful to think about fiction stories a child of the same developmental age and stage would be reading. How many words and how many pictures would there be? What language is used? How complex is it to understand? Then apply this knowledge to writing your life story book.

When you are writing a story for an older child, you will also integrate the work you have done together, and the process must be reflected in the product. You should also be able to incorporate the child's memories, perspective and feelings about the story, as explored in the life story work. Encourage the child to decide what they'd like to call the book, to choose the folder or to decorate it. They can decide how they want the front page to look, perhaps drawing a self-portrait or choosing a favourite photograph of themself or with their family. They might even like to write a brief introduction to their story. For example:

> My name is Charlie and this is a story all about me! I've had some help from my mum and Katie to understand what has happened in my life and it's all written right here. Some things I'd remembered but lots of things happened when I was a baby, and I needed a bit of help with remembering those bits. So, this is my life so far!

Present

1. Introduction to the child, their home and the family in which they are now living

This section should be a celebratory 'All about me' reflection of who the child is now, anchored in the present. You can integrate any work you have done together that celebrates their life, achievements, strengths and resilience. Include a general description of the child and photographs of them and their foster or adoptive family or special guardian. Describe the child with warmth and admiration. Focus on their qualities, also including comments from their carers or adopters. It is important that when they finish reading this part of the story, they are left feeling good about themself.

You might also introduce the idea of families and how different families come together at this stage – for example, some are born into their family, some are fostered, some adopted, and others live with extended family members or special guardians.

Past

As a bridge between the present and the past, I write:

> But it wasn't always this way and to find out why, we need to go right back to the beginning of this story to the day [insert child's name] was born. Let's go!

If there is a context to the pregnancy and birth or the birth parents' relationship that is relevant to the child becoming looked after, then you would write '...we need to go back to the beginning of this story, before [insert child's name] was even born'. Do the same if the child has older siblings to explain the environment into which the child was born.

2. The beginning

Begin with the basics around the child's birth if you have them – their date and time of birth, information about the pregnancy, labour and delivery, place of birth, who was present, due date, etc. How did the birth parents share the news of the birth with friends and family? How was the birth celebrated? It is so important, wherever possible, to share as many anecdotes about the story of their birth as we can. If there isn't much information available, we can assume that like all babies, this baby was born a 'gorgeous, lovely, adorable, loveable' little bundle (Rees 2017, p.45).

If known, include the reason why they were given their birth forenames. Who chose them? Were there other names on the shortlist? Was the child named after anyone, and if so who, and why? Even if the name was simply chosen because their birth parents liked it or it was the name of a character from a favourite TV programme, this should be stated. Remember that this is the kind of information children would learn from asking their parents if they grew up within their family of origin.

Also introduce the birth parents here by saying that all babies have a birth mum and a birth dad. I go on to refer to them by their first name, or whichever name the adoptee uses or adopters plan to use. Where the child has been adopted I stick to first names and don't give dates of birth. Adoptive parents should have this information for later in the child permanence report, but, as previously mentioned, we don't want to encourage unsupported searching on social media. I usually write how old parents were when the child was born. If the child has ongoing contact with the birth family there is usually no issue with using full names, including dates of birth and where they were living at time of the child's birth. But be sure to check if there is any potential risk to the child of disclosing this information. Also confirm how they refer to their parents – 'mam', 'mummy', 'mama', etc., and be consistent with this.

Again, the level of detail you go into about the birth parents here will vary – some information will be better saved for the later life letter – but at the very least include some descriptive and personal information about their physical appearance, self-perception and how they were viewed by other people. If there are shared talents, interests, personality traits or physical characteristics between the child and a birth parent, this is where to highlight these threads of positive connection. Add a couple of photographs of the parents, preferably with the child if you have them, unless they have been responsible for abuse so distressing that it might be re-traumatising for the child to include them.

I always remember that this is the child's life story book, so I don't want to over-fill it with too much information about the birth parents' own childhood and adolescence, education and employment history and life now. However, I'm also mindful that when links are severed there may not be another opportunity to share this information with the child. Some will show a great deal of interest and some very little at all, so you will need to make your decision on a case-by-case basis. The most important thing is to ensure that this important information is recorded somewhere. This might be in documents shared with adopters. It might be in the later life letter, or in an addendum to the life story book. Above all, do not allow this detail to overwhelm or dominate the story. Lengthy accounts about their birth parents' difficult childhood experiences, for example, and detailed explanations of why they were not able to give this child, or any child, safe love, are not necessary. A brief explanation will suffice, and you can use the prompts in Chapter 7 to help you with this.

You could include:

Childhood:

- education
- what they liked/disliked about school
- where they lived and who with
- happiest memories
- celebrations and holidays
- family rules or values
- cultural or religious beliefs
- favourite toys/books/TV programmes
- health.

Teenage years and adulthood:

- employment
- relationships
- friends
- music and fashion
- hopes for the future
- significant changes in their life
- interests and leisure activities.

Life now:

- who they live with

- what they do day to day
- interests and hobbies
- friendships
- relationships with family
- health and medical history
- achievements
- hopes for the future
- positive life changes (adapted from Nicholls 2005, pp.109–111).

You will also want to give information about maternal and paternal extended family members. You could illustrate this with a family tree, isolating a particular section of the tree from the rest of the structure to expand the detail. It is important for children to be told about their ancestry and family stories passed down through the generations, no matter how fantastical they may seem to you. They are the threads that bind families together within a shared identity.

Next I write about the birth parents' relationship. This might include:

- where they met and what they remember about the day
- what they liked about each other at first
- whether they ever lived together
- what they enjoyed doing together as a couple.

Where the couple relationship was or is negative, or where children are conceived through rape or incest, this can be discussed here (see also Chapter 7). Children need to know how they came to be born. The level of detail you include will depend on the child's level of understanding. Even very young children can understand that a relationship might not be happy or safe. You might need to talk about arguments, violence or addiction.

There should then be an honest, compassionate account of the child's journey to care. You will need to give a basic account of the decisions made by the social workers, police, the judge, etc., but you really do *not* need to list all the various child protection conferences and strategy meetings and give specific dates. For younger children this can be simply too confusing and detract from their understanding of their story. Rather than giving specific dates, I find that referring to the child's age at the time of the event is more meaningful – for example, 'When you were seven months old, your birth parents decided to separate because they were finding it so hard to get along.'

For an older child you will be able to give a more comprehensive account of the decisions made, but there must never be anything included in the book that you have not already explored and thought about together during the work. There should be no surprises and no major omissions, unless you have a good reason for this. It may be that there is information that, as a systemic network, you collectively decided not to share at this time, or the child decided they had done enough work before you had the opportunity to share it. In these instances, ensure that the parent or carer has been given the relevant information to share at a later point. On occasion I have written this as a short addendum to the book, or a letter to be shared with the child when appropriate. Remember that the child should also have a later life letter, which can offer more detailed information as they grow or begin to need or ask for more detail. The book is intended to be just the basic tool – information on which the parents or carers can build, at the child's pace.

3. Living with [insert foster carer's name]

Add information about short-term foster carers, and if the child has had more than one placement, explain each move. If you have made a moving calendar with the child, you could add this here. You need to talk about who else was living in the family, what they enjoyed doing together and who were frequent visitors. Where possible, integrate stories and memories directly from the carer that have depth to them. Include photographs of the carer, their house and garden, and the child's bedroom, if you have them. Again, this doesn't need excessive detail because hopefully there will also be a beautiful photo album and memory box from the foster carers that is a record of their life together.

4. The adoptive/special guardian's/long-term foster family [insert the surname] [delete where appropriate]

Older children might want to hear information about how adopters are chosen and prepared for adoption, or how long-term fostering matches are made, but this doesn't need extensive description within the text. You can add more if necessary in the later life letter.

In this chapter bring the child back to their current family. Describe meeting adopters/special guardians/foster carers and moving to their current home, with acknowledgement of how such a big change can bring many big feelings, especially as they are getting to know each other and becoming a family. You might mention all the different sights, sounds, smells, food and sensations to get used to, as well as a new bedroom. It's okay to write about the adults' excitement and joy, but also acknowledge the child's possible ambivalence and anxiety.

If adopters or foster carers have met birth parents before or after the child is placed, this can be included here. There may be a photograph of the meeting, in which case you can add that too. If either party was able to identify positive attributes in the other, then please mention that as well. It can help convey a powerful message to the child of acceptance on both sides.

5. Meeting the judge

This section covers going to court, applying for the adoption, care or special guardianship order, and what this means for the child. When exploring legal decision making it is important to stress that everyone had the chance to have their say, including the birth parents. Make it clear that decisions about residence and contact, whether direct or indirect, are adult decisions.

The decision about where the child should live and with whom took the judge a long time to make. That was because the decision was a very important one – important enough to really take time to understand what had happened and agree what the next best steps should be. If decisions are made about the nature of future contact with the birth family or to make different care plans for siblings, this will also need explanation. If you include details about family time, then you could add a few photographs with siblings or other birth relatives in the book.

In adoption you can also give details of the 'adoption celebration day', include any comments the judge made, and add photographs that show how the family celebrated the occasion.

Present

6. More about [insert child's name]

Bring the child back to the present and family life now. Perhaps mention rituals and routines that are unique to the family. How are religious festivals or birthdays celebrated? What are the child's favourite things to do? I often write about how well the parents know their child...so, for example, for a toddler you might write: 'They know John's favourite snack is peeled grapes. They know how he loves flying as high as he can on the swing at Harold Park. They also know he loves a super-tight squeezy hug.' For an older child it could be: 'They know Clare's favourite food is Chinese – she will keep going back to the buffet for more noodles. They know she is amazing on the monkey bars... So determined! They also know she is a super friend – loyal, kind and great at telling awful jokes!'

Future

7. The child's plans, hopes and aspirations, or their parents' or carers' hopes if the child is too young to contribute this

It is important to end on a positive note, by reminding the child that wherever they go and whatever they do they will always be loved by and be part of their family. Include the child's plans, hopes and aspirations for the future, and their parents' or carers' hopes where possible. This can be as lofty as high career aspirations or as simple as wanting to start swimming lessons when they're six.

I add some more photographs and stories at this point from the last year or so (less if the adoption order was granted more quickly) with the carer/adoptive parents, and might project forwards to consider family plans in the longer term, to reinforce to the child that their future is with this family. So this might be about plans for Christmas or a holiday next summer, for example, but gives a clear and hopeful message about permanence wherever possible.

The child might also want to reflect on their thoughts and feelings about their story or about having done life story work. I often sum up with testimonies about the child from people who know and love them – family, friends, education or social work staff – as well as something from you about what it has meant to do this work together. There are times when it will be appropriate to include messages from the birth family here too. I always hope that in more difficult times it will be a lovely part of the story to come back to, that reminds a child of their worth.

QUALITY ASSURANCE

As you come to the end of this incredibly important work, consider who is going to quality assure the work. You might find it helpful to run through a quality assurance checklist such as this. I always ask a colleague who doesn't know the child or their story to read it first. They need to sense check it – is the story coherent, even if they don't hold any knowledge about the child? Sometimes what you know implicitly as the author of a story needs to be made explicit for the reader. Your colleague also needs to check for grammar and spelling errors; sometimes the more you read, the less you see, so this is really important in terms of showing you value the child and their family. Then finally they need to be alert to anything that is written in a way that will be hard for a child to understand – acronyms or social work terminology that will need to be translated to meet the child's needs.

Task	Details	Date completed
Is there evidence of family history information? Is this comprehensive, including the maternal and paternal family?		
Is there evidence that birth parents have been consulted in the creation of family history information?		
Is there evidence of a carefully labelled memory box? Annotated photographic record of the child's life?		
Have life story work materials (memory box, photo album, life story book, later life letter) been provided by the child's foster carer? Are these of good quality? Are they annotated or labelled adequately?		

cont.

Task	Details	Date completed
Is there evidence of life story information/a book? Is this age and developmentally appropriate, and does it answer the questions the child is likely to have? Has someone checked it for content, spelling and grammar?		
Does the life story book contain a coherent narrative account of the child's journey?		
Is there evidence of a later life letter? Is this of good quality?		
Is there evidence that prospective adopters or carers have been consulted regarding the child's life story materials, and that their views have been taken into consideration?		
Where appropriate, is there evidence the child has been able to contribute to the life story book, or been offered the opportunity to engage in direct work? If not, why not?		
Are the materials ready to share within legislative time frames?		
Is the child/their parent or carer satisfied with the content of the life story materials?		

Once this step is complete, I share the story with the child's parent or carer. I like them to have it for a week or so and have time to read and re-read where necessary before I check back in. There are several reasons for this. I want them to fact check. When I've done life story work with a child, I might be relying on notes I've written after the session to translate into the story. Occasionally I might make an error in recording. I might inadvertently spell a name incorrectly or muddle up a date or place. It is important that anything like this is picked up before the book is shared with the child. I also want to feel confident that I have captured the essence of the child and their family, and that their parent or carer feels the language I have used is appropriate. A really simple example of this is where I had used the word 'poorly' and the parent told me they say 'ill'. These are simple fixes, but important in terms of a collaborative approach.

The final reason for sharing the completed book with the parent or carer first is so that I can be satisfied they feel comfortable with the content and are able to reinforce any messages therein before they use it to support their child. If they do not feel the story is suitable for whatever reason, they are less likely to share the book in the future. It is always better to amend the story at this stage, acting on feedback, so that it can be a useful resource for the family, rather than discarded or stored in the loft, out of sight. That serves no one well.

SHARING THE BOOK WITH THE CHILD

If you have written a story for a baby or toddler, ultimately it will be up to their parent or carer to decide when and how they share it with their child. If you have written a story for an older child who has actively been involved in the life story work, I take about four weeks after the final session to complete the write-up. I aim to be constructing the story as we progress through the work, but always need more time to make the final additions and quality assure it before it is shared with the child and their family. Rose prefers to send the child about 10 pages of the story at a time for them to edit, so it is more of a collaboration and the child takes more ownership of the narrative (Rose 2012, p.157).

Whichever process you decide is right for the child, think about the following:

- *Where* you share the story – it needs to be a safe, familiar space for the child.
- *Who* will be present when you share the story?
- *Choices for the child.* Where would they like to sit? Between you and the parent or carer? Would they prefer to listen to the story during or after their snack? Would they like you to read it aloud or would they prefer to read themself? Would they like to turn the pages? Simple options like this can help a child to feel in control, important, and part of the process, which, in turn, helps them to feel more present, relaxed and focused.

- The *timing* is also important, because although there should be no surprises, it would be foolish to underestimate the impact of having the story read aloud to you. There must be time allowed for processing (if the child wishes to), so try to make sure the family is not having to rush off to collect another child from school or race to swimming lessons, for example. Take the time the child needs and take breaks if necessary.

- Think about *comfort* – do you need blankets for snuggling, bean-bags, fidgets or a special teddy? Make sure there is an offer of something to drink and a snack because we know how hard it can be to focus and take in information if your basic needs are not met. If a child feels relaxed and calm, they will be more likely to have the capacity to really listen to the story.

- Agree how the child will let you know if they need *a break*. The story does not have to be read all in one go. Some might like to just flick through quickly and look at the photographs of themselves. Some like to read the chapters that focus on the present and skip the tricky bits. This is a tool to be used for years to come. There is no rush.

Rose describes the child recipient as 'editor in chief' of their story (2012, p.157). While they are not responsible for writing the book, they do have the right to contribute to what goes in and stays out. This includes photographs of people and places, as well as any artwork created during the direct work. Some children might find particular images from the past distressing, and where this is the case, you can save them in a separate photo album or memory box. If there is written content they would like to be removed, carefully consider the request. Simple changes like adding or removing an image or updating likes and dislikes are easy to address. Sometimes, however, it might be that they don't like or agree with what you've written, but the story might not make sense without it being included. While Rose would go with the child's wishes, I would be more inclined to explore the request with the child to understand their perspective, but I wouldn't automatically permanently remove the content. The child still has the option of unclipping and temporarily removing that section and giving it to their parent or carer for safekeeping. This is only possible with a loose-leaf design and construction of the life story book.

I print two hard copies if possible – one for the child, and a spare to keep safe just in case. If possible it is always better to share a digital copy, too, that can be saved to the parent or carer's computer, which will make it much easier for them to update in the future as required.

WHEN CHILDREN DO NOT WANT TO LOOK AT THEIR LIFE STORY BOOK

Even when the history is explained very gently, for some children it is so difficult and triggering that this approach may still be too direct and painful. Do not force it. Parents or carers might need to put the book to one side for a while – focusing more on the present and developing a sense of permanency is perhaps needed, before the child is able to make sense of what has gone before.

There are also many children's story books about fostering and adoption that could be used to help children explore aspects of their own story in an indirect way that feels less threatening. For stories about adoption see *We Belong Together: A Book About Adoption and Families* (Parr 2008), *Dennis Duckling* (Sambrooks 2009) and *Delly Duck: Why A Little Chick Couldn't Stay with His Birth Mother* (Marlow 2021). There is a long tradition of storytelling for healing, and in life story work there is often value in using generic therapeutic stories before introducing the child's own life story book. I often use Sunderland's *Helping Children with Feelings* series, which is a set of therapeutic stories for children aged 4–12, each accompanied by a professional guidebook. Each guidebook focuses on a particular feeling, with exercises and ideas to help children think about, express and focus on that feeling to the point of resolution.

However, it can be even more powerful to create a narrative that connects directly with the child's lived experience: 'Young people often dissociate from the strong feelings that have accompanied their trauma experience. Intense fear and sadness are too much to experience for an extended period of time and so, commonly young people learn to endure the abuse or neglect, disconnected from their emotions' (Shotton 2020, p.148). A third-person narrative can provide safety to explore difficult material, with story and metaphor helping to connect their thoughts and feelings to memories. The story still belongs to someone else. Such stories can help children understand relationships, come to know their feelings, and learn about their inner worlds (Golding 2014; Hammel 2018; Kagan

2009; Sunderland 2000). The hope is that they will also develop empathy for themselves and others as they look in on the story from a different perspective.

METAPHORICAL OR PARALLEL STORIES

If you are thinking about writing a therapeutic story, consider the purpose of the story and what message you want the child to hear. Usually these stories will reflect a child's experience, while providing enough *distance* that they feel safe enough to explore the issues raised in them. It is also important that the child feels a connection towards the protagonist, because a primary aim of a therapeutic story is for the child to relate to and empathise with the character and their experiences. This helps them feel less alone with the issues they have faced, and supports the validation of their own feelings and experiences. The story may also offer the language a child needs to explore their own thoughts and feelings, which may have been inaccessible previously.

Therapeutic stories can be an incredibly effective tool because children naturally relate and connect to the language of image, metaphor and story, often more easily than to a conversation about the same subject. Where life experiences have been traumatic, stories can help provide a safe distance from the issue, which can support children to stay with any difficult feelings and thoughts long enough to begin to process them, work out what this means for them and eventually reframe the experience. They can also be a wonderful starting point to allow for further processing through art, play, mask or puppet work, if these ways of working fall within your skill set and expertise.

A therapeutic story can therefore have multiple functions:

- Supporting the child to connect with their inner world, including how they see themselves and others, and perceive the world around them.
- Focusing on the child's resilient qualities, strength of character and any key protective factors in the face of adversity.
- Promoting a more positive self-concept as well as shifting how the child experiences others, and the world around them.

I often use metaphorical stories in my work with younger children or with children who might, understandably, still be caught up in the emotional experience of their trauma. We wrote about these stories and gave an example in our first book about life story work (Wrench and Naylor 2013, pp.84–89) in relation to the power of stories in helping children explore difficult issues. Hearing about a little prince or pussy cat who has similar problems to you can be less distressing than talking about your own history directly. The use of metaphor allows for distance from the child's own painful experiences so that the feelings can be more easily and safely thought about and discussed within a unique story that speaks directly to the child's own circumstances, but uses other characters to represent them or their family. Do not give these characters the same names as the child or their family.

I create a simple story that is developmentally appropriate and resonates with the child's experience. I also curate a little story toy sack that contains the characters from the story, because this means that rather than simply reading the story to the child, I can play the story out with the child as witness. I leave the sack with the family, together with the story book, and in this way the child has permission to explore their history through story *and* play. The child has a book to come back to whenever needed and their parent or carer also has a resource to facilitate conversations. In my experience it is unusual for a child not to recognise the story as their own, but they may need to revisit the story repeatedly to begin to internalise it. By retelling the story through play, they might also shift their perspective. New meanings can emerge by viewing the situation differently, or by having the opportunity to gain some control over the narrative: 'As children engage and empathize with the characters and the story, they also connect with their inner conflicts, thus finding solutions that they probably wouldn't reach in other circumstances' (Golding 2014, p.30).

In constructing the story, think about whether the child has a particular interest you could incorporate, such as dinosaurs or farm animals. Then create a simple story that is developmentally appropriate to the child. I usually use photographs of the small toys or figures in the story sack to illustrate the story. Remember to reflect the feelings of the characters as you go along, or to imagine into their experiences, which encourages the child to then do the same.

Here are some excerpts of stories to give you an idea of how they might read:

Once upon a time, which is how all good stories begin, Mr and Mrs Rabbit lived in a tiny burrow deep in woodland far, far away. Mrs Rabbit had only just grown up herself when she was delighted to find out she had a baby bunny growing in her tummy. When it was just the right time, baby bunny came into the world. They named her Betty. Betty Bunny had beautiful, brown eyes and the softest fur. Everybody who met her said she was the bounciest bunny ever to be born in the forest – she made every bunny she met smile from whisker to whisker.

Mama and Papa Monkey didn't always get along. Sometimes Papa Monkey would get very cross. He would shout at Mama Monkey and hurt her when their babies were watching. I don't know if you've ever heard monkeys getting angry with each other, but what a loud, screeching noise they make! This meant that sometimes the monkey nest was a scary place for the little monkeys to be, because there was always so much shouting and fighting. I wonder if Mama and Papa Monkey realised just how scared their babies would feel when they screeched so loudly in front of them?

One dark night, the little princess was woken from her sleep by shouting and a very loud bang. She was so scared she didn't know what to do. She felt like she was frozen in ice. She couldn't move. It sounded as if something scary was happening in the castle downstairs. It wasn't until the morning came that she discovered that the King had hurt the Queen so badly she died. Everyone was so sad. They couldn't understand how such a terrible thing could have happened.

One day a worried neighbour found Scout and Jude all alone in a very cold, dark and dirty den. She told Ellie Elephant about this because it was her job to keep baby animals safe in the savannah. Ellie Elephant decided she had to do something very quickly to keep these precious little ones safe. She had to find another family to take care of them just for now. It isn't safe for any little one to be left all alone. Ellie Elephant knew of a kind and gentle family of giraffes, who looked after baby animals who couldn't live with their own mummies and daddies. When they heard about Scout and Jude, they couldn't wait to meet them.

Mr and Mrs Unicorn didn't always remember to feed the baby, so she sometimes felt hungry. Mr and Mrs Unicorn didn't always remember to cuddle and play gently with the baby, and she spent too long all alone in her bed of hay. Mr and Mrs Unicorn didn't always come to help when their baby was crying. This is not what babies need at all! Poor baby unicorn.

DIGITAL MATERIALS

I am mindful that a book (that often doesn't even look like a book!) will not be right for every child, particularly given technological advances over the last 15 years. However, when working for a local authority, as I did for most of my social work career, options for recording and storage of digital material are likely to be limited. I didn't even have access to a smartphone until 2020! If you are working independently as a therapist undertaking life story work you may have more options available to you. This is not my area of expertise at all, but if you are interested in a different way of working, have a look at Hammond and Cooper's *Digital Life Story Work* (2013). Although I'm also mindful that technology has developed significantly since this was published, they describe projects that could augment the life story work process, particularly in adolescence, but stress the need to practice with any software or hardware *before* beginning work with the young person. Ideas include:

- Digitising old photographs, which then allows for editing and embellishing the images.
- Creating digital audio or video stories using a mobile phone or tablet to recount a short story from the child's life –you can then edit this using video-editing software installed on most laptops.
- Audio interviews of the birth family, foster carers or previous social workers; they can be conducted by the child with preparation or by the life story worker and then edited together.
- Life tracks – encouraging the young person to create a playlist of songs that link to events or feelings about things that have happened in their life.
- A photo collage – there are free websites and apps that allow you to create collages at no cost.
- A pod walk – engage the young person as a tour guide showing the adult facilitating the walk around places that are important to them, while sharing stories or feelings that are evoked by being there (Hammond and Cooper 2013, pp.13–37).

OBJECTS AND A MEMORY BOX

When you are collating life story materials or encouraging parents or carers to contribute, think about whether there are any unique objects that hold sentimental or special value for the child. It is important to think about what makes them so precious. Might it remind the child of a special memory? 'Memories are not just what we hold in our heads but also take concrete form and consist of documents, images and objects and this is true for individuals, families, ethnic groups and nations too' (Hoyle 2018).

Once you understand the object better, consider how to create space for it in whichever way seems to fit best. This could be adding it to a memory box, taking a photograph to include in an album, or even making a canvas from the image. These objects are an essential part of the child's story, so it is vital to add some brief text to remind the child of something someone may have said at the time, the name of a place or what they had for lunch on that day. Such objects can later be used to tell a story that keeps a precious memory alive by reigniting feelings that are unique to the child, because the object itself can trigger those memories. When a child interacts with the object, looks at it, feels it in their hands and connects with the texture, the story re-awakens.

A memory box should contain memorabilia significant to the child. Most commonly the child's foster carer or keyworker in a children's home will take responsibility for collation, and it should move with the child. It could include soft toys, letters, celebration cards, first drawings and paintings, and photographs or images of birth parents and other relatives or significant people. Any objects should have luggage labels attached to describe why they are important, or should be photographed and the story attached to them should be written on the back.

You can also support and encourage birth family members to make their own album, scrapbook or memory box, especially where the plan is adoption. They could complete a baby book for their child with photographs of themselves as children, of relatives, and copies of pregnancy scan pictures. Include information about the pregnancy, birth, choice of name, or first thoughts when they held the baby in their arms. If they are not comfortable with writing information down, they could record themselves on their phones to send to the social worker or foster carers. You might need to help them think of things to record and whether or not they have any objects or baby clothes they would want to share. At the very least you could photograph these items, because it's understandable that a birth parent might not want to let go of their baby's hospital bracelet or coming-home-from-hospital outfit. These items are as precious to them as they would be to their child.

An example of this is a partnership between women with lived experience of separation from their newborns at birth and a team from Lancaster University and Birth Companions to develop HOPE (Hold On Pain Eases) boxes. Their aim is to help mothers capture important memories of time with their baby prior to separation, and to promote the ongoing connection between them and their baby after separation and during care proceedings. Two boxes are created; one stays with the mother and the other follows the baby into kinship care, foster care or their adoptive placement if this is the final outcome, and can contribute to life story work with the child. The boxes include important items to both the mother and baby, such as photographs, footprints, cot cards and matching soft toys and blankets (CFJ n.d.).

It is a privilege to stand alongside a child and their family as they explore their story. I do hope this book helps you feel more confident in so doing.

References

Barber, E. and Barber, A. (2016) *Is Daddy Coming Back in a Minute? Explaining Sudden Death in Words Very Young Children Can Understand.* London: Jessica Kingsley Publishers.

Barefoot Books with D. Harter (illustrator) and F. Penner (narrator) (2021) *Animal Boogie: 1 (Barefoot Singalongs).* [Also available at www.youtube.com/watch?v=25_u1GzruQM]

Baylin, J. and Hughes, D. (2016) *The Neurobiology of Attachment Focused Therapy: Enhancing Connection and Trust in the treatment of Children and Adolescents* (Norton Series on Interpersonal Neurobiology). New York: Norton & Co.

Baylin, J. and Hughes, D. (2022) 'Moving from mistrust to trust: Social buffering, brain whispering and PACE.' *Foster* 13, 5–13.

Baynes, P. (2008) 'Untold stories: A discussion of life story work.' *Adoption & Fostering* 32, 2, 43–49.

Beacon House Therapeutic Services and Trauma Team (2019) 'Brainstem calmers.' https://beaconhouse.org.uk/wp-content/uploads/2019/09/Brainstem-Calmer-Activities.pdf

Beacon House Therapeutic Services and Trauma Team (2020) 'Psycho-education toolkit: How to help children understand and regulate their survival responses.' https://beaconhouse.org.uk/training/psycho-education-tool-kit-for-children-young-people

Beacon House Therapeutic Services and Trauma Team (2021) 'The Truncated Response.' https://beaconhouse.org.uk/wp-content/uploads/2021/10/The-Truncated-Response-1.pdf

Bell, J. (2017) *Benny's Hat.* Pomelo Pip. https://www.pomelopip.com

Bentrim, W.G. (2012) *Mommy's Black Eye.* Philadelphia, PA: Bearly Tolerable Publications.

Bernstein, S.C. (1991) *A Family that Fights.* Park Ridge, IL: Albert Whitman & Co.

Birch, E. (2023) '"Who can empathise with the big bad wolf?" Empathy and multiple narratives as an EP in a Children's Services context.' edpsy.org.uk Blog, 6 February. https://edpsy.org.uk/blog/2023/who-can-empathise-with-the-big-bad-wolf-empathy-and-multiple-narratives-as-an-ep-in-a-childrens-services-context

Black, C. (2018) *My Dad Loves Me, My Dad Has a Disease: A Child's View: Living with Addiction.* Las Vegas, NV: Central Recovery Press.

Bland, N. (2010) *The Very Cranky Bear.* London: Hachette Children's Books.

Blaustein, M. and Kinneburgh, K. (2010) *Treating Traumatic Stress in Children and Adolescents: How to Foster Resilience through Attachment, Self-regulation and Competency.* New York: Guilford Press.

Bowlby, J. (1969/1982) *Attachment and Loss: Vol. 1. Attachment.* New York: Basic Books.

Brodzinsky, D. (2011) 'Children's understanding of adoption: Developmental and clinical implications.' *Professional Psychology Research and Practice 42*, 2, 200–207.

Brodzinsky, D.M. (2005) 'Reconceptualizing Openness in Adoption: Implications for Theory, Research, and Practice.' In D.M. Brodzinsky and J. Palacios (eds) *Psychological Issues in Adoption: Research and Practice* (pp.145–166). Westport, CT: Praeger Publishers/Greenwood Publishing Group.

Brodzinsky, D.M., Singer, L.M. and Braff, A. (1984) 'Children's understanding of adoption: Developmental and clinical implications.' *Child Development 55*, 869–878.

Browne, A. (2007) *Silly Billy.* London: Walker Books.

Bruna, D. (2018) *Dear Grandma Bunny: A Miffy Book.* London: Simon & Schuster Children's UK.

Building Better Brains (2019) 'Our reaction to stress explained: How to use "The hand model of the brain".' https://buildingbetterbrains.com.au/hand-model-of-the-brain

Burnell, A. and Vaughan, J. (2008) 'Remembering Never to Forget and Forgetting Never to Remember: Re-Thinking Life Story Work.' In B. Luckock and M. Lefevre (eds) *Direct Work: Social Work with Children and Young People in Care* (pp.223–233). London: BAAF Adoption and Fostering.

CAMH (Centre for Addiction and Mental Health) (2009) *Can I Catch It Like a Cold? Coping with a Parent's Depression.* New York: Tundra Books.

Cammarata, D. (2009) *Someone I Love Died by Suicide: A Story for Child Survivors and Those Who Care for Them.* Jupiter, FL: Limitless Press.

Campbell, C. (2018) *Stewart's Tree: A Book for Brothers and Sisters When a Baby Dies Shortly after Birth.* London: Jessica Kingsley Publishers.

Carlson, R. Jr. (2012) *Please Stop Smiling: Story about Schizophrenia and Mental Illness for Children.* CreateSpace Independent Publishing Platform.

Carter, M. and Maclean, S. (eds) (2022) *Insiders Outsiders: Hidden Narratives of Care Experienced Social Workers.* Lichfield: Kirwin Maclean Associates.

Children's Commissioner (2023) *Siblings in Care.* London: Children's Commissioner. https://assets.childrenscommissioner.gov.uk/wpuploads/2023/01/cc-siblings-in-care.pdf

CJF (Centre for Child & Family Justice Research) (no date) 'Giving HOPE and minimising trauma.' Information Sheet. www.cfj-lancaster.org.uk/projects/giving-hope

Cohen, O. and Winter, K. (2005) 'Identity issues for looked after children with no knowledge of their origins: Implications for research and practice.' *Adoption & Fostering 29*, 2, 44–52.

Coram (2021) *Public Attitudes to Children in Care and Care Leavers.* London: Coram. www.coram.org.uk/resource/resource-public-attitudes-children-care-and-care-leavers-coram

CORC (Child Outcomes Research Consortium) (no date) 'Goal Based Outcomes (GBO).' www.corc.uk.net/outcome-experience-measures/goal-based-outcomes-gbo

Craig, G. (2011) *The EFT Manual.* Fulton, CA: Energy Psychology Press.

Craik, K. (1943) *The Nature of Explanation.* London and New York: Cambridge University Press.

Cross, C. (2022) 'Daisy's story: The child born of rape now fighting for the law to recognise her as a victim.' ITV News, 2 December. www.itv.com/news/central/2022-12-01/daisys-story-the-child-born-out-of-rape-now-fighting-for-the-law-to-change Accessed 29.12.22

Crossley, D. (2009) *Muddles, Puddles and Sunshine.* Gloucester: Winston's Wish.

Curcio, A. (2016) *Critters Cry Too: Explaining Addiction to Children*. Woodinville, WA: ICG Children's.

Dana, D. (2018) *The Polyvagal Theory in Therapy: Engaging the Rhythm of Regulation*. New York: W.W. Norton & Co.

Danielle (2021) 'Who am I? A blog about identity from an adoptee's perspective.' How to Be Adopted Blog, 9 June. https://howtobeadopted.com/blog/2021/who-am-i-a-blog-about-identity-from-an-adoptees-perspective

Daynes, K. and Pym, C. (2020) *Why Do Things Die?* London: Usborne Publishing.

DCSF (Department for Children, Schools and Families) (2010) *IRO Handbook: Statutory Guidance for Independent Reviewing Officers and Local Authorities on Their Functions in Relation to Case Management and Review for Looked After Children*. London: DCSF Publications. https://assets.publishing.service.gov.uk/government/uploads/system/uploads/attachment_data/file/337568/iro_statutory_guidance_iros_and_las_march_2010_tagged.pdf

de Thierry, B. (2019) *The Simple Guide to Attachment Difficulties in Children: What They Are and How to Help*. London: Jessica Kingsley Publishers.

Denborough, D. (2008) *Collective Narrative Practice*. Adelaide, SA: Dulwich Centre.

Denborough, D. (2018) *Do You Want to Hear a Story? Adventures in Collective Narrative Practice*. Adelaide, SA: Dulwich Centre.

Devine, R. (2022) 'Shame, Social Work, and Transformations: Reflections.' In M. Carter and S. Maclean (eds) *Insiders Outsiders: Hidden Narratives of Care Experienced Social Workers* (pp.146–152). Lichfield: Kirwin Maclean Associates.

Devlin, J. (2012) 'Telling a child's story: Creating a words and pictures story book to tell children why they are in care.' *Social Work Now*, February, 13–20.

DfE (Department for Education) (2011) *Fostering Services: National Minimum Standards*. https://assets.publishing.service.gov.uk/government/uploads/system/uploads/attachment_data/file/192705/NMS_Fostering_Services.pdf

DfE (Department for Education) (2013) *Statutory Guidance on Adoption: For Local Authorities, Voluntary Adoption Agencies and Adoption Support Agencies*. July. https://assets.publishing.service.gov.uk/government/uploads/system/uploads/attachment_data/file/270100/adoption_statutory_guidance_2013.pdf

DfE (Department for Education) (2015) *Guide to the Children's Homes Regulations Including the Quality Standards*. April. https://assets.publishing.service.gov.uk/government/uploads/system/uploads/attachment_data/file/463220/Guide_to_Children_s_Home_Standards_inc_quality_standards_Version__1.17_FINAL.pdf

Doel, M. (ed.) (2017) *Social Work in 42 Objects (and More)*. Lichfield: Kirwin Maclean Associates.

Doel, M. (2019) 'Displaying social work through objects.' *British Journal of Social Work* 49, 3, 824–841.

Dolfi, M. (2022) 'Relinquishment trauma: The forgotten trauma.' Adoption Educational. https://mariedolfi.com/adoption-resource/relinquishment-trauma-the-forgotten-trauma

Donovan, S. (2022) *The Strange and Curious Guide to Trauma*. London: Jessica Kingsley Publishers.

Doyle, R. (2009) *Her Mother's Face*. Abingdon: Scholastic.

Durant, A. (2003) *Always and Forever*. New York: Penguin Random House.

Ehlers, A. and Clark, D.M. (2000) 'A cognitive model of posttraumatic stress disorder.' *Behaviour Research and Therapy* 38, 319–345.

Evans, J. (2014) *How Are You Feeling Today Baby Bear? Exploring Big Feelings After Living in a Stormy Home.* London: Jessica Kingsley Publishers.

Fahlberg, V. (1994) *A Child's Journey Through Placement.* London: BAAF.

Fargas-Malet, M. and McSherry, D. (2020) 'The emotional nature of birth family relationships for care-experienced and adopted young people: A longitudinal perspective.' *Journal of Family Issues 41*, 10, 2263–2288. https://journals.sagepub.com/doi/pdf/10.1177/0192513X20978439

Fensham, E. (2005) *Helicopter Man.* Sydney: Bloomsbury Publishing.

Garcia, G. (2017) *Listening to My Body* (2nd edn). Skinned Knee Publishing.

Gilligan, R. (2010) 'Promoting Positive Outcomes for Children in Need.' In J. Horwath (ed.) *The Child's World: The Comprehensive Guide to Assessing Children in Need* (2nd edn) (pp.174–183). London: Jessica Kingsley Publishers.

Golding, K. (2014) *Using Stories to Build Bridges with Traumatized Children: Creative Ideas for Therapy, Life Story Work, Direct Work and Parenting.* London: Jessica Kingsley Publishers.

Gormally, E. (2011) *The Little Flower Bulb: Helping Children Bereaved by Suicide.* Dublin: Veritas Books.

Green, C. (2019) '"Contact" from the Birth Parents' Perspective.' In J. Alper (ed.) *Supporting Birth Parents Whose Children Have Been Adopted* (pp.132–148). London: Jessica Kingsley Publishers.

Green, J. (2013) *The Fault in Our Stars.* London: Penguin.

Greening, R. (2020) *The Very Hungry Worry Monsters.* Brampton: Make Believe Ideas.

Grollman, E.A. (1993) *Straight Talk about Death for Teenagers: How to Cope with Losing Someone You Love.* Boston, MA: Beacon Press.

Hammel, S. (2018) *Handbook of Therapeutic Storytelling: Stories and Metaphors in Psychotherapy, Child and Family Therapy, Medical Treatment, Coaching and Supervision.* London: Routledge.

Hammond, S. and Cooper, N. (2013) *Digital Life Story Work: Using Technology to Help Young People Make Sense of Their Experiences.* London: BAAF.

Harris, R.H. (2004) *Goodbye Mousie.* London: Simon & Schuster.

Heegaard, M. (1993) *When a Family is in Trouble: Children Can Cope with Grief from Drug and Alcohol Addiction.* Minneapolis, MN: Woodland Press.

Heine, O. (2019) *Rwandan Daughters: Photographs by Olaf Heine.* Berlin: Hatje Kanzt.

Herman, J.L. (1997) *Trauma and Recovery. The Aftermath of Violence – From Domestic Abuse to Political Terror.* New York City: Basic Books.

Hohnen, B., Gilmour, J. and Murphy, T. (2020) *The Incredible Teenage Brain: Everything You Need to Know to Unlock Your Teen's Potential.* London: Jessica Kingsley Publishers.

Howe, D. and Feast, J. (2000) *Adoption, Search and Reunion.* London: The Children's Society.

Hoyle, V. (2018) 'Creating memory boxes: A social worker's perspective.' UCL Blog, 15 November. https://blogs.ucl.ac.uk/mirra/2018/11/15/creating-memory-boxes-a-social-workers-perspective/#

Hoyle, V., Shepherd, E., Lomas, E. and Flinn, A. (2020) 'Recordkeeping and the life-long memory and identity needs of care-experienced children and young people.' *Child and Family Social Work 25*, 4, 935–945.

Hudson, K. (2020) *Lowborn: Growing Up, Getting Away and Returning to Britain's Poorest Towns.* London: Vintage.

Hughes, D. (2003) 'Psychological interventions for the spectrum of attachment disorders and intrafamilial trauma.' *Attachment and Human Development* 5, 3, 271–277.

Hughes, D. (2016) *Trauma*. London: CoramBAAF Adoption and Fostering Academy.

Hughes, D., Baylin, J. and Siegel, D. (2012) *Brain Based Parenting: The Neuroscience of Caregiving for Healthy Attachment*. London: W.W. Norton & Co.

Hunter, L. (2021) *What If, Pig?* London: HarperCollins.

Hussain, N. (2020) *My Monster and Me*. London: Hodder Children's Books.

Ironside, V. (2011) *The Huge Bag of Worries*. London: Hodder Children's Books.

Jay, C. (2014) *Seeds of Hope Bereavement and Loss Activity Book. Helping Children and Young People Cope with Change Through Nature*. London: Jessica Kingsley Publishers.

Jay, C. and Thomas, J. (2012) *What Does Dead Mean? A Book for Young Children to Help Explain Death and Dying*. London: Jessica Kingsley Publishers.

Jenkins, A. (2017) *Plot 29: A Memoir*. London: HarperCollins Publishers.

Johnson, L. (2019) '10 things adoptees want you to know.' HuffPost, 11 January. www.huffpost.com/entry/adoption_b_2161590

Kagan, R. (2009) *Real Life Heroes: A Life Story Book for Children* (2nd edn). New York: Routledge.

Lauerman, M. (2015) *Life Story Work: The Wider Context*. www.careknowledge.com/resources/special-reports/2015/scp/life-story-work-the-wider-context [for subscribers only].

Law, D. and Jacob, J. (2015) *Goals and Goal Based Outcomes (GBOs): Some Useful Information* (3rd edn). London: CAMHS Press.

Levine, P.A. and Frederick, A. (1997) *Waking the Tiger: Healing Trauma*. Berkeley, CA: North Atlantic Books.

Lloyd, S. (2016) *Improving Sensory Processing in Traumatized Children: Practical Ideas to Help Your Child's Movement, Coordination and Body Awareness*. London: Jessica Kingsley Publishers.

Lloyd, S. (2020) *Building Sensorimotor Systems in Children with Developmental Trauma: A Model for Practice*. London: Jessica Kingsley Publishers.

Lyons, J. (2022) 'Supporting infants as they transition into foster care.' *Foster* 13, 23–33.

Marlow, H. (2021) *Delly Duck: Why A Little Chick Couldn't Stay with His Birth Mother*. Holly Marlow. https://hollymarlow.com

Martin, P. (2007) *The Parent's Helping Handbook: A Practical Guide for Teaching Your Child Protective Behaviours*. Armadale, Western Australia: Safe4Kids.

Mellonie, B. and Ingpen, R. (1998) *Lifetimes: The Beautiful Way to Explain Death to Children*. New York: Bantam Books.

Mitchell, C. (2021) *I Am Here For You! A Story to Support Your Grieving Child Through Death from Suicide*. Brandon, MB: Puddle Jumper Publishing.

Mitchell, R. (2018) 'The sense of an ending.' BACP, March. www.bacp.co.uk/bacp-journals/private-practice/march-2018/the-sense-of-an-ending

Morwen, D. (2020) 'Compassion Fatigue and Secondary Trauma in Adoptive Parents.' Doctoral thesis, University College London.

Moundlic, C. (2012) *The Scar*. Somerville, MA: Candlewick Press.

Nacoa (no date) 'Frequently asked questions.' https://nacoa.org.uk/support-advice/for-children/faqs-2

Ness, P. (2015) *A Monster Calls*. London: Walker Books.

nicabm (National Institute for the Clinical Application of Behavioural Medicine) (no date) 'How the nervous system responds to trauma.' www.nicabm.com/how-the-nervous-system-responds-to-trauma

NICE (National Institute for Health and Care Excellence) (2013) *Looked-After Children and Young People*. Quality standard 31 (QS31). www.nice.org.uk/guidance/qs31

NICE (National Institute for Health and Care Excellence) (2021) 'Looked-after children and young people.' Guidance www.nice.org.uk/guidance/ng205

Nicholls, E. (2005) *The New Life Work Model: Practice Guide*. Lyme Regis: Russell House Publishing Ltd.

NSPCC (National Society for the Prevention of Cruelty to Children) (no date, a) 'Emotional abuse.' www.nspcc.org.uk/what-is-child-abuse/types-of-abuse/emotional-abuse

NSPCC (no date, b) 'Sexual abuse.' www.nspcc.org.uk/what-is-child-abuse/types-of-abuse/child-sexual-abuse/#what

Oakwater, H. (2012) *Bubble Wrapped Children: How Social Networking Is Transforming the Face of 21st Century Adoption*. London: MX Publishing.

O'Connor, D.S. (2009) *I Can Be Me: A Helping Book for Children of Alcoholic Parents*. Bloomington, IN: AuthorHouse.

Ottaway, H. and Selwyn, J. (2016) *No One Told Us It Would Be Like This: Compassion Fatigue and Foster Care*. Bristol: The Hadley Centre, University of Bristol.

Otter, I. (2019) *The Garden of Hope*. London: Caterpillar Books.

Parr, T. (2008) *We Belong Together: A Book About Adoption and Families*. New York: Little, Brown Books for Young Readers.

Pearson, M. (2023) 'Documenting narratives of strength and resource for young people in the context of social care services.' *Context, 188*, 9-12.

Percival, T. (2022) *Ruby's Worry*. London: Bloomsbury Children's Books.

Perry, B. and Hambrick, E. (2000) 'The neurosequential model of therapeutics.' *Reclaiming Children and Youth 17*, 3, 38–43.

Perry, B. and Szalavitz, M. (2017) *The Boy Who Was Raised as a Dog*. New York: Basic Books.

Porges, S.W. (1995) 'Orienting in a defensive world: Mammalian modifications of our evolutionary heritage. A polyvagal theory.' *Psychophysiology 32*, 4, 301–318. doi: 10.1111/j.1469-8986.1995.tb01213.x.

Porges, S.W. (2011) *The Polyvagal Theory: Neurophysiological Foundations of Emotions, Attachment, Communication, and Self-Regulation* (Norton Series on Interpersonal Biology). New York: W.W. Norton & Co.

Rawcliffe, C., Neil, E., Hancock, M. and Elias L. (2022) *Maintaining Relationships with Birth Families after Adoption: What Are Adopted Adults' Views?* Centre for Research on Children & Families. October. Norwich: University of East Anglia. www.pac-uk.org/wp-content/uploads/2022/10/Maintaining-Relationships-with-Birth-Families-Research-Briefing.pdf

Rees, J. (2009) *Life Story Books for Adopted Children: A Family Friendly Approach*. London: Jessica Kingsley Publishers.

Rees, J. (2017) *Life Story Books for Adopted and Fostered Children*. London: Jessica Kingsley Publishers.

Rees, J. (2018) *Life Story Work with Children Who Are Fostered or Adopted: Using Diverse Techniques in a Coordinated Way*. London: Jessica Kingsley Publishers.

Richards, D. and Lovell, K. (1999) 'Behavioural and Cognitive Behavioural Interventions in the Treatment of PTSD.' In Yule, W. (ed.) *Post-Traumatic Stress Disorders: Concepts and Therapy*. Chichester: Wiley.

Romain, T. (2023) *What On Earth Do You Do When Someone Dies?* Huntington Beach, CA: Free Spirit Publishing Inc.

Rose, R. (2012) *Life Story Therapy with Traumatized Children: A Model for Practice*. London: Jessica Kingsley Publishers.

Rose, R. (2017) *Innovative Therapeutic Life Story Work: Developing Trauma-Informed Practice for Working with Children, Adolescents and Young Adults*. London: Jessica Kingsley Publishers.

Rosen, M. (2005) *Michael Rosen's Sad Book*. London: Walker Books.

Rothman, J.C. (1996) *A Birthday Present for Daniel: A Child's Story of Loss*. Washington, DC: Prometheus Books.

Ryan, T. and Walker, R. (2016) *Life Story Work: Why, What, How and When*. London: CoramBAAF.

Sambrooks, P. (2009) *Dennis Duckling*. London: BAAF.

Saltzman W.R., Pynoos, R.S., Lester, P., Layne, C.M. and Beardslee, W.R. (2013) 'Enhancing family resilience through family narrative co-construction.' *Clinical Child and Family Psychology Review 16*, 3, 294–310.

Schofield, G. and Beek, M. (2018) *Attachment Handbook for Foster Care and Adoption* (2nd edn). London: CoramBAAF Adoption and Fostering Agency.

Shannon, B. (2019) 'Why language matters.' Rewriting Social Care Blog, 9 August. https://rewritingsocialcare.blog/2019/08/09/why-language-matters

Shepherd, E. (2022) 'Good practice in record-keeping in children's social care.' Research in Practice, 28 February. www.researchinpractice.org.uk/children/news-views/2022/february/good-practice-in-record-keeping-in-children-s-social-care

Shotton, G. (2020) *A Session by Session Guide to Life Story Work: A Practical Resource to Use with Looked After or Adopted Children*. London: Routledge.

Siegel, D.J. (1999) *The Developing Mind: How Relationships and the Brain Interact to Shape Who We Are*. New York: Guilford Press.

Siegel, D.J. (2010) *Mindsight: The New Science of Personal Transformation*. New York: Bantam Books.

Sissay, L. (2019) *My Name Is Why: A Memoir*. Edinburgh: Canongate Books.

Skandrani, S., Harf, A. and El Husseini, M. (2019) 'The impact of children's pre-adoptive traumatic experiences on parents.' *Frontiers in Psychiatry* 10, 866. doi: 10.3389/fpsyt.2019.00866.

Smid, E. (2015) *Luna's Red Hat: An Illustrated Storybook to Help Children Cope with Loss and Suicide*. London: Jessica Kingsley Publishers.

Smith, C. and Logan, J. (2004) *After Adoption: Direct Contact and Relationships*. Abingdon: Routledge.

Snel, E. (2019) *Sitting Still Like a Frog Activity Book: 75 Mindfulness Games for Kids*. Boulder, CO: Shambhala Publications Inc.

Solomon, M. and Siegel, D. (eds) (2003) *Healing Trauma: Attachment, Mind, Body and Brain*. New York: W.W. Norton & Co.

Spring, C. (2021) 'What grounding is and isn't.' Blog, 9 June. www.carolynspring.com/blog/what-grounding-is-and-isnt

Stein, D.E. (2022) *Don't Worry, Murray*. New York: Balzer + Bray.

Sunderland, M. (2000) *Using Story Telling as a Therapeutic Tool with Children*. Milton Keynes: Speechmark Publishing Ltd.

TACT Fostering & Adoption (2019) *Language that Cares: Changing the Way Professionals Talk about Children in Care*. March. www.tactcare.org.uk/content/uploads/2019/03/TACT-Language-that-cares-2019_online.pdf

Tait, A. and Wosu, H. (2015) *Direct Work with Family Groups: Simple, Fun Ideas to Aid Engagement and Assessment and Enable Positive Change* (Practical Guides for Direct Work). London: Jessica Kingsley Publishers.

Tottenham, N. and Gabard-Durnam, L.J. (2017) 'The developing amygdala: A student of the world and a teacher of the cortex.' *Current Opinion in Psychology* 17, 55–60.

Treisman, K. (2017a) *A Therapeutic Treasure Box for Working with Children and Adolescents with Developmental Trauma: Creative Techniques and Activities*. London: Jessica Kingsley Publishers.

Treisman, K. (2017b) *A Therapeutic Treasure Deck of Sentence Completion and Feelings Cards*. London: Jessica Kingsley Publishers.

Treisman, K. (2018) *A Therapeutic Treasure Deck of Grounding, Soothing, Coping and Regulating Cards*. London: Jessica Kingsley Publishers.

Treisman, K. (2020) *The Parenting Patchwork Treasure Deck: A Creative Tool for Assessments, Interventions and Strengthening Relationships with Parents, Carers, and Children*. London: Jessica Kingsley Publishers.

van der Kolk, B. (2005) 'Developmental Trauma Disorder: Toward a rational diagnosis for children with complex trauma histories.' *Psychiatric Annals*, 35, 5, 401–408.

Typpo, M.H. (1994) *Elephant in the Living Room*. Center City, MN: Hazelden Trade.

van der Kolk, B. (2015) *The Body Keeps the Score: Brain, Mind and Body in the Healing of Trauma*. New York: Penguin Publishing Books.

Vigna, J. (1993) *I Wish Daddy Didn't Drink So Much*. Park Ridge, IL: Albert Whitman Prairie.

Wachtel, T. (2016) 'Defining restorative.' International Institute for Restorative Practices. www.iirp.edu/images/pdf/Defining-Restorative_Nov-2016.pdf

Walker, H. (2020) 'Children deserve the best life story work we can give them. *Community Care*, 19 March. www.communitycare.co.uk/2020/03/19/children-deserve-best-life-story-work-can-give

Walter, N. (2023) 'My mother planned her own death for a long time. Why didn't I believe her?' *The Guardian*, 20 August. www.theguardian.com/books/2023/aug/20/mother-planned-own-death-natasha-walter-before-the-light-fades-suicide

Watson, D. (2015) 'We need to help children in care treasure the objects that tell their life story.' *The Guardian*, 9 April. www.theguardian.com/social-care-network/2015/apr/09/cared-for-children-treasure-objects-trove

Watson, D., Latter, S. and Bellew, R. (2015) 'Adopters' views on their children's life story books.' *Adoption and Fostering* 39, 2, 119–134. https://doi.org/10.1177/0308575915588723

Watson, D., Meineck, C. and Lancaster, B. (2018) 'Adopted children's co-production and use of "trove" (a digitally enhanced memory box) to better understand their care histories through precious objects.' *Clinical Child Psychology and Psychiatry* 23, 4, 614–628. https://doi.org/10.1177/1359104518776359

Watts, G. (2009) *Hear My Roar: A Story of Family Violence*. Toronto, ON: Annick Press.

Wells, L. and Robinson, M. (2018) *Only One of Me: A Love Letter from Mum*. Cardiff: Graffeg.

Wiener, C., Gregory, A., Rogers, M. and Walklate, S. (2022) 'Why victims of domestic abuse don't leave – four experts explain.' *The Conversation*, 15 February. https://theconversation.com/why-victims-of-domestic-abuse-dont-leave-four-experts-explain-176212

Winston's Wish (2020) 'How to explain suicide to children and young people.' 12 May. www.winstonswish.org/explain-suicide-to-children

Winston's Wish (2021) 'How to help bereaved children understand grief.' 20 July. www.winstonswish.org/how-to-help-bereaved-children-understand-grief

Wolfs, R. (2015) *Healing for Adults Who Grew up in Adoption or Foster Care: Positive Strategies for Overcoming Emotional Challenges.* London: Jessica Kingsley Publishers.

Wrench, K. (2016) *Helping Vulnerable Children and Adolescents to Stay Safe: Creative Ideas and Activities for Building Protective Behaviours.* London: Jessica Kingsley Publishers.

Wrench, K. (2018) *Creative Ideas for Assessing Vulnerable Children and Families.* London: Jessica Kingsley Publishers.

Wrench, K. and Naylor, L. (2013) *Life Story Work with Children Who Are Fostered or Adopted: Creative Ideas and Activities.* London: Jessica Kingsley Publishers.

Wrobel, G.M. and Dillon, K. (2009) 'Adopted Adolescents: Who and What Are They Curious About?' In G.M. Wrobel and E. Neil (eds) *International Advances in Adoption Research for Practice* (pp.217–244). Oxford: Wiley-Blackwell.

Subject Index

Author Index